# THE CHALLENGE OF TEACHING MEXICAN-AMERICAN STUDENTS

Dolores Escobar Litsinger

American Book Company

ACKNOWLEDGMENTS

The author wishes to acknowledge the assistance of many individuals who have demonstrated interest in improving the education of Mexican-American students. Of note is the support shown by colleagues in the Chicano Studies Department and the School of Education at California State University in Northridge, the encouragement offered by M.E.C.H.A. students on campus, and the cooperation of public school administrators and teachers who spoke freely of their concerns.

Special thanks go to: Dr. Rudolph Acuña, Dr. Julian Nava, Mr. Edward Moreno, Dr. Johanna K. Lemlech, Mrs. Mary Martinez, and Mr. Henry Lopez.

AMERICAN BOOK COMPANY

*New York  Cincinnati  Atlanta  Dallas  Millbrae*

COPYRIGHT © 1973 BY LITTON EDUCATIONAL PUBLISHING, INC.

# Contents

# About the Author

DOLORES ESCOBAR LITSINGER is a professor of education at California State University in Northridge. She attended UCLA where, as a PTA scholarship student, she graduated Phi Beta Kappa and earned her doctorate in education. As a student teacher, she worked with Mexican-American youngsters and learned techniques and skills that she eventually transformed into bilingual teaching strategies.

Dr. Litsinger was instrumental in establishing a bilingual-bicultural learning laboratory operated jointly by California State University in Northridge and the Los Angeles public schools. She brings to this book a wealth of training and experience in bilingual-bicultural education which can be extraordinarily valuable to teachers and prospective teachers of Mexican-American students.

Dr. Litsinger's other publications include numerous articles on bilingual instruction, teacher leadership patterns, and a textbook for teachers, *Social Studies Instruction at the University Elementary School, UCLA*. However, she feels that *The Challenge of Teaching Mexican-American Students* is her most comprehensive contribution, because it represents a personal search for identity as a Mexican-American, as well as an educator's attempt to be not only critical, but also constructive.

Dedicated to JOHN, SCOTT, LISA, and ELYZABETH

# 1

# WHY NOT A CHICANO HORATIO ALGER?

The plight of Mexican Americans in our society can be documented in the literature deal-ing with history, law, politics and labor in the United States. Recent investigations of urban and social problems have added startling statistics on the extensive deprivations suffered by Mexican Americans in health, housing, economics and education. As all seg-ments of society become increasingly aware of these inequities, educators are being asked to examine their role in determining the character of contemporary society. The profession appears to be experiencing a reawakening of social consciousness reminiscent of the thirties, though current approaches to educational reform rest more upon empirical re-search and there is less general agreement upon specific goals for education.

Nevertheless, educators look with great concern at large numbers of nonachieving and underachieving students who often become noncontributing adults. Questions are being raised about the relevancy and effectiveness of education for all students, but of special interest are students who are culturally, racially, or ethnically different. These students, too often nonachievers and dropouts, have become the subject of study and analysis. Frequently, however, these students are studied as separate entities—unrelated to the total society, curriculum, or pedagogy. Such an approach is unacceptable to many educators who feel that Mexican-American students' needs, problems, and strengths must be placed in proper perspective and then reflected in appropriate school curricula and teaching procedures. This book is an attempt to do just that. It presents the case for educational reform as objectively as possible from within the profession and from within the ethnic group itself. The text is written with three basic ideas in mind: (1) The Mexican-American student constitutes one of the greatest challenges to education in our time. (2) In order to meet the challenge, conflict and change are inevitable. (3) The present social and professional climate is conducive to meeting the challenge.

# The Mexican-American Student:
# An Educational Challenge

The Mexican-American student is a challenge because he has qualities which result in specific educational and personality needs. He is unlike Anglos and other minority students, and he differs from students of similar economic status who have culturally different backgrounds.

While most Mexican-American students cannot be stereotyped as to appearance, many are often physically and linguistically distinguishable. Many, however, are only subtly different in reactions or behavior.

"Just when I think I know exactly what Mexican-American students are like, one comes along to defy my definition," says one teacher. "All I know is they're different," says another. Just how unique the Mexican American is will become apparent as we examine dimensions of the challenge.

FAILURE OF THE SCHOOLS    Schools, for the most part, have been unable to meet the challenge posed by Mexican-American students. Among the generalizations that can be made about these students are the following: Mexican-American students have one of the highest dropout rates of any minority group in the United States; a disproportionately large number of them are classified as mentally retarded, and those considered to be of normal intelligence often do not achieve academically but fall progressively farther behind other students as they move through the educational system; few Mexican-American students go to college.

It is significant that these characteristics are particularly applicable to Mexican-American students living in Southwestern United States where they comprise a large percentage and, in some school districts, the majority of the students.

School failures are reflected in an abundance of statistics in which the educational attainments of Mexican-American students are compared to those of both Anglos and other minorities. Two such comparisons follow.

> In California in 1960, 54.8% of the Anglo high school students completed four years of high school, 39.8% of the Negro high school students completed four years of high school, while only 24% of the Mexican-American high school students completed four years of high school.[1]

> In Texas in 1950, there was a gap of 6.4 years in median education when Mexican-American educational attainment was compared to Anglo educational attainment. By 1969 the gap increased to 6.7 years; this, in spite of the fact that the Mexican population is now somewhat more urban and much younger than the Anglo population.[2]

The 1968 National Advisory Committee on Mexican-American Education reported the following:

> The average Mexican-American child in the Southwest drops out of school by the seventh year. In Texas, 89 percent of the children with Spanish surnames drop out before completing high school.
>
> Along the Texas-Mexico border, four out of five Mexican-American children fall two grades behind their Anglo classmates by the time they reach the fifth grade.
>
> A recent study in California showed that in some schools more than 50 percent of Mexican-American high school students drop out between grades 10 and 11.
>
> Mexican Americans account for more than 40 percent of the so-called "mentally handicapped" in California.
>
> Although Spanish surnamed students make up more than 14 percent of the public school population of California, less than $\frac{1}{2}$ of one percent of the college students enrolled in the seven campuses of the University of California are of this group.[3]

It is a basic premise of this text that these statistics *do not* represent shortcomings within students of Mexican-American heritage, but rather failures within the structure of educational institutions. And it is the author's contention that it is time that Mexican-American students cease to be considered a problem—that schools' inadequacies cause the problem, while the students, themselves, pose the challenge.

Part of the failure of schools to meet their challenge involves a lack of systematic knowledge about this ethnic minority as a result of indifference, inadequate methods or instruments to assess their capabilities, and limited communication between the school and the parents or community from which the students come.

Even more basic, the failure to reach Mexican-American students involves unwillingness on the part of individuals within school systems to change teaching techniques, curriculum, or school organization to utilize what is known about Mexican-American students. Though limited, the accumulated knowledge available from systematic research has seldom been effectively applied in the form of new school programs or teacher education courses designed specifically toward the needs of Spanish-speaking students. The inertia of decades is apparent when one reads questions asked by Herschel T. Manuel in 1934.

> How may the school become an active force for the improvement of the home of the underprivileged child?
>
> What elements of Spanish and Mexican culture should be saved to enrich our common store?

What modifications of curriculum are necessary to adjust to their peculiar background of experience and to meet their social needs?

How can their opportunities for mastery of English be increased?

How should they be taught so that their transition to English may be accomplished with the least possible loss?

How may the abilities of these children be adequately appraised?

What opportunities can be offered to the children of migratory families?

How can an adequate educational program be provided in communities that are now indifferent or antagonistic to these children?[4]

In the ensuing years, few, if any, of these questions have been adequately answered. The sensitive areas in the education of Mexican-American students remain: homelife or life-style, cultural preservation, school relevancy, linguistic ability, accurate student assessment, transiency, economic and minority status.

It can be said that professional education reflects the general society which has not, until recently, become vitally concerned with the education of culturally and economically "different" students. However, even with a shift in emphasis, the advent of special programs, expanded research, and increased governmental expenditures aimed at improving education of minority students, questions raised by Manuel remain formidable, because solutions to problems of minority education involve complex, philosophic, nonobjective differences of opinoin. Points of view concerning how these questions should be answered differ among educators, parents, and students, depending upon their attitudes.

Attitudinal or "affective" aspects of human relations and decision making are not well understood, but they cannot be ignored when considering the education of students who represent an ethnic minority. Attitudes about school, about teachers, about parents, about *self* come through as the most important single element affecting the behavior of Mexican-American students. Likewise, the way a teacher feels about Mexican Americans, the Mexican culture, and his own culture may well be the most critical element in an educational program.

Differing opinions and attitudes, which are by-products of unique socialization processes, are often an unconscious part of one's personality. When one is placed in contact with persons of differing values and attitudes, the stage is set for conflict. The corollary and second premise of this text is that educators must become sensitive to the conflicts inherent in the education of Mexican-American students. To become sensitive, they must know more about the group itself, but equally important, they must become more conscious of their own values and attitudes as they affect relationships with those who are culturally different.

# Conflict Over Educational Theories

The question of cultural assimilation versus cultural separatism is a key issue and probably the most controversial one affecting educators of Mexican-American students. Many educators and parents (Mexican-American as well as Anglo), concerned about the large number of Mexican Americans who do not achieve in school and who do not attain economic or social success in adult life, express the belief that the best means to success in the Anglo society is assimilation.

ASSIMILATION VS. SEPARATISM    Assimilation may involve less restricted integration into the economic, educational, or social aspects of the larger society. It may involve accommodation of individual behavior in ways that are acceptable to dominant mores. Defined in this manner, assimilation is more acceptable to Mexican Americans because it does not demand complete acquiescence of individual values in favor of those espoused by the dominant group.

Advocates of cultural assimilation, however, assume that the individual will modify or replace his cultural attributes with those of the dominant culture. In this group are individuals who feel that the major role of the school is to help students develop Anglo values and corresponding competencies which will enable them to compete more effectively in the larger society. They feel the schools must counteract the "foreign" elements of the Mexican Americans' culture which have resisted the "sensible" course of acculturation. As the quotations below indicate, cultural assimilation is often seen as the best means for individual success and as a necessity for the preservation of the dominant way of life.

> "Don't get 'hung up' on academics or philosophy," a principal recently told his staff. "Prepare them for the real world. They live in the United States, so give them what they need to live here!"

> "How can I teach them to think when they can't even speak English?" complained one teacher. "Teach them a trade, a vocation so they can earn a living."

> "They can't even talk in complete sentences. They don't need to learn about predicates, subjects, adverbs, adjectives, nouns; most of these children are never in their whole life ever going to use that sort of thing. We should have a simple book where we work on little stories, like the kindergarteners do," said a fifth grade teacher in an interview.

> "Why can't they be like other groups of immigrants, the Irish or the Germans? They become 'good Americans'; why won't Mexican Americans learn to speak the language and contribute to this society?" a student teacher recently asked.

"Our children have to learn the language and the ways of the Anglo world. In many ways they have to be 'Anglo' in order to get ahead," said one parent.

Opponents of the philosophies expressed in these statements claim that the "melting pot" theory has not worked to their advantage; they call for ethnic identification and preservation. Individuals in this group point out that, realistically, few Mexican Americans are totally accepted by the Anglo world, even when they try to be culturally assimilated. They feel the dark-skinned Mexican American who has classical Indian features (the "Prieto") will always be identified as "Mexican" by Anglo society. Culturally, the Mexican American may be "Anglicized", but he then runs the risk of being marginal in both cultures and accepted in neither. The Anglicized Mexican American ("Gringado"), they feel, is subject to discrimination in both cultures, and may face such serious identity problems as to preclude real personal success.

Proponents of ethnic preservation maintain that most Mexican Americans face three alternatives with regard to the dominant culture. They can attempt to assimilate culturally and accept the consequences, they can withdraw into the safety of their minority group and resign themselves to being dominated by Anglos, or they can adhere to some form of cultural nationalism which may range from complete cultural separatism to a selective, reciprocal "cultural exchange" between Anglo and Mexican-American society. The last alternative cited appears to be gaining popularity as the one which offers greatest self-determination and dignity.

A substantial number of Mexican Americans express the belief that their children must develop self-identity within their ethnic group in order to be secure and able to compete in the Anglo world. Furthermore, they contend that ethnic cohesiveness is essential to provide an effective power base for their individual members. They use the "real world" as evidence that Mexican Americans, as individuals, have not "made it" in the Anglo power structure either by cultural assimilation or by any other means. They cite, for example, the U.S. Bureau of Census Report, November 1969, which indicates that the average Mexican-American family earned $5,600, only 25% of the men had white collar jobs, and that their unemployment rate was almost double that of the rest of the population.

Proponents of cultural preservation feel that not only have they been systematically excluded from equal participation in American society, but also they have been ignored as a serious force in the history and social development of that society. They charge that social institutions, particularly educational institutions, have denied them equal access to opportunities while, at the same time, have attempted to destroy their cultural heritage and personal dignity.

ATTITUDES OF MEXICAN-AMERICAN COMMUNITY LEADERS    Most educators have considered themselves proponents of democratic principles and are often shocked at the bitterness of accusations by some Mexican Americans. However, most educators have their own definition of democracy tailored to fit their own values; the Mexican-American educator is no exception.

At a meeting to discuss how teacher training institutions could improve predominantly Mexican-American schools, some community leaders expressed the following points of view:

> "You speak of improving education for Mexican Americans. Actually you have been doing an excellent job of educating us for the purposes you have in mind. You've been doing a good job of it. If you sent us to college, who would pick your tomatoes, wash your cars, and clean your houses? There's no problem in the way we are being educated, the only problem is that we don't want to be only menial laborers any more."

> "The educational system in this country has been a monolingual, monocultural educational system primarily designed to exclude people who did not fit the mold; and it has worked very well with us. We don't fit the mold!"

> "Our schools are vocationally oriented. There's the attitude that you're good with your hands. Your name is Hernandez, go to shop. We're herded into shop courses, and we can't get out!"*

# Reappraisal of Responsibility for Minority Group Conditions

That the dominant society and its institutions have sustained and prolonged conditions which trap minority groups is a disturbing, if not threatening, idea. It is much easier to avoid conflict and guilt by assuming that the responsibility for failure (or success) lay with a minority group or the individuals who comprise it. From several sources, not the least of which is the burgeoning Mexican-American intellectual, it has become apparent that no longer can the dominant society, the school, or educators as individuals enjoy the luxury of absolution.

> "Peoples and cultures do not evolve or ever exist as isolated or isolable entities, participating only in their own histories, independent of the world around

---

* The author wishes to express appreciation to Mr. A. J. Gary Mitchell for the use of interviews on his movie sound track, "Chicano," BFA Educational Media, 2211 Michigan Av., Santa Monica, California 90404.

them, and therefore responsible only to themselves. . . . In this light it need no longer be said that historically, exploitation and oppression have required complicity with members of an exploited group of people. . . . In recent years the mystique of culture has been expanded to imply the poverty-stricken of society. Hence the suggestion has been made that the ways of poverty are also insolable and, therefore, evolving an independent history. Any slum-dwelling pimp or prostitute knows better as they look over their uptown clientele, pay off the police, and work the nightclubs."[5]

The use of stereotypes about Mexican Americans' inherent characteristics or cultural traits cannot be used to explain the economic hardships and educational failures of Mexican Americans. More and more Anglos are joining Mexican Americans in rejecting such theories and propounding the concept that the responsibility for social conditions rests with those in power. The "new" Mexican American's definition of democracy includes the idea that the dominant group shares responsibility for the life-style of minorities.

Many studies and investigations have clearly shown that the failure of the Mexican-American school child cannot be blamed on the *pupil* who cannot learn, the *family* that does not care, or the *group* that will not acculturate. Rather, such studies indicated that the educational establishment must assume a large share of the responsibility—*teachers* who are ineffective, the *school system* which is too slow to restructure itself to meet pupils' needs, the *profession* which has not developed adequate theory and teaching models.

To be sure, Mexican Americans have clung to their life-style with unusual tenacity. The question, then, is why haven't they adopted a Horatio Alger pattern of success typical of other immigrant groups. Some Mexican Americans will offer an historical answer. They will remind us that they were not immigrants to the Southwest; their forefathers settled the territory. The "Americano" intruded, conquered and occupied their land, and ultimately excluded them from participation in the new society.

Others will point to the contemporary economic scene and proximity to Mexico as being major factors in keeping their Mexican culture alive. Easy access across the border from Southwestern United States allows frequent visitation and renewal of family ties and tradition.

Because of its proximity and internal economic conditions, Mexico provides American industry and agriculture with a willing and continuous source of cheap labor. These new immigrants not only transplant and adapt their Mexican culture in the United States, but also renew such Anglo stereotypes of Mexican Americans as their being foreign, uneducated, unskilled, and dependent. As these traits are generalized to apply to all Mexican Americans, the group continues to occupy a low social status.

Within the Mexican-American community, the new immigrants create a complex dilemma. They may be relatives whom native-born Mexican Americans feel obligated to protect and assist. At the same time, the immigrants depress the standard of living of the entire community by working for lower wages. The cycle of poverty, segregation, and powerlessness may be repeated for generations, and the traditional mores of a folk culture may be maintained out of necessity.

However, most Mexican Americans agree that they retain certain of their cultural values and traditions by choice. For example, most Mexican Americans believe that it is a good thing to value one's family above business or career, that to have an emotional experience and express feelings openly is healthy, or that one should value the individual over the institution. They feel these values are superior to alternatives even if the alternatives may be conducive to material success in the Anglo culture.

# The Case for Cultural Pluralism

Whether it is by necessity, circumstance, imposition, or choice, a Mexican-American culture exists, and schools are being asked to recognize this culture formally through curriculum content, educational programs, and instructional techniques.

Many Mexican Americans and other minority groups are requesting public schools to educate toward cultural pluralism, rather than cultural conformity. These Mexican Americans feel the democratic code which emphasizes majority rule has been overworked and that concern for the individual must be reinstated. Educators are being asked to apply to minorities the democratic principle that *each individual* be developed to his highest potential so that he may enrich the general society. For many Mexican Americans, this potential includes an understanding of his heritage, command of the Spanish language, and the academic skills to assume leadership roles in adult society.

To insure that his unique qualities are recognized and nurtured, Mexican Americans are demanding effective and significant participation in the decision making process at all levels of planning. The conflicts possible in such areas as educational objectives, curriculum emphasis, teacher selection, and training and promotion are obvious, considering the various points of view which may be represented.

CONFLICT OVER METHODS AND PROCEDURES    However, there is still another area of conflict which will become apparent as the challenge of the Mexican-American student is explored. This area involves professional judgment and preference concerning curriculum development, teaching techniques, evaluation, instructional aids, and school organization. No complete body of research exists to validate which teaching method works best with Mexican-American students, whch type of curriculum best motivates these students to learn, which class organization best results in increased achievement. Therefore, most practical suggestions for teachers have to be inferred from what is known about Mexican-American students through available research and experience.

The suggestions and ideas which follow in this guide are, therefore, open to criticism and disagreement. This book does not attempt to be a panacea to resolve all the conflicts involved in working with Mexican-American students. Rather, it is intended to stimulate teachers, administrators, and parents to become involved and concerned with educational processes which may be unfamiliar to them. In doing so, it is hoped that teachers and parents will devise new and better procedures to meet local needs, and that this guide will be only one of many constructive efforts to meet the challenge.

# Conditions Conducive To Meeting the Challenge

Though conflicts are inevitable, the third basic premise of this text is that conditions in the general society and within the profession are conducive to meeting the challenge of culturally different students.

CONDITIONS CONDUCIVE TO CHANGE    In the general society, two outstanding changes have occurred which should aid efforts to meet the challenge. The first involves the organization of Mexican Americans into effective pressure groups able to make their needs known and bring about change. Secondly, and closely related, is the awakening of national interest and concern over the plight of Mexican-American citizens. Increased federal and state legislative appropriations to stimulate and maintain innovative educational programs are beginning to have some impact upon school systems.

Today, questionable stereotypes of passivity and disorganization cannot be applied to Mexican Americans. Throughout the United States, and most noticeably in the Southwestern states of California, Texas, New Mexico, Arizona, and Colorado, where Mexican Americans comprise 13 per cent of the total population, Spanish-speaking citizens are organizing. From farms and migrant camps to elementary schools and college campuses, one senses a singleness of purpose, a commitment to improve their situation. Often individuals of Mexican descent who may have left the Mexican-American community are being drawn back to work for *La Causa* (the cause).

Though there has always been a form of organization in the Mexican-American *barrio* (neighborhood), that organization is becoming more visible and vocal within the larger community. The social, economic, and educational problems long felt in the barrios are being voiced, particularly in matters concerning employment, education, and politics.

HELP FROM THE FEDERAL GOVERNMENT    The fact that voices from the barrio are being heard at top levels of government became apparent in 1967 when President Lyndon B. Johnson established a Cabinet Committee on Opportunities for Spanish-Speaking People. And the importance with which national leaders are now approaching problems of Mexican Americans is reflected in the committee's membership: the Secretaries of Agriculture; Labor; Health, Education, and Welfare; Housing and Urban Development; and Treasury; the Attorney General of the United States; the Director of the Office of Economic Opportunity Commission; the Administrator of the Small Business Administration; and the Commissioner of the U. S. Equal Employment Opportunity Commission concerned with Spanish-Speaking Americans.

The purpose of the committee, to which the President named Vincente T. Ximenes as chairman, were: (1) to hear solutions to problems of Mexican Americans; (2) to assure that Federal programs were reaching Mexican Americans and providing the assistance they needed; (3) to seek out new programs that were unique to the Mexican-American community.

In 1969, this committee became a statutory Cabinet committee and President Nixon reiterated federal concern:

"In signing this bill, I reaffirm the concern of this government for providing equal opportunity to all Spanish-speaking Americans . . . Many members of this significant minority group have been too long denied genuine, equal opportunity . . ."[6]

Under the Nixon administration, the committee was strengthened by: (1) removing it from complete presidential control and making it responsible to the Congress for a period of five years after which it must be reestablished through legislation; (2) providing funds to assure its continuity; (3) broadening its scope to include all Spanish-speaking citizens.

At the same time, however, the committee became essentially an advisory one, and therefore open to biting criticism from many Mexican-American leaders and legislators, such as Henry B. Gonzalez, a Texas Congressman, who called it:

"A token, a false hope and a vague promise. This bill provides no substantive programs; all it does is create a committee to research, to study and to advise. It has no powers to act and none to compel action . . . It may well be that this agency will in fact imprison hope and freeze into permanence the injustices that afflict the Spanish surnamed."[7]

Whether the committee will achieve its goal as chief advocate for the betterment of the Spanish-speaking peoples of the United States or formalize injustice remains to be seen. Nevertheless, it is clear that the term "invisible minority" once used to describe Spanish-speaking citizens is no longer applicable.

IS POLITICAL INVOLVEMENT THE ANSWER?   Today, there are many who believe that Mexican Americans, themselves, will probably supply most of the stimulus and many

**11**

of the resources to meet the challenge of educating their children effectively. In the terms of a Mexican-American parent who expressed her belief:

> "As you can see, some of us are going into politics. And there will be more coming because we're good! Little by little things will change. We'll be able to express our own feelings, what we really need, and what we really want."

The young Chicanos in high school and college express what is happening in somewhat different terms. They rely on different means for bringing about change.

> "The Chicano is beginning to realize the value of education; he's walking out *not* because he doesn't want education, but because *he wants it more*. He knows he's getting a second class education, and he won't stand for it any more."

> "We know how to get action! Take the East Los Angeles High School walkouts. After the disciplinary action of the police, the Mexican-American community came to the defense of the students; they realized the need for unity. Sometimes *it takes a riot* to bring people to their senses."

A MULTI-RESOURCE APPROACH TO MEET THE CHALLENGE    The means selected for change by the majority of Mexican Americans in the decades to come will depend to a large extent upon the effectiveness of education. To be effective, educators need to draw upon all the resources available, including the Mexican-American community; they need to think in terms of preparing all teachers to meet individual differences of their students. In the Southwest, this means providing all teachers opportunities to become acquainted with and sensitive to the cultural background that over two million Mexican-American students bring to the classroom.

Consistent with that goal, this book is offered as a tangible effort to speed the process of change. Its major purpose is to help teachers and administrators realize the nature and depth of the challenge provided by Mexican-American students and to suggest some practical means for meeting this challenge in ways that are sensitive to the students' personal and social needs.

In order to do this, we will first consider the Mexican-American student in relation to the school and the teacher. Who is he? What might his cultural background be? How and why is he different from other students? Can any good teacher work successfully with Mexican-American students? How does the school often prevent the Mexican-American student from learning? Who is the "new" Chicano student? The exploration of these questions will comprise the first section of the text and will provide a background for suggested changes in school organization, methodology, and curriculum.

The second section will include practical and specific suggestions to teachers. Special emphasis will be given to two areas of the curriculum which are critical to Mexican-American students—language development and understanding of self and heritage in

12

relation to the total society. The principles of education and methodology suggested will be illustrated through a series of lessons suitable for upper grade or junior high school students. The lessons will be developed in Spanish as well as English so as to encourage bilingual techniques of instruction.

The major goals to be implemented in these lessons are: (1) curriculum content relevant to Mexican-American students; (2) continuity of learning activities toward specified, short-term educational objectives; (3) activities oriented toward language development; (4) inquiry strategies of teaching; (5) motivational activities designed with specific concern for affective learnings or attitude development.

Finally, a major portion of the text is designed to help teachers create other teaching strategies to meet their local needs. At strategic points, teacher and student bibliographies will be included along with sources for instructional aids and media to motivate students who have reading handicaps.

In attempting to suggest effective education for Mexican-American students, it is hoped that many of the ideas, teaching strategies, and resources will be useful to other students and teachers who wish to develop intercultural understanding.

# 2

# WHO IS THE MEXICAN AMERICAN?
## An Historical Perspective

## I Am Joaquin

I am Joaquin,
Lost in a world of confusion,
Caught up in a whirl of an
          Anglo society,
Confused by the rules,
Scorned by attitudes,
Suppressed by manipulations,
And destroyed by modern society.
My fathers
  have lost the economic battle
and won
  the struggle of cultural survival.
And now!
  I must choose
         Between
the paradox of
Victory of the spirit
despite physical hunger
         Or

    to exist in the grasp
of American social *neurosis*,
sterilization of the soul
  and a full stomach.

Yes,
I have come a long way to nowhere,
Unwillingly dragged by that
  monstrous, technical
  industrial giant called
         Progress
and Anglo success. . . .
  I look at myself.
    I watch my brothers.
      I shed tears of sorrow.
      I sow seeds of hate.
  I withdraw to the safety within the
Circle of life. . . .
         MY OWN PEOPLE

In his epic poem, *I Am Joaquin,* Rodolfo Gonzales captures the essence of the Mexican-American today—his pride, history, strength, diversity, confusion, and economic and social plight. Other stanzas from the poem appear later to illustrate important historical elements from the Mexican American's background which provide insights to the question: Who is the Mexican American?

Three other perspectives of the Mexican American will be provided as background to answer this question. The second area considers the larger, contemporary social milieu of

14

which the Mexican-American student is a part; it is the cultural-ecological perspective (Chapter 3). The third and fourth areas to be presented in Chapter 4 deal with the teacher's perspective of the American student and the students' perspective of themselves. Together, these differing perspectives form a rationate for the suggested changes in curriculum and methodology which the author proposes.

# Old and New Worlds Meet

A PROUD HERITAGE   The Mexican American is a true blend of the Old and New Worlds, so an historical perspective must begin in both Spain and America. His is a proud heritage that traces its roots to both the diverse races and rich cultures of the Hispanic peninsula and to the highly-developed Indian civilizations that existed in Mexico long before Columbus and other early Spanish explorers came to the New World.

SPANISH ORIGINS   In Spain, successive waves of Celtic, Phoenician, Greek, and Roman conquerors mingled with Iberian peoples and created a culture that was further enriched by the Moslems and Sephardic Jews. Unification of the peninsula under Ferdinand of Aragon and Isabella of Castile led to a cultural and intellectual development unparalleled in Europe during the 16th and 17th centuries.

INDIAN ORIGINS   The Spanish heritage brought to the New World by the Conquistadors continued to emerge and change as it came in contact with the highly developed Mesoamerican Indian civilizations. Though one can appreciate the intellectual life and political glories of Spain, it was the Indian peoples of the New World who provided the base of culture and life from which contemporary Mexican Americans emerged. Numerically, it was inconceivable that the Spanish culture or the "pure Spaniard" could be maintained. A relatively small group of Spaniards existed among over six million Indians. Though the Indians were defeated, they adapted and blended the Spanish culture with their own. A Mexican culture evolved; a Mexican of various racial mixtures emerged.

A NEW RACE EMERGES   Essentially, three races combined to form the new race or La Raza.* The Indian and Spaniard united to form the Mestizo (the largest racial group

---

* Literally means "the race" but a variety of meanings are involved in the concept. One meaning is derived from the works of José Vasconcelos, a noted Mexican author and educator. In *La Raza Cósmica*, Vasconcelos espoused the theory that miscegenation forms vigorous races. In his *Indolgía* he applied the theory directly to the people of Mexico. Other meanings go beyond race to include a common bond of culture and heritage between Spanish speaking people. In the Southwest "la raza" refers to those individuals who are actively engaged in the movement to improve social conditions of the Mexican American.

today); Indian and Negro produced the Zambo; Spaniard and Negro, the Mulatto. Consistent with Spanish culture, the Spaniard born in Spain, the Gauchupín, retained the highest social status. Criollos, Spaniards born in the New World, occupied the next highest social status, while those of mixed racial parentage remained at the bottom of the social scale. The centuries of suffering endured by the Indians at the hands of the Spanish, have made Cortés, symbol of the Conquistador, a victor but not a hero in Mexican history.

Traditionally, some Mexican Americans perpetuated a similar social stratification. Other Mexican Americans, particularly in New Mexico territory, culturally related to Spain rather than Mexico because geographic isolation throughout the colonial period resulted in cultural isolation from Mexico.

Even today, traditions, language patterns, music, and foods in New Mexico are reminiscent of archaic Spain. It is one reason why New Mexicans of Spanish descent wish to be known as Hispanic Americans, not Mexican Americans. However, it is realistic to assume that many Mexican Americans throughout the United States call themselves "Spanish" because it is politically, socially, and economically wise to do so.

Today, more and more Mexican Americans are beginning to recognize with pride the Indian cultures which are a part of their heritage. They point out that while the Iberian Peninsula was being invaded by waves of different peoples, and Roman Legions finally united the peninsula only to lose it again to the barbarians from the north, great civilizations existed in the New World. Cities like Teotihuacán were established that made European cities look like villages by comparison. There were philosophies of thought, highly structured social systems, governments, numeration systems, sciences, and highly developed art forms. There were statesmen and heroes. To have descended from these great civilizations is now a source of pride. And to be racially mixed, a member of *La Raza*, is considered a source of virility and strength.

# The Role of Mexican History in Shaping the Character of the Mexican American

---

Unquestionably, many significant events in Mexican history helped to shape the character of the Mexican people and, of course, of their descendants, the Mexican Americans. Many of the attitudes, convictions, and ideas about freedom, equality, justice, and economic opportunities which many Mexican Americans are discussing today are probably an inheritance, at least in part, from such great Mexican leaders as Father Miguel Hidalgo y Costilla and Benito Pablo Juárez.

Mexico's early history as a colony of Spain is also particular meaningful to Mexican Americans because it was during that time that the Spanish-Mexican colonists laid cultural foundations which have persisted to the present. It was a significant period also because Old World animosities, distrust, and rivalries were transplanted to the New World. The barriers of language and religion were reflected in differing philosophies and ways of life that even today distinguish a Protestant Anglo culture from a Catholic Mexican-American culture.

INTERNAL TROUBLES AND WAR WITH THE U. S. FOLLOW INDEPENDENCE    Mexico's struggle for independence from Spanish and Criollo oppression has special significance for Mexican Americans. It begins the movement of a brave people toward freedom and provides them with some of their greatest heroes. The Revolution of 1810, led by Father Hidalgo, began with a rebellion on September 16th. Although Father Hidalgo was a Spaniard, he deplored poverty, inequality, and injustice in Mexico and called for land reforms, liberty, justice, and equality for the common people. Though a period of revolt and militarism followed and actual independence did not come until 1921, Father Hidalgo's cry to arms, *El Grito,* is a revered event. September 16th is still a celebrated holiday for both Mexicans and Mexican Americans.

The troubled times which followed independence from Spain were complicated by the Texas Wars which started in 1836 and culminated with the declaration of war between Mexico and the United States in 1846. During the war and the period that followed, the foundation was laid for the mistrust and hatred that would characterize Mexican (later Mexican American) and Anglo relationships for generations to come.

The Treaty of Guadalupe Hidalgo in 1848 granted to the United States 525,000 square miles of territory, and Mexican citizens in that territory became citizens of the United States.

> "The Mexicans in the territories aforesaid, . . . shall be incorporated into the Union of the United States, and admitted as soon as possible, according to the principles of the federal constitution, to the enjoyment of all rights of citizens of the United States. In the meantime they shall be maintained and protected in the enjoyment of their liberty, their property, and civil rights now vested in them according to Mexican laws. With respect to political rights, their condition shall be in an equality with that of the inhabitants of the other territories of the United States. . . .

> Article LX
> Treaty of Guadalupe Hidalgo

In spite of the terms of the treaty, most new Mexican Americans were treated more like a conquered people than like citizens. Most of the new citizens lost their political power and wealth, and, eventually, many were even denied the right of the ballot. Too often Anglos considered the Mexican Americans to be lazy, cowardly, and villanous. Histories of the period, written from a U. S. point of view, generally perpetuated the stereotypes, a gross distortion of history which ignored the Mexicans' acts of valor and the contributions that these new citizens of the U. S. made in the states carved from the territory the U. S. gained through the Treaty of Guadalupe Hidalgo.

> *Equality is but a word,*
> *the Treaty of Hidalgo has been*
> *broken*
> *and is but another treacherous*
> *promise*
> *My land is lost*
> *and stolen,*
> *My culture has been raped,*
> *I lengthen*
> *the line at the welfare door*
> *and fill the Jails with crime*
> *These then*
> *are the rewards*
> *this society has*
> *For sons of Chiefs*
> *and Kings*
> *and bloody Revolutionists.*

INVASION INTERRUPTS REFORM   The period immediately after war with the U. S. was rich with reform (*La Reforma*), but torn by internal strife, civil war, and foreign intervention. Benito Juárez became one of the most renowned Mexican heroes of all time. A Zapotec Indian, he became president for the first time in 1855 and symbolized the rise of the Indian to a position of leadership in Mexico. In 1857, a new constitution was written to solve some of the country's problems; it called for land reform, separation of church and state, and protection against foreign intervention. However, reform was interrupted by a French invasion which had the tacit approval of the governments of both England and Spain.

Before Juárez became president, Mexico had become deeply indebted to France and several other European powers. In an effort to alleviate an economic crisis that gripped his country, Juárez stopped payments on loans to the European nations. In retaliation, France invaded Mexico and established Maximilian, an Austrian Archduke, as Emperor.

Mexicans again heard a call to arms and rose up to drive out Maximilian and the French troops. The defeat of the French troops in Puebla on the Fifth of May (*Cinco de Mayo*) gave Mexico a famous, almost legendary victory. A poorly equipped, poorly trained, but brave Mexican army defeated a highly trained army that was considered one of the finest in Europe. And *Cinco de Mayo* became one of Mexico's great holidays—a holiday also widely celebrated by Mexican Americans, for it represents the brave and valiant efforts of an oppressed people to throw off the yoke of a foreign power.

DICTATORSHIP AND ANOTHER REVOLUTION    After the defeat of the French, Juárez was again elected president and continued his reform. A few years after his death, however, Porfirio Díaz seized power and brought political stability under a virtual dictatorship. From the time he assumed the presidency in 1876, Mexico reaped the benefits of a stable government. The political unrest and intrigue that had followed the death of Juárez was ended, but Mexico paid the price of a capitalistic economic base founded largely upon foreign investors. A new class society developed with the educated, elite, and privileged-class Criollos at one end of the scale and the uneducated masses, usually Mestizo or Indian, at the other. Díaz' presidency ended in 1910 when the people of Mexico began a long, bloody, ten-year struggle against tyrannical government and economic oppression. Guerilla armies organized and roamed across Mexico, and colorful legendary heroes, such as Emiliano Zapata, Pancho Villa, and Alvaro Obregón rose to lead the people. The literature, history, and art forms of Mexico recorded many acts of valor in what some historians have called the Epic Revolution of Mexico.

# Immigration in the Twentieth Century

Significantly, the first great wave of Mexican immigration to the United States in the twentieth century began the same year as the Epic Revolution. There seems little doubt that political unrest, violence, and economic deprivation were key factors that motivated many of the immigrants in the early years of this century. Many of the members of the privileged classes left seeking refuge from the revolutionaries, probably intending to return from exile as soon as it was safe to do so. Others, however, left to escape the depressed economy, hoping to find a new home and better way of life in the U. S.

THREE WAVES OF IMMIGRATION    Immigration of Mexicans to the U. S. was concentrated in three waves of relatively short periods each (1910-1920, 1920-1930, 1950-1960) that corresponded to periods of economic growth and depression in the United States and Mexico. Each successive wave brought a different type of immigrant from varied geographic regions and social strata in Mexico to work in specific vocations and locations in the United States.

The first wave of immigrants came in response to a large land reclamation project in the Southwest that opened up new agricultural lands and increased the need for more laborers. Most of these refugees from economic depression and political uncertainty and unrest in their country were unskilled, rural inhabitants who became field laborers in the United States. Only a few found their way to northern cities like Chicago, Gary, and Detroit where they were employed in steel mills, meat packing plants, and automobile factories. The few nonagricultural jobs available to Mexicans in the Southwest were connected with the railroads.[1]

The depression years in the United States (approximately 1929-1940) resulted in large scale deportation of Mexican-American families. Many times family members who were American citizens were deported without concern for individual rights. The bitterness and fear of deportation developed at that time remains a matter of grave concern in Mexican-American communities today.

The two world wars and resultant labor shortages led to another type of Mexican who lived and worked in the United States and who often immigrated permanently through legal or illegal means. Special government programs and, finally, federal legislation encouraged the use of Mexicans as contract labor. In 1942 and 1943, Mexican farm and railroad laborers were brought to the United States under agreements negotiated through the U. S. Farm Security Administration and the Mexican government. From 1943 through 1947, the program was administered by the War Food Administration and "some 361,500 workers, only a few thousand of whom were not Mexicans"[2] came to the United States.

During these years, the two governments set standards for housing, wages, transportation, length of employment, working conditions, and treatment of laborers. Some states were blacklisted by the Mexican government for discriminatory practices; but, in general, the *bracero* distinguished himself as a valuable worker. However, controls over the program proved increasingly difficult to enforce; conditions deteriorated, and the program was terminated in 1951.

That same year, however, Congress enacted Public Law 78, The Bracero Act, which formalized the use of Mexican labor. Each year the number of Braceros entering the United States increased. In 1956, 460,000 entered; in 1959, 445,000 more were admitted to work, particularly in the fields of California.

According to the law, braceros were to be used in "essential crops" and paid the "prevailing wage." Transportation, work guarantees, housing, insurance, medical care, subsistence when illness occurred, were provided. Resistance to the program by domestic labor and farm groups was consistent and, at times, dramatic. Finally, in January, 1964, the program was terminated.

However, during the following year, 1965, it is estimated that at least 20,000 more Mexican agricultural workers were brought to the United States to work as aliens under the Immigration Law, Public Law 414.[3] This law enabled a farmer to request a Mexican National to work for him as a permanent entrant. Issued a green identification card, this worker became known as a "green carder."

> "The green card worker is a permanent resident alien not under the protection of an inter-governmental agreement. He is initially brought into the country at the request of an employer but is essentially on the same competitive basis as U.S. workers . . . (He) may remain in the United States indefinitely and . . . may bring his family with him.[4]

Still other arrangements to obtain laborers from Mexico provide permits to aliens who cross the border frequently or who commute each day between the United States and Mexico. These aliens are issued a blue card ("blue carders") and enter in considerable number along the border.

Another type of entrant is the "white carder" who holds a visitor's permit and may stay in the United States for only 72 hours. Though a "white carder" is not supposed to work, it is believed that many do when the opportunity presents itself.

THE EFFECTS OF CONTINUOUS IMMIGRATION    The effects of these recent and continuous immigrations on the standard of living of second and third generation Mexican Americans, especially farm workers, domestic workers, and others in unskilled jobs, is particularly important. Recent Mexican immigrants, eager for jobs of any kind, will often work for less pay, and thereby depress the wage scale. Throughout the Southwest, it is an open secret that many employers prefer to hire Mexicans whom they know are illegally in the United States, instead of Mexican-American citizens. Under constant fear of exposure and deportation, these Mexican citizens will work for less pay and cause the employer little trouble. They constitute a source of labor that can readily be exploited to the detriment of Mexican-American citizens who need jobs.

There are also subtle effects of continuous immigration upon the Mexican-American community which are equally important. There exists within the community a social system apart from Anglo society. Often, established Mexican-American families do not interact with immigrants who are not family members from their locality in Mexico, or of equal social status. At times, newer immigrants are exploited by those who preceded them. Historically, for these and many other reasons, internal organization of Mexican Americans has been difficult, and, therefore, power to implement demands within the general society has been virtually impossible.

# The Mexican American in American Society Today

A MOVE TOWARD COHESIVENESS    In recent years, the organization of Mexican Americans into a cohesive and effective ethnic group has been meeting with increasing success for three reasons. The first is related to the changing attitudes about Mexican Americans who served in World Wars I and II and the conflicts that followed. The second is an outgrowth of their more active role in the labor movement, and the third is their involvement in the civil rights movement through which they struggle for equality and justice in the dominant society.

> *Now*
> *I bleed in some smelly cell*
> *from club.*
> *or gun.*
> *or tyranny.*

*I bleed as the vicious gloves of hunger*
   *cut my face and eyes,*
*as I fight my way from stinking Barrios*
   *to the glamour of the Ring*
      *and lights of fame*
         *or mutilated sorrow.*
*My blood runs pure on the ice caked*
*hills of the Alaskan Isles,*
*on the corpse strewn beach of Normandy,*
*the foreign land of Korea*
               *and now*
                     *Viet Nam.*

*I shed tears of anguish*
*as I see my children disappear*
*behind the shroud of mediocrity*
*never to look back to remember me.*
*I have endured in the rugged*
   *mountains of our country*
*I have survived the toils and slavery*
   *of the fields.*
         *I have existed*
*in the barrios of the city,*
*in the suburbs of bigotry,*
*in the mines of social snobbery,*
*in the prisons of dejection*
*in the muck of exploitation*
*and*
*in the fierce heat of racial hatred.*
*And now the trumpet sounds,*
*The music of the people stirs the*
               *Revolution,*
*Like a sleeping giant it slowly*
*rears its head*
*to the sound of*
            *Tramping feet*
            *Clamoring voices*
            *Mariachi strains*
      *The smell of chile verde and*
      *Soft brown eyes of expectation for a*
                     *better life.*

THE MEXICAN-AMERICAN SOLDIER: A CHANGE IN SELF-IMAGE   Mexican Americans have distinguished themselves as soldiers of the United States. During World War II and the Korean War, they had a very impressive record with 17 Congressional Medal of Honor winners and recognition as being one of the most highly decorated ethnic groups. Their participation in every major conflict has continued. Because of their low economic status and comparative youth, a disproportionate number of Mexican Americans have been drafted, and they have suffered a higher percentage of casualties than any other population group. In 1961-1962, Mexican Americans comprised 20 percent of the total American losses in Vietnam, while they comprised only 11 percent of the population in the Southwest.

In spite of the suffering and the losses, Mexican Americans gained certain advantages from military service. First, they were no longer "Mexicans" to the general population, nor to themselves. They were hypenated "Mexican-Americans" to many and just "Americans" to others at home and abroad. In some ways, they had reached the point of no return; they were no longer a part of Mexican society and had to become a member of American society. Though there were some setbacks during the war, such as the Zoot Suit riots of 1943, the military service afforded a means for more positive identification and the opportunity for social mobility.

Following the war, many Mexican Americans took advantage of postwar benefits in education and business. For many, these benefits accelerated cultural assimilation and acceptance into Anglo society. At the same time, however, the growth of Mexican-American organizations in politics, education, and labor indicated a growing ethnicity and awareness of the need for organization in order to work effectively within Anglo society.

> *Here I stand*
> *before the Court of Justice*
> *Guilty*
> *for all the glory of my Raza*
> *to be sentenced to despair.*
> *Here I stand*
> *Poor in money*
> *Arrogant in pride*
> *Bold with Machismo*
> *Rich in courage*
> *and*
> *Wealthy in spirit and faith.*
> *My knees are caked with mud.*
> *My hands calloused from the hoe.*
> *I have made the Anglo rich*

INCREASING INVOLVEMENT IN THE LABOR MOVEMENT  Many Mexican Americans feel that the most critical area in which they need organization in order to improve living conditions is labor. While Mexican Americans have a long history in the American labor movement, it is only in recent years that large numbers of them have become active in labor organizations. The first involvement of the Mexican Americans in the labor movement was in 1883 when cowboys in the Panhandle of Texas went on strike. In 1902, sugar-beet workers went on strike in California. In 1922, Mexican field workers sought to organize in Fresno and eventually formed *La Confederacion de Uniones Obreras.* Strikes followed in 1928; and in 1933, seven-thousand Mexican-American agricultural workers struck in Los Angeles County. During the 1930's, Mexican Americans were striking in Arizona, New Mexico, Texas, Idaho, Colorado, Washington, and Michigan. Other labor movements in the coal mines of New Mexico resulted in a labor union called *La Liga Obrera de Habla Espanola* with a membership of 8,000. Still other strikes involved the ranches of Texas and citrus groves in California. Thousands upon thousands of Mexican and Mexican-American workers actively sought to better their working conditions against overwhelming forces and a constant threat of deportation.[5]

However, the most recent movement to organize Mexican-American agricultural workers has received national and international attention which, to a great degree, can be attributed to the charismatic leadership of Cesar Chavez. A migrant worker with a seventh grade education, Chavez has become one of the most powerful union organizers in the nation. He demonstrated the ability to capture the loyalty and cooperation of his followers against seemingly impossible odds. An advocate of nonviolence, and an opponent of organization along racial lines, Cesar Chavez has devoted his life to unifying workers around the common cause of unionism.

Perhaps Cesar Chavez' own statements, which have been eloquent and clear, are best used to describe his philosophy. In answering groups which urged him to use violence to speed settlement of the 1968 grape strike, he said, "If we had used violence, we would have won contracts long ago, but they wouldn't be lasting, because we wouldn't have won respect."[6] In explaining his own life of dedication to *La Causa,* this statement has become a classic:

> "I am convinced that the truest act of courage, the strongest act of manliness is
> to sacrifice ourselves for others in a totally nonviolent struggle for justice. To
> be a man is to suffer for others. God help us to be men."[7]

In spite of his idealistic philosophy, Cesar Chavez has proven to be a tough, effective crusader. Since 1962, when he organized the National Farm Workers Association, he has successfully led its membership through the 1966 strike against grape growers, the grape boycott of 1967-1970, and the lettuce boycott of 1971. During that time, his union has received national support and successfully negotiated contracts with some of the largest growers in the nation. Equally important, his crusade has dramatized the plight of all agricultural laborers.

Whether his efforts are sustained will depend upon the outcome of court battles surrounding the legality of the boycotts and the effectiveness of his opponents, who see him as a troublemaker and a violent, power-hungry racist. Nevertheless, his leadership has made him a special kind of hero to Mexican Americans, young and old. A young Chicano student recently analyzed Cesar Chavez' appeal in the following manner:

"Cesar Chavez is not so much respected for his ideology, but because of his personal appeal, his sincerity, his humbleness, and his humanity. A lot of Chicanos don't agree with all of his ideas. He espouses the non-violent approach, such as the boycott, and I'm not so sure that technique is effective. Some Chicano students see him as an old person, and that means he's out of it.

"What's most important is that he is very acceptable to the Mexican-American community. Chavez is a good Catholic, and the Mexican people are engrained with the Catholic church. Chavez believes that a good Catholic doesn't have to tolerate the injustices of the system."[8]

*"Basta"*—A CHICANO MOVEMENT IS BORN   Many young Mexican Americans feel that the most exciting, promising, and progressive period of their history is currently being written. They point out that they are a young population group with an average age of 20.5 as compared to 28.0 for the total population of the United States. Furthermore, they feel they are a generation aware of their minority group status with all the concommitant social and psychological problems that accompany it. Their attitude is one of *"Basta"* (Enough) and the militancy that was born with the civil rights movement of the sixties has become characteristic of the group of Mexican Americans who prefer to be known as Chicanos.*

Chicanos explain the goals of their social reform movement *(El Movimiento)* as basically the improvement of the economic and social well-being of all Chicanos in a manner that preserves their cultural and personal dignity. Inherent in this goal is the Chicano's identification with the poor, their close involvement with the community or barrio life, which inherently possesses Mexican culture, and a realistic recognition that socialization processes in the United States have produced neither Mexicans nor Americans, but a mixture of both. In the words of one Chicano leader:

"Chicanos are not identified with all Mexican Americans but basically with the poor Mexican Americans. We are identified with the worker; Chicanos want to do something to eliminate the injustices of the system as these work against the Mexican American. American society as it exists today lends itself to group association, to class association, to class struggle, not to individual struggle. You see we are Mexican Americans; we are a member of the group. We are labeled as a group by the rest of society, and more important, we are a member of a

---

* Once a derogatory term signifying poor, uneducated individuals without culture—Mexican or Anglo, Chicano was derived from "Mexicano" with the first syllable dropped and the "x" pronounced "ch." Today it is used to apply to those Mexican Americans actively involved in social reform, a member of "The Movement" *(El Movimiento)*.

class, usually the lower economic class. Therefore, we are not just involved in an individualistic struggle, but in a class struggle.

"We are going to have to work in the barrios and have our own professionals, who have been trained in the general society, go back to the barrio and make sure that the people are enjoying the rights of citizenship as provided under the constitution."[9]

The *Movimiento* involves a cultural as well as a class struggle that is clearly defined in the following statement:

"Chicanos identify with Mexico, not as a nation but as a culture. We are socialized here in this environment by Anglo institutions. We can't be molded into Mexicans, our personalities are different, our behavior is different, our outlook on life is different from the Mexican. We cannot reject ourselves and part of us is Anglo whether we admit is or not. We are Americans. Although we want to change the existing system with a new ideology and a new economic system, we cannot change our personality.

"We want to accept ourselves as having historical roots in Mexico, of being descendants of a culture that is not inferior. We want to appreciate those things of which we are descendants, but also, we will have to appreciate those things which are not Mexican."[10]

The methods by which Chicanos seek to bring about their social revolution varies with their leaders and the situation. Some Chicanos work through existing social structures of government, church, and educational institutions. Others advocate the "any means necessary" approach to bring about change. One leader put it as follows:

"Violence can be used as the last means to achieve certain ends but not as an end in itself. The 'Revolution', as far as Chicanos are concerned is not an attempt to pick up arms and fight to regain territory, as much as it is a quest to seek a new perception of one's self and to create within the larger society a new image for one's group."[11]

Chicanos, however, recognize some basic problems facing their movement, not the least of which are internal unity, the maintenance of identity within the dominant society apart from the Black American's struggle for civil rights, and the constant dilemma of maintaining ethnic identity while still being able to move freely within the total society. A Chicano leader recently told the author:

"The Black movement really has more unity and more white support. No Black person can escape being black; therefore, he is in some way a part of the movement. Whereas, in the Mexican-American community, you can escape. You can move over more easily into the establishment or into the dominant culture. Furthermore, we cannot identify ourselves so much with a racial background because we are mixed: White, Indian, and Black. We cannot say we are a Brown race. We have to identify with a culture, not with a color. We cannot hate all whites; nor can we condone attacking whites because they are white.

"Our movement has suffered because there has always been present the danger of deportation. This is not a danger in the Black movement. Furthermore, the Black middle class has offered major portions of support in the form of money, organizations, attorneys. We have little support; that's why we can't afford to be as militant as the Blacks.

"A real impetus for the black movement comes from portions of the white community. Whites have opened up the doors for the Blacks because they have a greater sense of guilt about the Blacks. The Chicanos don't have this going for them; they don't make the same impact upon the general society.

"A most basic difference between our two movements is the fact that Blacks are caught in the Black-White syndrome the same as the Whites are. They don't understand the Mexican American—his needs, his low economic position, etc., any more than the Anglos do."[12]

Chicanos and other Mexican Americans recognize the problems involved in trying to maintain ethnic identification and still enjoy social mobility. It is a basic problem for all society and was brought out earlier. Some Chicanos are more optimistic than others about changing the larger society to allow such individual choice. They look upon the barrio as an essential part of preserving that choice, in fact, as the only means to the betterment of life for all.

"The dilemma is to keep the barrio intact and still enable people to filter out into the general society. Unless there is a major change in the social attitude of the general society, the barrio can be destroyed through rezoning, through industrialization, and through urban renewal. This the Chicanos feel would be a great loss.

"On the other hand, if we move into the barrio and attempt to build them up, there is suspicion in the general society that we want separatism. The Chicanos feel that we can exist in our barrios and still be Americans. We want to maintain our cultural individuality, but we want to develop our economic solidarity or conformity. We feel we can become an economic force and a social force for our own betterment. We tried being individuals and moving into the general society and it hasn't helped our people. It's been a long struggle, and we are at the bottom."[13]

27

It remains to be seen whether the Chicanos will be successful in convincing the majority of Mexican Americans that their course is better. Nevertheless militant organizations are growing: *La Raza Unida.* The Crusade for Justice, *Movimiento Estudiantil Chicano de Aztlán, Católicos Por La Raza* are only a few. Leaders are emerging who are particularly appealing to young Mexican Americans: (1) Reies Tijerina, who led the raid against a county courthouse in New Mexico to make a citizen's arrest of the district attorney and claim the land under a Spanish land grant; (2) Rodolfo (Corky) Gonzales, cultural nationalist, who founded the militant organization, Crusade for Justice, and at the first National Chicano Youth Conference proclaimed "The Spiritual Plan of Aztlán" in which Chicano youths claim the Southwest and pledge their revolt against existing conditions in the name of Aztlán, legendary land of the Aztecs; (3) Jose Angel Gutierrez, who founded the independent political party, *La Raza Unida,* in Texas.

Of great significance is the development of the intellectual centers and a body of literature and expression through arts that are Chicano oriented.* These media may provide the means for productive communication and dialogue between Chicanos, middle-class Mexican Americans, and members of the dominant society.

> *And in all the fertile farm lands,*
> *the barren plains,*
> *the mountain villages,*
> *smoke smeared cities*
> *We start to MOVE.*
> *La Raza!*
> *Mejicano!*
> *Expañol!*
> *Latino!*
> *Hispano!*
> *Chicano!*
> *or whatever I call myself,*
> *I look the same*
> *I feel the same*
> *I cry*
> *and*
> *Sing the same*
> *I am the masses of my people and*
> *I refuse to be absorbed.*
> *I am Joaquin*
> *The odds are great*
> *but my spirit is strong*

---

* See Bibliography for Teachers Appendix A, for sources of Chicano literature.

*My faith unbreakable*
*My blood is pure*
*I am Aztec Prince and Christian Christ*
*I SHALL ENDURE!*
*I WILL ENDURE!**

*Rodolfo "Corky" Gonzales*

OTHER CONTEMPORARY ATTITUDES OF MEXICAN AMERICANS    While many Mexican Americans are not active in militant organizations, most take their Mexican heritage seriously and are in agreement with militants on many essential points. Though Mexican Americans played major roles in building the Southwest and maintaining the agriculture on which it is dependent, they feel that Mexican Americans in that area have been economically exploited and often denied equality and justice.

Though they have a rich history in Spain and Mexico, they feel that they have been unrecognized and unappreciated in the United States. They feel either ignored in history or inaccurately recorded as bandits, robbers, romanticized people of the California missions and ranchos, or as Pachucos. Like the militants, those who prefer to be called Mexican Americans feel strongly that equality, economic opportunities, and justice are long overdue. And they feel that distortions of history must be corrected.

WHO, THEN, IS THE MEXICAN AMERICAN?    In summary, from an historical point of view, the Mexican American is:

An individual who has a long, rich history that may be relatively unknown to the average teacher due to language barriers, the long separation of Latin and Anglo cultures, and general historical neglect.

An individual whose group has contributed to American life and letters but has experienced discrimination and little recognition.

An individual who is a composite of many races and civilizations.

An individual who may represent diverse socioeconomic and cultural backgrounds, both in Mexico and the United States.

An individual who represents one of the many waves of immigrants to come from Mexico; a first, second, or third generation American.

An individual who through his music, holidays, and heroes is emotionally identified with the history of Mexico, though he may have little objective or intellectual knowledge of that history.

An individual who may be sensitive to and suffer as a result of historical accounts written in a manner that is biased in favor of Anglo Americans.

---

* The excerpts on this page and the preceding pages in this chapter are taken from "I Am Joaquin," the narrative poem by Rodolfo "Corky" Gonzales, The Crusade for Justice, 1567 Downing Street, Denver, Colorado, and are used by permission of the author.

An individual who may be experiencing a renaissance of pride in his Indian, Spanish, or Mexican beginnings.

An individual who at this point in his history faces more than ever before the dilemma of whether to cut cultural ties with the Mexican portion of his culture and become Anglicized, or maintain that part of him which is Mexican and strive to make the larger society accept his uniqueness.

Against this historical perspective, the contemporary Mexican-American student can be better understood. To a great extent, his present status is a result of his history. However, a concise perspective of his present cultural-ecological characteristics is necessary in order to adapt curriculum and teaching techniques to his needs.

# 3

# A CULTURAL-ECOLOGICAL PERSPECTIVE OF THE MEXICAN-AMERICAN STUDENT

The Mexican American is a part of the total social fabric of the United States, and yet he is an identifiable and sometimes separate part of that structure. He is both a part and set apart. He is a member of a somewhat nebulous entity, a subculture, which has meaning only when compared to an even more abstract set of norms descriptive of the dominant culture. Stated another way:

> The terms "Anglo" and "Hispano" are the heads and the tails of a single coin, a single ethnic system; each term has meaning only as the other is implied. The terms do not define homogeneous entities; they define a relationship.[1]

Relationships between the dominant culture and the Mexican-American subculture have been studied from a variety of viewpoints, and discussions of differences involve such basic concepts of culture as value systems, degree of acculturation, family relationships, and language patterns. In the case of the Mexican-American subculture, it is essential to consider economic status, place of residence, and recency of immigration, as well.

## Factors Influencing Subculture Characteristics

Most important for teachers is the *interpretation* given general subculture characteristics as they are used to afford insights into existing conditions and individual behavior. It is this interpretation of cultural, ecological, and economic characteristics that will be stressed in pursuing an answer to the question "Who is the Mexican-American Student?"

A MATTER OF VALUES    Values involve the individual's beliefs concerning the world and his position in it. They are often generalized ideas closely related to group norms. Sometimes they are almost unconscious assumptions people make about the appropriateness or inappropriateness of ideas and actions. Values, therefore, have a universal referent and a judgmental character. Most important, values generate attitudes and, finally, actions.

Related to school achievement, values have been found to affect student behavior by determining: (1) "the goals toward which his activity is directed; (2) the activities which he sees appropriate for the attainment of these goals; (3) his perception of the feasibility of performing the activities necessary to achieve these goals; (4) his perception of their ultimate attainability."[2]

The Mexican-American student has been described, characterized, and explained in terms of a value system said to be characteristic of his subculture. This "Mexican-American" value system often is compared to an "Anglo" value system and the differences give rise to an infinite number of implications, explanations, and rationalizations. For a number of reasons, this practice has become highly suspect, particularly among Mexican Americans. First, Mexican Americans charge that such comparisons are derived from studies that have employed inadequate sampling techniques or other research designs that can be challenged. Second, a list of contrastive values may encourage stereotyping; individuals may be classified or expected to have the characteristics of the group rather than be recognized as individuals. Third, unqualified lists of value comparisons may lead to an oversimplification of the situation by inferring that there is only one "Mexican-American culture" and one "Anglo culture," when in reality it is usually an Anglo middle class core of values that characterizes one culture and a Mexican folk culture or lower socioeconomic value structure that represents the other. For example, the following comparison of Mexican-American values with Anglo values is derived from several studies and serves to illustrate typical value comparisons.

| *Mexican-American Values* | *Anglo Values* |
| --- | --- |
| Immediate and extended family relationships and responsibilities extremely important. | Family responsibility tempered with duties toward school, work, nonfamily associations. |
| Father's authority considered unquestionable. Authority of elders and church personnel great. | Extensive use of reason in control exercised by parents and other authority figures. Questioning valued. |
| Worth of individual based on family membership and other ascriptive characteristics. | Worth of individual measured upon achievement; universalistic rules which apply to all. |

| | |
|---|---|
| Individual welfare most important. | Welfare of group often placed above individual. Particularistic orientation with exceptions to the rule based upon individual need or status. |
| Orientation toward the satisfaction of present time needs, enjoying life of the present. | Orientation toward satisfaction of future or long term goals. |
| Distinct sex roles with male dominance. | Less distinct sex roles with less restrictions for females. |
| Acceptance of life as it exists. Spiritual and social aspects of life valued. | Emphasis on cause and effect with control over life as it exists. Material aspects of life valued. |
| Affective, emotional relationships valued. (Expressive orientation.) | Objective relationships with purpose valued. (Instrumental orientation.) |

A positive or negative quality can easily be inferred from such lists. For example, Anglo values can be interpreted as positive values because they lead to success within the United States, while Mexican-American values may be given a negative connotation. Consequently, the people who possess said values are also awarded positive or negative qualities; they become superior or inferior human beings. As Octovio Ignacio Roman pointed out in an article in *El Grito: A Journal of Contemporary Mexican American Thought,* comparisons of values can lead to such attitudes as those described below:

> Members of minority groups who have joined in the exploitation of their own group, or in the exploitation of other groups, traditionally have made use of certain words to describe the condition and behavior of those who are beneath them in the social order. . . . Once they occupy some position or role in society that is above abject poverty, they all too often speak of those who remain in such straits as people who are fatalistic, resigned, apathetic, tradition oriented, tradition bound, emotional, impetuous, volatile, affected, non-goal oriented, uncivilized, unacculturated, nonrational, primitive, unorganized, uncompetitive, retarded, underachieving, underveloped, or just plain lazy. . . . They thereby place the reasons or causes of "inferior" *somewhere within the minds, within the culture of those who are economically, politically or educationally out of power.*

> On the other hand, no matter from which group they come, those in power describe their own station in life as resulting directly from goal-oriented behavior, a competitive urge, responsibility, rationality, a long cultural tradition, etc., in short, they place the reasons or causes for their 'success' *somewhere within themselves.*[3]

It is important, then, to interpret carefully social science research data concerning the values of any subculture. Only when such data are combined with other cultural dimensions can it be an effective aid to understanding the Mexican-American student. Never can such data alone be used to rationalize the student's academic and social status or predict an individual's behavior.

DEGREE OF ACCULTURATION    Patterns of belief and behavior which characterize any culture or subculture are dynamic, and the rate of change is accelerated by increased contact and interaction with other cultures. Therefore, one must expect degrees of "Mexicanness" (or "Anglization") to exist among Mexican Americans.

The degree to which Mexican Americans take on the ways of behaving common to the dominant culture depend upon several major conditions. Recently, there has been concerted effort among some Mexican Americans to resist acculturation and retain portions of their Mexican culture, such as their language, art, literature, music, and humanistic values. Generally, however, cultural assimilation of the Mexican American seems to be related to recency or "wave" of immigration, geographic location, ecological patterns within cities, and economic status. All these conditions, in turn, are related to the receptivity of the larger society and the opportunities afforded for assimilation.

Students whose families have recently immigrated from Mexico naturally would be most "Mexican" in cultural orientation. However, even among the "new" arrivals there are important distinctions to be made because they represent various economic and social classes within Mexico. Nevertheless, length of time in the United States or "generation"* is one clue to understanding the cultural characteristics of Mexican-American students; but it is not the single most important variable. Statistics indicate that most Mexican Americans living in the United States are native born (85% in 1960); yet, there are marked differences in acculturation that cannot be related to the "generation" classification.

Ecological patterns within cities and geographic location in the United States appear to be even more critical to the assimilation patterns of Mexican Americans. In certain states and sections within urban centers, the social milieu is more open and assimilation occurs more rapidly. For example, comparative studies between cities within the Southwest reveal that "a second generation Mexican-American man in Los Angeles is generally far more acculturated than a second generation person in a Texas City, such as Corpus Christi. As a consequence, generations of Mexican immigrants are difficult to compare from one city to the other. The social milieu of some agricultural towns, on the other hand, is so repressive and offers so little opportunity for economic or social movement that change from one generation to another is almost imperceptible."[4]

The concept that "generation" is a matter of "place" is helpful in understanding

---

* A useful definition of generation is given by Dr. Joan W. Moore in her book *Mexican Americans:* (1) Third generation, native born of native parents; (2) Second generation, native born of foreign or mixed parentage; (3) First generation, foreign born.

Mexican-American students. Where cultural interaction is not necessary or allowed by either the minority or majority, cultural assimilation does not occur. As an example of the former condition, many Mexican-American families in New Mexico trace their family lineage back to the sixteenth century and consciously keep their Hispanic culture alive. They may be more Hispanic and Mexican in culture than a second generation family in Los Angeles.

In the urban centers, those living within the barrio retain the Mexican culture more than those living in integrated neighborhoods. However, since the maintenance of barrios is largely dependent upon the will of the larger community, assimilation or segregation must be seen as a function of the total environment.

Regardless of conditions thwarting or fostering cultural assimilation, two important concepts emerge. First, Mexican-American students represent various and different stages of acculturation. Therefore, they cannot be classified as having one "Mexican-American" culture. Second, for the individual, the process of acculturation is laden with personal conflict and associated problems. As one Mexican American put it:

> The student's culture, values, identity demand that he be something other than the school or the larger culture desires. Therefore, he has do one of two things, change himself and become an Anglo, which means he has to reject his parents, reject himself, reject his peers and attempt to be someone else. Or he has to remain a "Mexican" and join the ranks of the unemployed, segregated people. Either way is psychologically crippling. There's got to be another way.

Individuals have, indeed, found a variety of ways to live with the conflicts of acculturation; some of the ways are socially acceptable, others are not. Some Mexican Americans become excellent students, still others overcompensate and in adult life become "Super-Anglos". Many seek the security of the barrio. The youth may become part of a "gang" which often is alienated from both cultures. Some individuals vent their frustrations through hostility, aggression, withdrawal, and other antisocial, delinquent, even illegal behavior. Still others make the necessary adjustment with few if any ill effects, though statistics indicating school failure, unemployment, and arrest indicate that a disproportionate number do not. It is essential that educators recognize the seriousness of the conflict and consider the consequences of acculturation to the individual and society.

THE LANGUAGE BARRIER    The Spanish language is often one of the most obvious cultural characteristics of Mexican-American students. In November, 1969, 6,700,000 persons reported Spanish as their native language, and of these, 72.6% were born in the United States. Almost five million persons reported Spanish as their *current* language rather than English. Considering the number of persons using Spanish and that fact that they tend to live in concentrated areas throughout the United States, the chances are good that Mexican-American students will have some degree of familiarity with the language. Though they may speak a dialect of Spanish or may be linguistically handicapped in both Spanish and English, there is a high probability that the students' sound system, vocabulary, and syntax will be largely Spanish or some combination of the two languages. Most important, those people close to the student during his early life are likely to speak Spanish and some form of nonstandard English, if they speak any English at all.

The Mexican-American student's linguistic capabilities obviously are significant to his personal and social adjustment in the school environment. His feelings about himself and his family as well as his academic achievement are dependent upon his ability to communicate. The frustration aroused because of a communication barrier between student, teacher, and parent is well documented.

Too often the English language is considered such an essential skill to future success that the Spanish language is considered a problem to be irradicated as quickly as possible. Language must be seen as a very important and personal aspect of the student's total culture. For many Mexican-American students and their families, the Spanish language is a symbol of the dignity of their culture and a part of their heritage which, they feel, should be nurtured and developed for the benefit of the total society. The demands for bilingual-bicultural education are predicated on the belief that schools should formally recognize this heritage by using the Spanish language as a medium of instruction and developing it as a language art.

The effect upon the individual resulting from cultural differences reflected in the language barrier is graphically portrayed as a Mexican-American educator, Mr. Leonardo Olguin, recalls his own school experience:

> A Mexican-American kid is born in a bicultural setting; he's born right on top of a red brick and adobe wall. For the first five or six years of his life, all he sees, all he feels, all he experiences is the adobe side. As life begins to pour into his psyche, he hears things like *Pon, Pon, Pon, el dedito en el buton!* or *Ay viene la luna, tirando cascarones.* . . . He doesn't hear Little Jack Horner, sat in a corner. . . . He hears beautiful, soft sounds that mean nice things in his comfortable world; he hears the system of a language that affects him all his life.
>
> Then he goes to school—eager, happy to join his brothers and sisters. He walks in and discovers that the teacher can't talk! He can't understand a thing, and no one can understand him. He can't talk either! It's horrible! The school is make-believe and the real world is at home.
>
> I went through the first two years of school in a cloud—going to school, eating lunch, and going home. I didn't know until the second grade that there were *two* complete languages. I just thought I didn't know all the words!

The student who can survive spending the first and formative years of school life "in a cloud" is fortunate. When inability to communicate because the native language is Spanish is further complicated by a home environment which exists in poverty, the student's chances of school success are even more limited. Poverty is so prevalent among

Mexican Americans that it must be considered as an element in their cultural characterization.

A MATTER OF ECONOMICS    The Mexican-American student is likely to be a member of an economically disadvantaged family; his parents probably earn less than $3500 a year, receive welfare, and possess many problems related to poverty, i.e., sub-standard living conditions, low educational attainment, poor health and nutrition habits, high delinquency rates, etc. (See Table 1 below.)

TABLE 1.*    Frequency of Low and High Family Incomes in the Southwest

|  | Families with Incomes Under $1,000 | | Families with Incomes of $10,000 or more | |
|---|---|---|---|---|
|  | General Population | Mexican American | General Population | Mexican American |
| Arizona | 5.9% | 7.2% | 14.4% | 4.6% |
| California | 3.3 | 4.5 | 21.8 | 10.8 |
| Colorado | 3.5 | 6.4 | 14.6 | 4.8 |
| New Mexico | 6.9 | 11.3 | 14.3 | 4.5 |
| Texas | 7.6 | 8.8 | 11.8 | 2.7 |
| Southwest | 4.9 | 8.8 | 17.6 | 6.6 |

* Herschel T. Manuel, *Spanish Speaking Children of the Southwest* Austin: University of Texas Press, 1965, p. 48.

In the Southwest, the percentage of Mexican Americans who earn less than $1,000 per year is twice as great as the general population. While at the other end of the scale, the percentage of Mexican Americans who earn more than $10,000 per year is less than half the percentage of those who earn that amount within the general population. Complicating the low annual income status is the fact that a greater proportion of Mexican Americans have significantly larger families than the general population. (While 19.2% of the Mexican-American families have seven or more members, only 5.8% of the general population have seven or more members.) The fast rate of growth among this segment of the population means an increase in problems related to poverty and increased pressure upon the school to help solve those problems.

Probably the most economically deprived Mexican Americans are the migrant agricultural workers who set out each year from a home base, a rural village or a barrio on the outskirts of a city in Texas, Arizona, California, or Florida. The families (on the average, 6.4 members) follow a fairly regular path dictated by the cultivation and harvest patterns of key crops throughout the country. A typical migration from a home base in

37

Texas would begin in April or May. The family may travel north to work in the truck farms of the midwest, go on to the sugar beet fields of the northern states, or head west to harvest cotton in California. By early autumn, many families move far north and west to bring in the fruit harvest of Wisconsin, Michigan, Minnesota, Washington, and Oregon. By Christmas or the New Year, these families return home after traveling thousands of miles and, if they are lucky, having earned $1,000. "The average yearly income from farm labor of the migrant worker has been reported as less than $1,000 over recent years, and every year it is becoming increasingly difficult for most of them to find steady employment."[9]

Increased mechanization is forcing migrant laborers to seek employment in the cities, and they bring with them their problems and life style. An account of the daily life of one migrant family illustrates the kind of background that some Mexican-American students bring to school.

Xavier Sanchez' home is one of the mass-produced grey brick structures in Indio's Riverside county-run labor camp for farm workers and their families. It has five small rooms. The Sanchez home is cluttered, but not with furniture. The sofa's stuffing's are coming out, its springs exposed. A worn blanket is spread across it. This morning, the three worn chairs have been placed around the small table, with its peeling linoleum top. Ordinarily, the family's 7 year old portable television is on the table, to be moved off only at mealtime. . . .

The family's welfare check comes, $186, twice a month. Of this $372 total, $55 a month goes for rent; the rest for clothing, food for the family of nine; utilities and gasoline for the car.

The children (the four youngest), out of deference, hurriedly finish (breakfast) when they see their father and rush out to their day at play. A ball, an old deck of cards, and a few children's books are their only toys. They chatter like all children at play, only in Spanish. The entire family speaks Spanish almost exclusively except for a few English phrases mixed in. . . .

Xavier Sanchez, 48, seems smaller and older than he really is. He looks 55 or 60. Years of farm labor have taken their toll—he has worked in the fields since he was 11. . . . Heavily muscled about the neck and shoulders, he cannot stand at full height. A hernia and poor kidneys (which he has never had the money to see a doctor about) both pain him. His weak, sagging pot belly is more a product of his badly stooped posture than of poor eating habits. He squints often, since years of "too much dust, hot air and glare" almost blinded him recently. . . . The eye sickness put Sanchez suddenly out of work just five months after he had moved to California from New Mexico, in the hope of earning better pay as an operator of tractors and other farm machinery. Sanchez applied for welfare—for the first time in his life. "I wish we did not have to go to *la Ayuda*—the welfare, but what could I do? At least now they are paying the doctor for me."

A small, round woman, (Ofelia) has borne Sanchez 12 children in 29 years of marriage. "People always ask why I had so many children," Mrs. Sanchez added, "but what can I say? We are Catholics, and I could never have confessed to something like birth control, never! God gave us these children and He will give us a way to take care of them. . . ." Now with heart trouble and in need of a bladder operation she works at raising the seven children still at home. . . .

Mrs. Sanchez works alone. Her daughters are too young to help, and Mexican culture considers it unmanly for even a young man to work in a kitchen. . . . The teenagers watch TV. . . .

For Richard, and his brother, Pedro, 16, to be young and strong, yet out of work, is frustrating. The only jobs that come to mind are in the fields. . . . Any private or public agencies that might help them—such as the Neighborhood Youth Corps—have remained unknown and unused. . . .

It was another fruitless day when Richard returned home, it was still morning, and he settled into watching television.

"I'm sorry, but we're all set to shut down for the next two months." (The foreman seemed genuinely sorry.) "With the damn grape picking over early," Richard said, "it's hard to get work anywhere else. The market was so bad that the growers gave up picking early. You can't blame the dudes. It isn't a bad way to live," he continued, "if you can find work. I suppose that once I get out of high school, and spend some time in the Navy, I'll come back and work at it. I mean, all my ancestors did.". . .

"Not much to do," Robert sighed, to no one in particular. . . . A lack of transportation has almost totally kept them from mingling with any Chicano or white youngsters outside of the camp. . . . They sneak an occasional cigarette, but use no drugs. They consider fighting with anything other than fists as "chicken". . . . "It's been a long time since I threw some *chingasos* (blows), you know. . . . The last time was in high school when me and some black dudes whipped some gringos!" Pedro said.

Pedro, full of belligerent Chicano pride, boasts of the many times he has fought to defend it against both blacks and the *gringos* he dislikes.

Yet Pedro and his brother are largely ignorant of the ferment currently spreading among Chicano youngsters in urban barrios and on campuses. "All I know is that I don't like *gabachos*," (whites). Those dudes think they're too damn smart," Pedro says.[5]

Other accounts of the living conditions of migrant workers indicate that the Sanchez family is fortunate to live in a state that provides government housing, welfare, and medical compensation for at least a portion of the workers who migrate to California each year. In general, migrant workers do not enjoy the same protection and security under the law as other citizens.

> . . . At the time of this writing (1967) the seasonal farm laborer has no protection under the national minimum wage laws, the National Labor Relations Act, or from abuses of child labor in certain areas.

> The argument is constantly advanced that labor legislation for farm workers should be a matter of state action . . . the states where this is most needed are the states that do not and will not act of themselves . . . Protective legislation . . . is nonexistent in 12 of the United States. Yet these 12 states use 47 per cent of the total seasonal labor force, including Texas, Kansas, Nebraska, and North Dakota, states which use Spanish-speaking labor almost exclusively.[6]

If the Sanchez family follows the usual pattern, they will go to a city in search of a better life. There they will probably live in a barrio, remain unemployed, and become part of the urban problem. The local school will inherit these educational handicaps resulting from migrant life:

1. Students who have experienced sporadic school attendance due to frequent moves;

2. Parents who have had to rely upon the immediate income of their children and who probably have not developed a realistic understanding of the value of education;

3. Students and parents whose language and cultural patterns are so different as to block traditional means of communication;

4. Students who have few previous school records due to the lack of interstate and intrastate cooperation between school districts;

5. Students whose total background makes traditional curriculum and grade placement meaningless and irrelevant;

6. Students who cannot be evaluated accurately with traditional evaluation instruments, and who might not respond to traditional teaching techniques;

7. Students and parents who may evoke negative attitudes and feelings on the

part of educators, administrators, and peers with whom they come in contact.*

Given these conditions, the prognosis for the Sanchez children's successful adjustment to school and city life is not favorable. Not only are they incompetent to compete effectively for further schooling, and eventual employment, but also they will be subjected to more contacts with others outside their social and ethnic group. Cultural conflict, discrimination, personal frustration may result in a variety of responses, such as those described below, some of which may bring them in conflict with the law.

Lack of satisfying human relationships increase a feeling of inadequacy, privation or thwarting. Delinquent behavior may result when frustration is sufficiently strong. The clash of cultures experienced by the Mexican youth is seen as increasing the amount of experienced frustration as well as lessening one of the major socializing forces, anticipation of punishment. There is an ever-widening gap, as Americanization proceeds, between the socioeconomic conditions under which the Mexican youth is forced to live and the standard of living created by American advertising.[7]

Not all Mexican-American students who live under poverty conditions become delinquents; however, delinquency is a problem highly correlated with low socioeconomic and minority group status. In the minds of some people, delinquency is almost synonomous with Mexican American. A principal of a predominantly Mexican-American school recently remarked, "We don't have a school; we have an honor farm for delinquents."

In an attempt to explain conditions, some studies have tried to establish relationships between Mexican-American cultural characteristics and delinquency, i.e., Mexican American males try to be *Macho* (manly, aggressive); they fight for honor or family name; the culture sanctions masculine camaraderie which, in turn, encourages the formation of gangs.

This type of logic is inaccurate; the extreme antisocial behavior which characterizes delinquency is as unacceptable to Mexican-American values as it is to Anglo standards. Furthermore, a recent analysis of the general characteristics of delinquent Mexican-American males as compared to non-delinquent Mexican-American males shows little that could be classified as "inherently Mexican." Rather, their characteristics could be descriptive of any ethnic or racial group. The delinquent Mexican-American male is:

less responsible, conscientious, and dependable;

---

* In 1971 the federal government awarded $57,608,680 to state programs for migratory children. Approximately 52% went to states in the Southwest indicating a concentration of migrant families and apparent need for special programs in education. For complete list of allotments to state programs see Appendix B.

tends to be more resentful, headstrong, and rebellious;

more impulsive, or lacking in self-control;

self-centered, and less concerned with how others react to him;

less cooperative and industrious, less secure, and more easily disorganized under stress or pressures to conform . . . at least to roles prescribed by the majority society, though he may adopt a "negative identity" or role;

defensive, shallow, unambitious, and lacking in self-direction and self-discipline;

unable to accept or identify with authority figures;

passive, and feels he is a hapless victim of circumstance or society, whose problems are not to be solved by his own efforts;

less able to "let go" and express himself, and may when called upon to do so, take refuge in either a sterile and noncommittal response, or "cover up" by crude humor and clowning.[8]

The problem of delinquency among Mexican-American youth must be considered in the total social and psychological environment involving culture conflict, poverty, and minority status. For example, the Mexican-American community often complains that they are victims of police harassment, or that they do not have adequate agencies and facilities to handle youths who have problems.

> The large numbers of the group's offenders referred to the police and the probation departments may be, in part, a reflection of this fact . . . delinquency rates of certain groups are substantially influenced by the absence of the kind of welfare agencies that certain other ethnic groups with low rates, notably the Jews, maintain and which assume responsibility for many problem cases that would otherwise go through official channels.[9]

It is apparent that the problems of Mexican-American youth are the problems of all youths in similar circumstances. Even the patterns of delinquency, the types of offenses, are becoming less distinctive for particular ethnic and racial groups. In 1956, a study initiated by the Welfare Planning Council, Los Angeles Region, concluded that:

1. Nearly 30 percent of all Mexican-American delinquents were charged with minor violations, a proportion somewhat smaller but close to that of Anglo whites.

2. Mexican-American delinquents come from almost as many broken homes as Anglo whites, but were over-represented among children from families broken by death.

3. Mexican Americans have a higher proportion of youngsters charged with felonies involving actual or threatened bodily harm than Anglo whites, but the over-representation for such offenses was smaller for Mexican Americans than Negroes.

4. Mexican Americans were over-represented in offenses which have been lumped together in this report as Human Addictions (acting out of bio-dynamic and psycho-dynamic needs in socially deviant behavior—narcotic offenses, violations of liquor laws, sex delinquencies). This fact is largely due to the relatively high proportion of drug offenses, which exceeds that of Negroes and Anglo Whites in a ration of about three to one.

5. Mexican-American youngsters were under-represented in violations affecting property other than autos.

6. Mexican Americans were like other ethnic categories in their proportion of offenses involving major traffic violations. There were no significant variations between these three ethnic groups in this type of offense.

7. Mexican Americans were like Negroes in the proportion referred for rape and homosexuality and like Anglo Whites in the proportion charged with illegitimate sex relations. Unlike both groups, however, the ratio of girls to boys referred for illegitimate sex relations was very low: 1 to 1.2.

8. Mexican-American girls were like Anglo Whites in having a high proportion of female offenses accounted for by runaway and incorrigibility charges. They were like Negroes in the fact that nearly one in every ten was referred for petty theft.[10]

Recent statistics from the Los Angeles County Probation Department indicate some interesting trends. A review of twenty-four categories of offenses of juveniles under pre-court investigation and initial court petitions (Table 2, page 44) indicates that:*

1. Mexican-American delinquents still tend to be involved in acts involving aggressive physical behavior. Furthermore, there has been an increase in offenses involving violations against property, i.e., burglary, petty theft, receiving stolen goods.

---

* The author is indebted to Mr. William K. Salstrom, Research Division of the Los Angeles County Probation Department, for supplying the statistics upon which this discussion and Table 2 is based.

TABLE 2.   Mean Distributions of Selective Juvenile Offenses for Three Ethnic Groups
July 1967 through December 1969, Los Angeles County Probation Department

| TYPES OF OFFENSES | Anglo-White | | Mexican American | | Negro | |
|---|---|---|---|---|---|---|
| | Number | Percent* | Number | Percent | Number | Percent |
| *Acts Involving Actual or Bodily Harm* | | | | | | |
| Murder | 3 | .03 | 12 | .23 | 4 | .13 |
| Robbery | 122 | 1.0 | 306 | 5.6 | 49 | 1.4 |
| Resisting an Officer | 27 | 0.2 | 27 | 0.5 | 21 | 0.6 |
| Forcible Rape | 12 | 0.1 | 17 | 0.3 | 7 | 0.2 |
| Assault | 72 | 0.6 | 98 | 1.8 | 45 | 1.4 |
| Assault/Weapon | 77 | 0.6 | 141 | 2.6 | 65 | 2.0 |
| *Violations Affecting Property* | | | | | | |
| Burglary | 1165 | 9.6 | 755 | 13.7 | 333 | 10.0 |
| Petty Theft | 522 | 4.3 | 370 | 6.7 | 151 | 4.5 |
| Receiving Stolen Goods | 49 | 0.4 | 33 | 0.6 | 16 | 0.5 |
| *Human Addictions* | | | | | | |
| Drunk | 1265 | 10.5 | 334 | 6.1 | 433 | 12.9 |
| Glue Sniffing | 110 | 0.9 | 11 | 0.2 | 78 | 2.4 |
| Possession Marijuana | 859 | 6.9 | 213 | 3.8 | 122 | 3.6 |
| Possession Marijuana for Sale | 53 | 0.4 | 9 | 0.1 | 5 | 0.2 |
| Narcotics Violations (possession, for sale, use, prescription, forgery, miscellaneous) | 1140 | 10.3 | 64 | 1.2 | 231 | 7.3 |
| Prostitution | 3 | 0.0 | 15 | 0.3 | 1 | 0.0 |
| In Danger of Leading Lewd Immoral Life | 332 | 2.8 | 69 | 1.3 | 63 | 1.9 |
| Other Sex Offenses | 84 | 0.7 | 37 | 0.7 | 14 | 0.4 |
| *Major Traffic Violations* | | | | | | |
| Auto Theft and Joyriding | 646 | 5.4 | 523 | 9.5 | 280 | 8.5 |
| Drunk Driving | 169 | 1 4 | 30 | 0.6 | 56 | 1.9 |
| Hit and Run | 32 | 0.3 | 8 | 0.1 | 12 | 0.3 |
| *Minor Violations* | | | | | | |
| Disturbing the Peace and Disorderly Conduct | 117 | 1.0 | 102 | 1.9 | 50 | 1.6 |
| Riot | 4 | 0.0 | 7 | 0.1 | 2 | 0.1 |
| Incorrigibles | 1154 | 9.5 | 364 | 6.6 | 208 | 6.2 |
| Runaway | 1346 | 11.0 | 423 | 7.3 | 321 | 9.6 |
| Truancy | 361 | 2.8 | 56 | 1.0 | 106 | 3.1 |
| | T = 9724 | | T = 4024 | | T = 2673 | |

* Computed upon total arrests during stated period: Anglo-White N = 36,655, Mexican-American
N = 16,461, Negro N = 10,012.

2. For the given time period (July 1967–December 1969), Anglo and Negro youths surpassed Mexican-American delinquents in human addictions like drunkenness, glue sniffing, narcotics, lewd or immoral actions.

3. Automobiles have become an important force in the delinquency of Mexican-American youths. They outnumber other groups in auto theft and joy-riding; however, they have less violations involving drunk driving or hit and run.

4. Mexican-American delinquents tend to exceed other groups in disturbing the peace and riot, but have less tendency to be incorrigible, runaway or truant.

Some of these trends are contrary to popular opinions about Mexican-American youth. A longer, more thorough study would be needed to confirm these trends; however, all conclusions concerning delinquency among Mexican-American youth must take into consideration the fact that Mexican Americans are a very youthful population group (44% are under age 15, as compared to 30% of the general population). Delinquency is a very real problem in the Mexican-American community and the school must recognize the probabilities of working with students who may experience conflicts with the law. Most important, educators must be concerned with the causes that underlie the conflicts.

A MATTER OF INDIVIDUALS    At no time can an historical or cultural perspective of a group be used to classify an individual. "Then why learn about these characteristics?" a student teacher asked the author. The answer involves a basic concept of good pedagogy, the anticipation of student need, interest, and response and the preplanning to meet the demands effectively in a manner that results in learning.

An historical-cultural perspective of the Mexican American should serve as a backdrop, a set of hypotheses with which to try and understand the student. As an illustration, the essential elements of the cultural perspective of the Mexican-American student might be presented in the form of a grid. For each element of culture, there is a continuum of possibilities upon which the individual might be placed. Taking the variables of economics and acculturation, a classification scheme with assocated characteristics might be illustrated as on the grid on page 46.

Other elements of culture might prove to be more important in local situations; also new relationships between elements of culture may be demonstrated; nevertheless the use of a grid or some similar classification allows more flexibility in summarizing generalized cultural characteristics and their interrelationships. It is possible to keep the individual in the foreground and plan for specific needs. For example, pupils "A" and "D" might both be Mexican American, but each would need a very different kind of educational program.

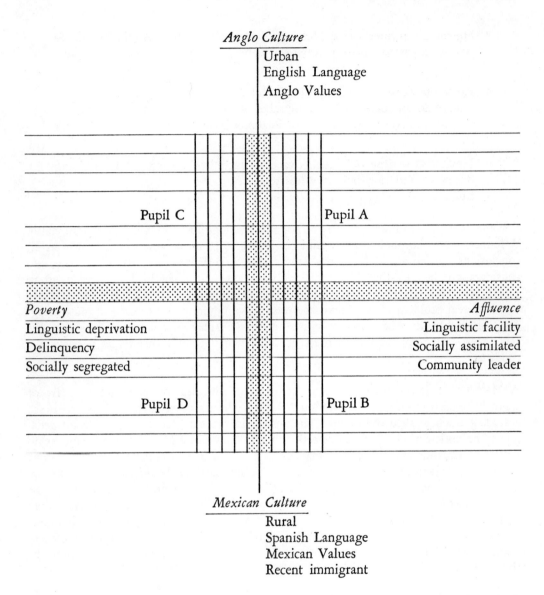

*Anglo Culture*

Urban
English Language
Anglo Values

Pupil C                    Pupil A

*Poverty*                                                    *Affluence*
Linguistic deprivation                          Linguistic facility
Delinquency                                     Socially assimilated
Socially segregated                              Community leader

Pupil D                    Pupil B

*Mexican Culture*

Rural
Spanish Language
Mexican Values
Recent immigrant

To summarize the cultural characteristics of the Mexican-American student, it is possible to say that the Mexican-American student is:

1. An individual who represents a heterogeneous cultural group composed of various geographical, sociological, and economic subgroups;

2. An individual who may be in various stages of acculturation from traditional

Mexican culture to Anglo culture, dependent upon his length of residence (generation) and geographic location within the United States;

3. An individual who probably has some facility with the Spanish language varying from minimum comprehension to fluency, and who is likely to have some difficulty with English;

4. An individual who is rapidly becoming an urban dweller;

5. An individual who probably has experienced social segregation and possibly discrimination as an identifiable minority;

6. An individual who is probably a member of the lower socioeconomic group within the United States;

7. An individual who is vulnerable to psychological pressures related to minority status, linguistic barriers, and acculturation.

Along with generalized knowledge about the ethnic minority known as Mexican Americans, the effective teacher must understand himself—his attitudes, his beliefs, and his capabilities. He must also have insight regarding the pupil's perception of a teacher, school, himself, and his world. Self-assessment is no easy task, but some knowledge about oneself can accrue from comparing our feelings with the reactions of others in similar situations. To learn about students' perceptions of school and themselves, we need but ask and listen.

# 4

# A TEACHER AND STUDENT PERSPECTIVE OF THE CHALLENGE

## Some Crucial Questions About Attitudes

How do teachers feel about Mexican-American students or their parents, and how do students feel about their teachers and school? Do these attitudes affect student achievement? These are important questions which involve some of the most basic issues in education, such as the goals of education, discipline, problem areas, curriculum and methods of teaching.

Questions about attitudes are difficult to answer because they involve not only a multitude of individual experiences, but also feelings which may be below an individual's threshold of consciousness. Relationships between attitudes and achievement are equally complex because many variables can affect the success or failure of students in school.

Nevertheless, attitudes remain a critical element in teacher-learner interaction during the learning process. No teaching material, no fool-proof program or means of grouping exists to replace the importance of the human relationships between teacher and learner. When the critical moment of decision arrives—to reteach or go on, to discipline or ignore, to cooperate or antagonize—attitudes often determine which action is taken. In the education of an ethnic or racial minority, attitudes held by teacher and learner may be the single most important element which determines frustration or success.

The first section of this chapter considers teacher-student attitudes concerning basic questions inherent in the education of Mexican-American students. The reader is invited to examine his attitudes about the areas discussed. The second part of the chapter will be broader in scope and draw upon the knowledge gained through systematized research which attempts to establish relationships between attitudes of teachers, students, parents and school achievement. The third, and last section, will deal with the attitudes of a small but vocal group of Chicano students who are emerging as leaders in a movement dedicated to social reform in which the school occupies an important role. A discussion of attitudes of Mexican-American students would be incomplete without this Chicano point of view because it is a part of the reality teachers will face working in a predominantly Mexican-American school or community.

STUDENT AND TEACHER ATTITUDES ARE REAL    In talking to teachers and students, it is apparent that they are willing to discuss their school experiences freely; and as they talk about critical issues, individual attitudes can be inferred. The diversity in points of view among teachers and students is startling. Even more significant are the differences of perspective between student and teacher when they discuss the same issue.

To illustrate representative points of view of both students and teachers, statements have been selected from taped interviews and organized around the following questions:*

1. How do Mexican-American students and their teachers feel about each other?

2. What do Mexican-American students and their teachers feel are the major problems in school?

3. What do Mexican-American students, their teachers and parents perceive as the major responsibilities of the school?

4. How do Mexican-American students and their teachers feel about discipline?

5. What type of teacher preparation do Mexican-American students and their teachers consider appropriate?

Answers to the questions are candid, critical, bitter, annoying, and sometimes shocking. In most cases, expressions appear as they were given because they represent "the way it is" for students and teachers. Some statements will be easy to identify with, while others will be completely foreign or antagonistic to one's point of view, but most statements will serve to stimulate discussion, debate, and, above all, self-assessment. How do you feel about the comments that follow?

*How do Mexican-American students and their teachers feel about each other?*

### Mexican-American students respond:

A: "I think that there are only some teachers that try and motivate students. Most really don't care."

---

* The author wishes to express appreciation to Mrs. Mary Martinez and Mr. Henry Lopez for their assistance in obtaining some of the interviews used in this chapter.

B: "If we don't learn, the teachers have a very biased attitude toward us, especially the ones that have been here for years and years and years."

**Are students A and B correct? How do you feel about students who don't learn?**

C: "I worked with the newspaper, so I could drop into classes anytime. These teachers were sitting on their asses. The students were struggling with papers that were the simplest thing in the world to do. They were actually breaking their heads, while the teachers were sitting there reading. You ask them to help you, and they tell you to read the book. That's where you get your instructions from."

**Are teachers that student C describes really teaching? What is a teacher's role in the classroom?**

D: "I hassled with the teachers because I walked out during the semester. They had a really bad image of me—troublemaker. They didn't want me. Then they said, 'You missed seven days, Maria. If you miss one more, you are going to get an automatic fail, no matter how much work you do.' I was trying to do something, and it was just a lot of hassle. So I quit."

**How do you feel about student D or activists who strike or walk out?**

E: "My teacher smiles at the other kids but not at me."

F: "The instructions go to the entire classroom as a group. And I guess she takes it for granted that they are all on the same level. And their conscience feels justified because they say, 'I told them all if they needed any help to come to me.' Yes, and yet she has that stern look that says, 'Don't bother me now. I'm busy.'"

G: "This counselor just can't stand Mexicans, so she puts them in EMR classes. She can't stand them because they all look retarded to her. God knows how many she's put in EMR."

H: "They are trained to teach middle class kids. They are not trained to teach Chicanos or Blacks. They're just not. So what they try to do is to stimulate a student the same way, and it's impossible because we're different."

I: "It doesn't matter if the teacher is Anglo or Chicano. It all depends. To me, it really doesn't matter so long as he doesn't put you down."

J: "He's a very good teacher. He knows the Chicano, like during the walkouts, he helped us. He took us to his home to study the whole thing and to analyze the pueblo, and everything else. He is very receptive toward the Chicano; he knows more Chicanos than most of the Mexican-American administrators and teachers. He's a good guy."

**In what ways are students F, G, H, I, and J indicting the system? In your judgment, is their perception accurate?**

K: "There was this one guy Mario. He would come into class about once a week on reds. He would come in and drool over everybody and start bothering the girls. This biology teacher wouldn't call the pig the first thing off. He took time to talk to the guy. He told him he was getting tired of his coming into class like that. He didn't give him any moralistic junk that it's bad for you because every kid knows what grass or speed or whatever will do to them."

How would you help a student who came into your class high on drugs?

### Teachers respond:

A: "I'm beginning to think there is a real difference between Black children and Mexican children. A black child, most of mine at least, are really concerned about their grades and education. But this group of Mexican kids that I have don't seem to care about their education, and I get the feeling that their parents don't either."

**Do you feel there are differences between Black students, Mexican-American students, and Anglo students? Identify them.**

B: "They are no longer respectful, they are no longer obedient. We're having sit-downs out on the yard. We were having all kinds of petition-carrying kids in the 4th, 5th, and 6th grades. They never used to think about that. They were calm; they were nice; they were humble. Now they're more inclined to be overbearing, rude, and force-ful."

C: "Seems to me they are only interested in using their intelligence to cause trouble. They are not really interested in learning."

D: "On the whole, these children don't want to talk to other people. They're so embarrassed or something. They feel so inadequate. They're afraid to talk to the teacher about a problem. They don't want you to know about it. They're embarrassed about it."

E: "The people I'm dealing with don't have a real Mexican culture. It's the Baja, California, type of thing, which is altogether different."

**How would you respond to teachers B and E? Role play a faculty meeting where teachers B, E, F, and J discuss school problems.**

F: "Can you tell me why so many Mexicans get into this country? They come in and the first week they're here, they get on welfare, free lunches, free breakfasts. Why don't they pick up a few of them and take them back to Mexico, instead of raising all our taxes?"

**How might teacher F reflect her attitude in the classroom?**

G: "Let's face it—I'm 'whitie' even if I am their teacher. They're not going to re-spond to me beyond a certain point. I can understand this, but it's unfortunate. If they won't accept help from 'whitie', then where are they going to get it? Most of the teachers in the world are white like me."

H: "I came to this school and was very favorably impressed. These are clean kids. They come to school immaculate. Their clothes are pressed; they take pride in their personal appearance. You'll never know that these kids have any problems or a lack of money. Yet, I know some don't have enough food to eat."

I: "These kids don't ask questions. I'm not saying that it's passiveness, because I think they are full of questions. They really want to ask, and they really want to know. It's because at home they don't. In this room, there are two personalities—the girls and the boys. The girls sit here and say, 'Give me my paper, and I'll do my work.' Off they go. The boys, they tumble and do all kinds of things. They are children; they are excited about things. Really, sometimes it's exasperating, but I don't want to put them down because this is what I want."

Teachers G, H, D, and I teach the same grade level students. How has each adjusted to teaching in a Mexican-American, lower socioeconomic school?

J: "Mexican-American parents, like any others, really appreciate it if you take an interest. Many times I'll call them at night and discuss a problem with them because they can't get in during the day. They have other children, or they work. I'm always concerned that I'll interrupt their dinner or that they are busy, but they never seem to feel that way. Before we've hung up, they say, 'Thank you for calling and for being so concerned about my child.' "

Do you agree with teacher J? Are there some universal principles of teaching and human relations that are effective in any situation? Identify them.

*What do Mexican-American students and their teachers feel are the major problems for Mexican-American students in school?*

Mexican-American students respond:

A: "In the barrio, you have no money. You have nothing to do. You have no transportation, and it's depressing. You have this messed-up house, messed-up neighborhood. You are ashamed of yourself. I can see my sister's family—their mother can't get involved in their school activities, just as when I was young. She has a house full of children to raise and a baby. It's not the school's fault. It's the home environment, too—how your parents respond to you and school. It's not just enough to tell you to do your homework; you also need the understanding."

B: "Their fathers were running the entire town. And here my father was ignorant. He was in the cannery, and we worked in the fields every day after school. You start being ashamed of your own parents, you know—not inviting them to the PTA. You want them to come, and yet . . ."

C: "It's worse for people with brains. I could have had A's, but, shoot man, I was struggling trying to keep up with those kids. One thing about me is that I never had the encyclopedias, and I don't have a library card. We lived out in the country, and we couldn't stay after school. I didn't have the materials to make a project of my own. They were teaching us o. k., but, hell, when you don't got the materials at home and you don't have the money at home, you just get your C's and that's it. You are discouraged."

**What might be the motivational patterns of students A, B, and C in school? What teaching methods should be used for these students?**

D: "We had an exceptionally large family. We had bussing over there. We had to take lunch, while the other Anglo kids went to the cafeteria or went home. I used to be really ashamed and embarrassed when my mother would have to make *burritos* because she can't afford to make bread and bologna sandwiches for us."

E: "It's terrible being the only person in your whole classroom not coming to open house. Your whole class is Anglo. It makes you feel weird, inferior. I wasn't accepted by them, and I was not accepted by the Mexicans."

**Can the school be concerned with social or cultural characteristics of home life reflected by students A, B, D, and E? What can teachers do?**

F: "Over here, we are all categorized in two levels. Either you are a college-bound student or you're not. That's all there is. If you are college bound, you have potentials. If you're not college potential, forget it."

G: "My little sisters are not dumb, you know. I told that teacher, 'They come from two highly intelligent parents, so they have to be intelligent. Why aren't they learning? And Stella is only reading a fourth grade reader, and she is in sixth grade. What's the problem, man? He says, 'Well, the problem is this. Most of the kids are bilingual. They talk Spanish and English, and it's really a big problem to teach them because we're Anglos and we do not speak Spanish. I'm sorry I can't help you.'
"I go, 'Yeah, that ain't the problem. My little sisters don't speak Spanish. My mother talks to them in Spanish and they communicate, but the problem is that they aren't learning English very well in school. They're not learning English, and they can't read.' They're putting it all on bilingualism and that's ridiculous."

H: "We didn't grow up in the city. This made the difference. We had organizations we joined. This kept people active and I guess your mind also. But here in the city, the students have nothing to motivate them. This is one thing that has to start from the elementary level. If you don't get this motivation, you just don't care. It just dies and you quit."

I: "My little sisters are absolutely not learning, I swear to God. It frustrates me. They still do their homework because they have to do it; otherwise, my mother will get on their asses. They have that 'I don't care attitude.' They've given up. Really! And they are only 9, 10, 11. Why are they like that?"

How correct is the insight expressed by students G, H, and I? Does bilingualism thwart motivation and school achievement? Why have 9, 10, and 11 year olds given up?

J: "I don't think there is any problem right now. I don't have any. I'm getting pretty good grades and things."

Why might student J have no problems in school?

Teachers respond:

A: "I think they don't work. It isn't because they don't have brains enough to work. Something has happened to kill the desire for an education."

B: "I've too many children. There is only one thing that I ever would want. That's 20 children in the room. I don't care, you can have the most fantastic material, but if there are too many children in the classroom, the teacher has lost his effectiveness."

C: "I'll tell you one thing. You can't do a damn thing for any of them unless you get them early enough. And what happens? These kids are poured through the mill. My whole reason for wanting to be a teacher was to come to a ghetto school and try and help. Now I am able to do nothing!"

D: "It's so discouraging. There is so much welfare and depression. A kind of defeatist attitude comes through from the home. In the home, it's 'let's get them for whatever we can get.' There's no motivation to do anything or to learn."

E: "I think the biggest problem I have to overcome is their not questioning. They come to school and are told by their parents, 'You do what the teacher says.'"

F: "They don't have the same positive attitudes toward school as the children in a middle class area. Your middle class children hear from their parents: 'You're going to do well. You're going to study when you come home from school. What did you do today? Let me help you with your homework.' Mexican-American children are not getting any of this at home. They come to school, and it seems that after kindergarten and the first grade, the magic sparkle of school seems to go away. They really don't want to come."

What have the analyses of teachers A, C, D, E, and F in common? In their perceptions, where does the problem lie?

G: "I think the worst thing of all is the testing program. It doesn't give a true picture of their intelligence, nor is it a true picture of their achievement. They know they are going to get the lowest scores and they feel stupid. If I were to go to Mexico and take a test, I would be a Stanine One, too."

H: "I have never thought of myself as a Mexican American or anything else—just a human being. It's hard for me to understand all this Chicano business. Now everybody looks at me and says, 'Oh, you're Mexican.' I think the problem is in categorizing people."

**Do you think that classifying students into ethnic and racial groups causes more problems than it solves? Why? Why not?**

I: "I think sometimes the problems and frustrations are within me. I'm trying to impose my standards upon them."

**Defend or refute the statements made by teachers H and I. Should the teacher impose his standards upon pupils?**

J: "I don't have any frustrations working with Mexican-American children. I use two basic rules. The first is: We never laugh at one anothers' mistakes. Number two is to speak to me in the language you are comfortable in."

**Can teachers implement their own philosophies and still work within the system?**

*What do Mexican-American students and their teachers perceive as the major responsibilities of the school to Mexican-American students?*

### Mexican-American students respond:

A: "When it's time for reds, you see them all over campus and you see the school swinging all at once. It's just that you're escaping; all it is is an escape gate. You know some kids go on real happy. Most of them are super drunk and cocky. But it is not a trip seeing them loaded on reds, and that's why it frustrates me. I don't like it, especially when I have friends that take them all the time. This is exactly what the schools should be worrying about."

B: "I don't know why Chicanos get loaded on that stuff, except maybe because it's right there in front of their eyes. One day, Gomer and I were going to class, and this guys offers us reds, five for a roll. This one rides around in a Riviera in a suit and is really suave. And so we went over and told Mr. B. 'Look Mr. B., right there in front of your mind, you have a drug pusher. He's pushing reds, how much plainer can we put it to you?' I go, 'We're concerned. You just look at us like we are a bunch of agitators. We really want something done in this school. It's our school, you know. This is exactly what *you* should be doing especially your narc agent, you know."

C: "They close the restrooms during class time because they get messed up and over-flooded. Some kids break the mirrors and things like that. We want something to be done about that. It's bad to hold your urine. So we went down and told Mr. D. 'Look, Mr. D., you know damned well who the hell breaks the windows. You know it's the niggers. And there are only 50 in the whole school, why should all of us suffer? You got to face reality. You say you went to high school here, and there were the same problems when you were here. They didn't close all the restrooms, did they?' He said, 'No, but things were different at that time.' Well, things aren't any different now. So you know what he did? We got two more restrooms, but the whole school was restricted. They hired about 11 security guards. I mean, grown up men acting like policemen.''

How would you defend the system and its established procedures or define the broader ramifications of the problem described by students A, B, C, and D?

D: "We only have two lawns open. Now there's not much grass at school and 3,000 students just don't happen to fit on those two small lawns. The cafeteria can only hold 324 people. So what do you do with all the rest? We told him, 'Do something about it, man! Where do you expect all of us students to go? Hell, do you expect the impossible? This is how you are going to start a lot of fights if you keep the people crowded. It's going to start looking sloppy. You are going to have more people jumping the fence and getting in trouble.' They installed a new P.A. system instead. The whole situation was disgusting. So we walked out."

If you were the principal discussed by students B, C, and D, what would your course of action be?

E: "I wasn't classified as college bound, but I wanted to go to college. I didn't care how, but I was going to make it. I was going to go to college! I wanted to take three classes, because there was no competition in the classes I had and I wanted to go and learn. But they told me, 'No, you don't have the grades.' I told them that at my other school I was put in level $y$ and I couldn't get higher than a B. And so all I had were C's and B's. I was getting A's in my work even though they didn't give me A for the class. And she didn't believe me. So what happened. I remained there for another semester. It shouldn't be that way!"

F: "We look to school as the institution that develops all aspects of the person. To some extent, it will develop his self confidence, or lack of it. What's more important is the extent to which the school recognizes and develops the person. The school must help us become more competent and confident."

G: "The Chicano student wants the school to help him become aware of himself, his culture, his history, his place in this country. The Chicano is not even intellectually knowledgeable about himself. His culture can't be all Mexican, and it can't be all American. It's in between. The school should help us find ourselves."

How can the schools fulfill the responsibilities assigned to it by students F and G?

**Teachers respond:**

A: "I want to turn them loose to be normal questioning children. I don't think their parents could object unless they turn around and do the same thing at home. I don't want children to take 'no' for an answer. I don't care who says it. I want them to know 'why' and 'how come.' I try never to resort to 'because I said so.' "

B: "Here we have to build up their confidence and skills, so they can and will be able to compete. Now is *not* the time to compare them with the kids who have traveled all over the world, who live in other parts of the city, or come from fine homes. I make my own curve, and you would be surprised how normal a curve they fall into. I judge them on how they are doing with their peers and how much they've improved over the pre-test."

**How can teacher B justify using a class curve instead of standard norms in assigning grades to his students?**

C: "I think if they are really going to make it, they are going to make it on their own. Now is the time they have to start to be dependent. If they keep relying on the home, then the cycle keeps repeating."

D: "I am an individualist. Usually, my class gets split up because I want them to all be independent. I think it's too early to have them be groupies. I think all too soon they get stuck in our little cubbyhole."

**What kind of teaching methods must teachers A, B, C, and D employ in order to implement their philosophies?**

E: "First of all, we must impress upon them that they must accept responsibility not only for themselves but for their group. They must choose where to begin and the one that volunteers to be chairman knows he has to accept the responsibility for the job and his group."

*How do Mexican-American students and their teachers feel about discipline?*

**Mexican-American students respond:**

A: "Wow! She's bad. If you talk to someone, she goes 'whap' with the ruler. She shakes us. She could get much more out of us if she was nice."

B: "I wanted to learn. They just didn't want to teach or something. Maybe the teachers weren't qualified to teach. The students controlled the teachers. It was ridiculous. The students would jump out of the window, and say, 'I don't want to be in this classroom today.' The teachers acted like them at times too. 'Children, children, control yourselves, before I send you to the principal's office.' Nobody wanted to go there, damn."

C: "He's a friendly guy. He's not a teacher that will strictly abide by the rules. He's not just there to teach you something and that makes learning fun. That's what I like about this guy. He likes the kids, too. He likes the kids just as much as his subject. You can joke off in his class, but he will teach you what he wants you to know. He balances it out."

### Teachers respond:

A: "I've tried being permissive. I've tried being understanding. I've tried a gamut of everything, and the only thing they respond to is when I'm very strict and very structured."

B: "I think I'm an average teacher, probably better than average in one sense, I'm never satisfied. I don't like a lot of movement in my room—kids just walking all over the place randomly. I tried saying to them, 'You know when you can get out of your seat'—and they were all over the room. I have to keep it so strict in there now, that they can't get out of their seat to pick up a pencil if they drop it."

C: "I am freer than I was, but I think that all kids need a certain structure. They need to know that there are limits on what they can do. Within those limits, anything and everything goes."

### What kind of discipline do you think works best with Mexican-American students?

D: "Several of our classes went down to the mission and some of the children were playing in the fountain. So I made a comment to this Anglo teacher. (I wasn't thinking of the children as being of Mexican descent. To me they were children, period.) I asked, 'Why do you let the children play in the water?' She said, 'Oh, it's such a hot day; anyway they don't get to play out very often.' I said, 'Let me ask you a question. Suppose they were Anglo children, would you allow them to play in the water?' 'I don't think so,' she said. Then I said, 'You had no right to let those Mexican children in there. They can't go far with this idea of being different.' I hate this difference, this separatism."

### Do you think teacher D is correct in holding all children to the same standards of behavior?

E: "Usually when friends find out that you are working in one of these areas, they say, 'Are the kids hard to control?' I found that, actually, the opposite is true. These kids are not harder to control, because they have a respect for authority. Also, they don't harbor a grudge. They have a wonderful openness about them. These kids get it out of their systems, and they forget about it. I think it's a very healthy attitude. Furthermore, they understand teachers. They know that sometimes teachers get mad, and they know that the teacher is going to get over it too."

### How do you feel about "getting mad" in the classroom?

F: "I had one little boy that was so excited because he had stolen a bottle of Old Spice for his dad, and his dad was delighted. Now when you approach that problem, you don't say, 'You stole; you're bad.' It's very touchy. You can say, 'Well, how did you feel about it? Did you feel that you deserved that because you got away with it? Is that good? Have you accomplished something you are really proud of?' In this case, he said, 'Yeah!' Sometimes you have to kind of drop it. And then think about getting back to it in another way. Now maybe, something comes up where he loses something . . . or something is done to him. Now you back-track and say, 'Hey, remember when you did such and so . . .' "

**Role play the situation described by teacher F. How would you teach children virtues of honesty, fair play, etc.? What if the values of the peer group or family are different?**

G: "I give them a choice. If they take part in the activity, they must follow the rules they've helped make. I say, 'If you go there, you have to follow the rules. The first few times, it's your choice. If you don't folow the rules, then it is my choice.' It works."

**If you were teacher G who believes in giving students a choice over their actions and students made the wrong choice, what would you do?**

*What type of teacher preparation do Mexican-American students and their teachers feel is appropriate?*

**Teachers respond:**

A: "When I started school, I didn't speak English, only Spanish. Living in the barrio, a community where all Spanish-speaking people lived, we listened to the Mexican radio; and when we went to the movies, we went to a Mexican movie. I can understand these children and their problems."

**Do you think fluency in Spanish is a prerequisite for a successful teaching experience in the barrio?**

B: "I have 200 units, a 3.5 average, and a master's degree in educational psychology. I know nothing from educational psychology that can help me here, but I can sit and argue with the best of them."

C: "There's no substitute for actual experience in this kind of school. I think I have become more compassionate, realistic about everybody and myself. . . . It's so easy to sit in your ivory tower and say, 'I just can't understand why there is this riot or that riot.' I still get mad at it, but I understand it."

**Should teachers automatically serve some period of their professional life working with minority groups students in order to understand the problem?**

D: "What I had done was to look at these children as different because of their language barrier. After actual experience, they are the same in their need for their teacher to relate to them, to provide meaningful experiences and models, to give them their culture, their language, and a good self-image. No special planning for that was really necessary, but special training was necessary. I am not inadequate but uneducated to some of their needs—especially their language needs."

Do you feel special schools staffed by teachers with special training will solve the educational problems of Mexican-American students? Why? Why not?

Mexican-American students respond:

A: "You know, I think in order for a teacher to teach in the barrio, he's going to have to be trained how to teach and to know our problems. You got to know how we live, and be sensitive to us. Teachers have to feel some of the hurt of the pain in the barrio. They've got to get personally involved in the barrio and with the kids."

To what extent do you feel teachers should be involved in the community? How can an Anglo teacher become involved?

B: "Teachers should never stop going to school. They should never think they have learned enough. They seem to forget everything they learned and were taught during the time they were getting their teacher's credentials."

C: "I think the best way to approach the Mexican-American student is to understand his background, his culture, his personality, his differences."

What type of special training do you think is necessary to work in the barrio? Should only Mexican-Americans teach in the barrio?

It is clear from these statements that students and teachers are reflective about what is happening in and around their classrooms. Students, particularly, go to great lengths to relate what they perceive as their problems. Whereas teachers think in specific terms about professional problems, students think about themselves in relation to the world or society e.g., getting a job, finding themselves, etc. When discussing school, students most often refer to the personalities of teachers and respond either positively or negatively to the teacher as a person. Both students and teachers are extremely concerned with motivation for learning, and a sense of urgency for change is apparent and will be even more prevalent in the comments of Chicano students who are active in "the Movement."

Though there seems to be less disagreement than we might expect about goals for Mexican-American students among teachers, few educators seem to have made the transition between stated goals and means of achieving these goals. Teaching strategies are needed to develop such goals as independence, self-confidence and other goals expressed by teachers. It is precisely toward this end that suggestions for changes in curriculum and methodology are offered in succeeding chapters. However, these changes will not be instituted until and unless educators and students seek to understand the relationships between attitude and achievement, and then work together to develop the learning environment which will encourage attitudes conducive to learning. At any rate, many of the intuitive impressions expressed by both students and teachers are documented in systematic research studies which should offer guidance in the selection of effective educative practices for Mexican-American students.

# The Relationship Between Teacher Attitudes and Student Achievement

What is the relationship between teacher attitude and student achievement? How are prevalent attitudes of educators reflected in general school policy and what are the effects upon Mexican-American students? The teacher's professional, ethnic, and racial background as well as his attitude are implied in the first question. School district organization, special programs, grading policies, and general goals are considered in the second question.

Research studies have shown that there is a high relationship between the Mexican-American student's achievement level and what he perceives his teacher's feelings toward him to be. In fact, "the influence of the teacher is greater for Mexican-American students than for most other minority groups as well as the majority group."[1]

THE EFFECT OF TEACHER ATTITUDES ON ACHIEVEMENT    Generally, teacher influence is greatest at the early years of education and decreases as the student becomes older. This is dramatically documented by Robert Rosenthal and Lenore Jacobson in their book *Pygmalion in the Classroom*. Intrigued by results of experimentation with animals, the authors sought to test the theory that:

> If animal subjects believed to be brighter by their trainers actually became brighter because of their trainers' beliefs, then it might also be true that school children believed by their teachers to be brighter would become brighter because of their teachers' beliefs.[2]

This study was conducted in a public elementary school in a lower-class community of a medium size city in which Mexican-American children comprised about one sixth of the total school population. A standard nonverbal intelligence test was administered school-wide, and eighteen teachers from grades one through six were notified that the scores of about 20% of the children indicated they would "bloom" during the following academic year. The teachers were told to expect dramatic intellectual growth from these children. Actually, the "bloomers" were chosen at random. "The difference between the special children and the ordinary children, then, was only in the mind of the teacher."[3]

The school utilized an ability tracking system to divide each grade level into slow, average, and fast groups. Grouping procedures depended largely upon reading ability, and Mexican-American children were over-represented in the lower groups. After the "gifted" children were identified, they took their places in various classrooms. The total school population was retested three times—one semester, a full academic year, and two full academic years later. Teachers were asked to rate their children on intellectual curiosity, personal and social adjustments, and the need for social approval. Correlations between test results and ethnic group status were made, and some interesting findings were reported.

1. The younger children whom teachers expected to bloom showed a significant expectancy advantage in IQ from pretest to retest. 19 percent of the control group gained twenty or more total IQ points. 47 percent of the "gifted" gained twenty or more total IQ points.

2. During subsequent retests, the first and second grade children lost some of their advantage; but the middle and upper grade "gifted" children maintained their expectancy advantage in IQ.

3. The "gifted" children made substantial gains in reading ability, the greater the gains in IQ, the greater the gains in reading scores.

4. The children in all ability groups showed an expectancy advantage in IQ and in reading ability; however, those in the medium or average track showed the greatest advantage from having their teachers think they had an intellectual advantage.

5. The more "Mexican" a child looked, the more he profited from his teacher's positive expectations. "These magnitudes of expectancy advantage were then correlated with the 'Mexican-ness' of the children's faces. After one year, and after teachers' positive prophecies, teachers' pre-experimental expectancies for these boys' intellectual performance were probably lowest of all. Their turning up on a list of probable bloomers must have surprised their teachers. Interest may have followed surprise and, in some way, increased watching for signs of increased brightness may have led to increased brightness."[4]

6. Teachers graded the "gifted" children more rigorously than they did the other children. "It is a possibility to be further investigated that when a teacher's expectation for a pupil's intellectual performance is raised, she may set higher standards for him to meet . . . The fear has often been expressed that the disadvantaged child is further disadvantaged by his teacher's setting standards that are inappropriately low . . ."[5]

7. Teachers rated the "gifted" Mexican-American children (particularly the boys) lower in intellectual curiosity than their Anglo counterparts, even though the Mexican-American children showed the greatest gain in IQ, reading scores, and overall school achievement. "It seemed almost as though, for these minority-group children, intellectual competence may have been easier for teachers to bring about than to believe."[6]

8. Teachers rated classroom behavior of the special children in the fast groups more favorably than those in the slow groups. The more intellectually competent the children in the fast group became, the more favorably they were rated by their teachers. However, the *more intellectually competent the children in the slow group became, the more negatively they were rated by teachers.* "Teachers may require a certain amount of preparation to be able to accept the unexpected classroom behavior of the intellectually upwardly mobile child."[7]

This study is particularly significant in demonstrating the importance of teacher attitude upon pupil achievement because no special programs, extra time, special personnel, extra field trips, nor special materials were utilized to increase achievement.

By what she said, by how and when she said it, by her facial expression, postures, and perhaps by her touch, the teacher may have communicated to the children of the experimental group that she expected improved intellectual performance. Such communications together with possible changes in teaching techniques may have helped the children learn by changing their self concept, their expectations of their own behavior, and their motivation, as well as their cognitive style and skills.[8]

Some educators and many minority group members feel that the only answer to the problem of teacher attitude is to have more teachers who are, themselves, members of the minority group. Mexican-American teachers, many feel, might at least know the language, be familiar with the culture, provide a positive role image for the student, and be able to communicate better with parents. Realistically, however, Mexican-American teachers for Mexican-American children cannot be the only solution. In the eight largest school districts in California where Spanish surnamed pupils and Negro students comprise one-third of the kindergarten through twelfth grade enrollment, only 1,091 teachers out of 48,277 are of Spanish surnames.[9]

Nor will there be a great change in this proportion if indications from teacher training institutions are valid. Furthermore, there is no assurance that all Mexican-American teachers are any more sensitive to the needs of the students than Anglo teachers. They may, in fact, be more middle class than teachers who have not struggled so hard to achieve their professional role. Not only must recruitment procedures encourage Mexican-American students to become teachers, but also teacher education programs must sensitize *all* teachers to the needs of minority-group students.

It is only when the majority of teachers and administrators are committed to improve conditions for minority students that district policies and procedures will change. At present there is considerable evidence that existing policies, particularly those involving evaluation and those resulting in segregation, place Mexican-American students at a disadvantage in school.

TEACHER ATTITUDES REFLECTED IN SCHOOL POLICY    Some of the most disconcerting evidence is provided by a five year U.S. Office of Education study at U.C.L.A. The major purpose of the study was "to explain why the achievement and aspirations of Mexican-American pupils tend to be lower than those of Anglo pupils and to determine the sources of influence on the absolute level of achievement and aspirations within each ethnic group."[10]

Pertinent conclusions from this study document the ways a school system contributes to the academic failure of Mexican-American students. Junior high schools and high schools in Los Angeles use different criteria in grading Anglo and Mexican-American students. Junior high schools in middle socioeconomic neighborhoods give Anglo children grades based on achievement compared to national norms (universalistic criteria), while junior high school in lower socioeconomic neighborhoods give Mexican-American students grades based on peculiaristic norms which often reflect conformity or social conduct rather than academic achievement (ascriptive criteria). This results in an unrealistic assessment of Mexican-American students and, perhaps, indicates that the schools have already concluded that Mexican Americans are probable dropouts who will not proceed within the system and will not need to compete with students of other junior high schools.

This practice also avoids the necessity of redesigning the educational program to bring Mexican-American students up to national norms. The result is continued retardation and perpetual academic incompetency. In this way, consciously, or unconsciously, the school allocates to Mexican-American students an inferior adult role by *not developing their abilities to compete* for preferred roles.

# The Effects of Segregated Schools

Mexican-American students attend schools in which they often comprise a high percent of the student population so that, in effect, they attend racially and ethnically segregated schools. A National Educational Opportunities Survey conducted by the U.S. Office of

Education in 1966 disclosed that in counties where Mexican-American and Anglo children live and attend public schools:

> At the first grade 30 percent of Mexican-American students attend schools in which they comprise the majority of the student body (50 to 100 percent of the students). By the twelfth grade, however, only two percent of Mexican-American students attend schools in which they comprise the majority.[11]

The low percentage of Mexican-American students attending segregated high schools must be considered a result of high drop out rates—30-50 percent in some areas. Nationally, "at the 16-17 year age level more than 20 percent more whites than Mexican Americans are enrolled in school."[12] Therefore, one would expect the percentage of Mexican-American students attending segregated high schools to decrease.

Surveys of schools receiving special federal and state aid also indicate that there is a high percentage of Spanish surname pupils enrolled in these schools; indirectly, this also indicates the extent of segregation which exists for the Mexican American. In California alone, 48 percent of all Spanish surname elementary school pupils attend target schools receiving compensatory funds from the federal or state government.[13]

CAN SEGREGATION BE BLAMED FOR LOW ACADEMIC ACHIEVEMENT?  That most Mexican-American students attend segregated schools is not difficult to establish; but to confirm a relationship between segregation and low academic achievement is not so easy. Most studies attempt to analyze two aspects of school life and levels of achievement, the physical plant with its educational program and the social aspects or interpersonal relations within the school.

Because of federal and state funds, some segregated schools which receive compensatory education funds do fare rather well by comparison. Often they have excellent physical facilities, such as media centers, teaching machines, libraries, and extra school personnel. Yet, national surveys reveal that students who attend segregated schools generally have significantly fewer educational facilities than those who attend integrated schools.

> White students who live in the same county as Mexican-American students have more special programs for especially skilled and talented and the physically handicapped, more state and regionally accredited schools, fewer students in part time attendance and fewer nonwhite teachers and principals.[14]

At the same time there are differences between the types of educational programs offered at schools which host a high Mexican-American student body population.

> At the elementary level, Mexican-American students have more free lunch programs, more frequent art sessions and less access to free kindergartens and nursery schools than do whites in the same county. At the secondary level

Mexican-American students have fewer college preparatory, commercial, and industrial arts curricula and more agriculture; they less often receive standardized intelligence, achievement, and interest tests but have newer textbooks.[15]

These differences in facilities and educational programs may reflect the differentiated needs of Mexican-American students; however, they could also reflect different assumptions educators hold about Mexican Americans, as implied in the U.C.L.A. study. The crucial question is what are the consequences of segregated, differentiated educational climates for the student? Inequality or equality of education must be measured less in terms of the school's and the community's inputs into the educational process (per pupil expenditure, school plants, library, quality of teacher, racial composition), and more in terms of the intangible characteristics of the school (teacher morale, teachers' expectations, interest of the student body in learning).

According to a recent discussion by James Coleman, the most important input in the educational process is provided by the educational backgrounds of fellow students, with teacher quality, school facilities and curriculum occupying positions of lesser importance.[16] The importance of peer group influence places the focus back upon other students and their families as the most crucial element in the socialization of an individual student.

For all grade levels attributes of the student body tend to be more highly related to achievement than do any other aspects of the school. . . . It was found that as the proportion of white students in a school increases, the achievement test scores of Mexican-American students also increases and that this trend becomes more pronounced for the latter school grades. This improvement in achievement is not attributable to better facilities and curriculum but rather, perhaps wholly, related to effects associated with the student body's educational background and aspirations.[17]

THE INFLUENCE OF SEGREGATED SCHOOLS ON THE COMMUNITY    The ethnically or racially segregated school reflecting a segregated community becomes a powerful vehicle for maintaining the cycle of segregated adult life. In general terms, the school maintains the ethnic cleavage dictated by the larger community. As an example, bussing students to bring about racial and ethnic integration in the school is opposed by both the minority community that wishes to sustain its culture and the majority community that wishes to maintain the status quo. Eventual solutions to the question of integrated or segregated schools will depend upon the courts, political power, ecological patterns, and the will of the majority.

Nevertheless, educators must face the negative consequences of maintaining segregated schools with differentiated educational programs which are inferior or sustaining standard educational programs which are insensitive to the students' needs. These consequences involve immediate student competency as well as the long-term quality of society. Which consequences we choose to live with or which changes are to be made will in large part depend upon the attitude and feelings of the educators, legislators, and citizens who affect decisions. Regardless of the alternative chosen, segregated or integrated schools, we must be prepared for the accusations of militant Chicanos who attack a system which perpetuates their low social status. We must devise a new solution, or we must seriously consider meeting their new demands which no longer request integrated schools, nor separate but equal schools, but separate and *better* schools.

# Is There a Key to Academic Success?

What are the relationships between student personality, motivation, and values and academic achievement? This question includes consideration of the student's social and emotional adjustment, effects of cultural assimilation, and self-image. In these very personal areas, can the school play as important a role as the family in developing attitudes conducive to academic success?

There is little disagreement that student personality, attitude, and values are the most critical factors related to school success. Numerous investigations have sought to determine "characteristic" attitudes of Mexican-American students and they relate these characteristics to achievement levels. For example, it is well documented that Mexican-American students often feel academically inferior to their Anglo peers. Furthermore, they often express a sense of frustration, fear, or confusion from the pressures of acculturation or from being a part of two distinct cultures unable to perform satisfactorily in either. These feelings often result in withdrawal from one or both cultures or, at the very least, avoidance of competition.

Do Problems of Acculturation Influence Motivation?   The behavior which these feelings generate is often perceived as lack of motivation which, in turn, is cited as the cause for poor academic performance. Yet a recent study of rural Mexican-American students (preschool through twelfth grade) indicates that Mexican-American students *begin* school with certain characteristics that should give them some advantages in a learning situation. They are shown to be more socially mature and responsible than Anglo students, although they are behind the normative population in perceptual-motor and language development.[18]

The same study indicates that Mexican-American students' feelings of inadequacy increase sharply in grades five and nine where major changes in curriculum occur, and that the feelings of social adjustment are considerably below the average in all grades except the twelfth. With such feelings of personal inadequacy, it seems unlikely that students would appear highly motivated toward school work. Those students who compensate for these feelings by trying harder and becoming outstanding students often have other factors working for them, i.e., they are extremely gifted, physically attractive, have a teacher who is personally interested in them, etc. Generally, theories of motivation and personality suggest that the organism is more concerned with satisfying basic personal needs of security and acceptance than expending energies competing for the rewards of a grading system. Grades and school achievement can be considered higher order needs, and "higher order needs cannot emerge as effective determiners of behavior until more basic needs have been satisfied in some way."[19]

Lack of motivation, then, is a symptom which may have complicated causes difficult to remedy. Many teachers blame home environment, most students blame the school, and both often blame cultural clash. As one student states it: "Man, we can't relate to this competition for grades bit. We don't like the dog eat dog idea, just to get ahead. That's not our way."

This is not to say that Mexican-American students do not aspire to do as much with their lives as any other student. In fact, the evidence is to the contrary. When Mexican-American students are questioned about their ultimate aspirations, the majority express a life goal and ultimate social status similar to that of an Anglo student. Mexican-American students desire to succeed within the social system; even studies done among rural Mexican-American populations show no significant differences between Mexican-American and Anglo students' aspirations.[20]

However, it can be said that Mexican-American students have learned not to expect too much of life. There appears to be definite differences between Anglo and Mexican-American students as far as their expectation levels are concerned. The Mexican-American student indicates that when he views his chances of attaining his life's goals realistically, he is less certain of success than the Anglo student is. This attitude would naturally affect the manner and intensity with which a student pursues long term goals.

However, some Mexican-American students do attain success in the dominant society; and this adult success is usually preceded by academic achievement in school. It might be beneficial, therefore, to look at the differences between the attitudes of achieving and non-achieving Mexican-American students and to ask whether the school could assume more responsibility for developing these attitudes without violating personal freedom. If the answer is affirmative, then educators can develop suitable programs, curriculum, and teaching strategies.

WHAT ARE THE ATTITUDES THAT DETERMINE ACADEMIC SUCCESS?   The Mexican-American Study Project at U.C.L.A. isolates attitudes which distinguish academically successful from academically unsuccessful Mexican-American students. The successful students possess:[21]

1. Personal congruence with the goals toward which the school tasks are directed. The student sees the goals of the school consistent with his goals. The tasks the school asks the student to perform is seen by the student as relevant to his goals.

*Relevant goals:* What are the goals of the Mexican-American student? Which of these goals can the school legitimately reinforce? What goals can the school legitimately inculcate?

2. Rational rather than emotional orientations toward goal attainment activities. The achieving Mexican-American student is generally less emotional or expressive toward school. He sees the rational cause and effect rather than unexplicable emotional basis for events.

*Rationality:* Can the school develop in learners habits of rational behavior? How?

3. Generalized confidence in mankind which allows for effective interpersonal relations in the tasks required by the school. The achieving student has a feeling of confidence and security during the learning activities designed to develop competencies.

*Confidence:* Can the school insure a certain amount of success in performing school tasks so as to build confidence? How?

4. The achieving Mexican-American student has an optimistic definition of the life situation which includes the view that through personal activity, goals can be attained.

*Personal control:* Can the school provide experiences where personal control of environment brings success? How?

5. The achieving student has greater concern for peer rather than adult disapproval, but relative independence from the opinions of peers.

*Independence:* Can the school provide learning experiences which develop independence? How?

WHAT IS THE SCHOOL'S RESPONSIBILITY IN INCULCATING VALUES?    To say that the successful Mexican-American students had developed Anglo values is an oversimplification. These are attitudes built upon values that can be generalized beyond cultural boundaries. They are acceptable attitudes to most people because they are conducive to further growth. They emphasize the individual as a thinking, dignified, competent, human being; they characterize a type of individual who would be respected by any society regardless of the language or the customs. Whether the school can go further to inculcate a standard set of values and attitudes among all students is highly controversial. However, the school can do considerable service by developing among students an understanding of his own culture and that of others. More important, the school can encourage cultural plurality by allowing cultural choice, based upon understanding. The school can help the individual become knowledgeable of reasonable alternatives and consequences of culture, so that he can consciously choose, without penalty, those aspects of any culture he wishes to retain.

HOW DOES CULTURAL PLURALISM AFFECT ACADEMIC ACHIEVEMENT?    Cultural pluralism probably is more common than realized, especially among minority group members who become successful in the general society but have retained their ethnic identity.
A Mexican-American teacher, who is successful by Anglo as well as Mexican standards,
relates this experience which illustrates conscious cultural choice:

> "I can truthfully say that I think like a Mexican. I'll tell you what I mean. In
> college I took a test in a psychology class and I'll never forget how I felt about
> one question. It was a multiple choice and went like this: 'When you get mar-
> ried you should— a) remain closely tied to your family; b) leave your family
> and establish a home of your own.' Now I know I should have chosen "b" but
> I chose "a", and later I told the instructor why. I love my family—my mother
> first because she gave me life, my children because I gave them life, and my
> wife because she makes life worth living. I don't think I should have gotten the
> question wrong, do you?"

One can assume that this teacher's choice was determined largely by the cultural
teachings he received at home. Another important assumption is that in spite of his
thinking like a Mexican, this teacher has been able to achieve academic and professional
success. To what extent did his family help or hinder his success? Or, generalizing from
this case, to what extent does the home environment of Mexican-American students determine their academic success?

The question of family influence upon academic achievement is an intricate one that
involves personal conflicts which occur when there are cultural, socioeconomic, and linguistic differences in the school population. Studies which seek to establish cause and
effect relationships indicate that no one family characteristic, alone, causes the Mexican-
American student to lag behind the Anglo in academic achievement; rather, the elements
of family life are interrelated, and various elements emerge as most important in different
studies. Those factors which have been isolated as most important to student achievement are the family's language patterns, cultural affiliation, socioeconomic status, and
educational attainment.

The relationship between the family's language habits and achievement has been
studied more than most, because language patterns are easily identified and considered
essential to academic achievement. Most studies indicate that Mexican-American children coming from English-speaking families show more initial school achievement than
those coming from Spanish-speaking families. However, it has not been clearly demonstrated that the use of Spanish in the home, *per se,* is the factor most detrimental to
school achievement. The Spanish-speaking home has to have other cultural factors in
order for the language to deter learning.

If, for example, Spanish language patterns are well developed at home, school achievement is enhanced because the child is prepared to handle abstractions and conceptualize
experience through language. Furthermore, his progress would be accelerated if the

school were prepared to instruct him in his native language and systematically teach him a second language (English). However, even if he were left to make the transition to the second language by himself, he would learn if "other" conditions were positive.

"Other conditions" were isolated in a study by Ronald Henderson and published under the title "Environment Stimulation and Intellectual Development of Mexican-American Children."[22] Potential high achievers scored high on both Spanish and English vocabulary, and families that had recently arrived from Mexico had as many high potential achievers as those families that had been in the United States a generation or more. Access to books, newspapers, opportunities for travel, and social interaction appeared to offset the initial disadvantage of coming from a Spanish-speaking home, particularly when the school provided intensive language experiences in English. These factors of family life reflect its socioeconomic and educational level which are more basic to school achievement than ability to speak English.

Language, then, becomes significant as it represents life style or general cultural attitudes of the family. The use of Spanish in the home often indicates adherence to Mexican or Hispanic culture, while Mexican-American homes in which English is spoken may indicate a greater degree of acculturation. However, again it is not a simple matter of Anglo versus Mexican culture which enhances school achievement. The Mexican culture values education, and children coming directly from Mexico often become high achievers.

The real barrier to achievement seems to occur when values espoused in the home and subsequent behavior are in opposition to those values and behavior needed to achieve in the school, e.g., competition versus cooperation, questioning versus acceptance of authority. When value systems of the home and school are not mutually supportive, the student is at a disadvantage because he may be unable to operate consistently enough to achieve in either system. His feelings about himself and his family become the crucial barrier to school achievement.

> "The truth is that the language problem is but a superficial coating over a much deeper problem which encompasses culture, self concept, attitudes, and values. It is an important aspect of the overall problem but learning to speak English is no answer . . . It's not just the language problem. It includes the gathering of information, comprehension, the ability to handle symbolic reproduction— all of these are important in the learning process. Most important of all is the feeling the child has about himself."[23]

The critical question becomes: what can the school do to lessen the problems felt by students who come from homes which do not or cannot reinforce the attitudes and skills necessary for scholastic achievement? Experiments throughout the country with bilingual programs of education in which instruction is offered in Spanish and English should produce some useful guidelines for helping students from non-English speaking homes. Even more promising are programs taking a bilingual-bicultural approach. In these programs, there is concerted effort to promote cultural understanding as well as linguistic

71

skill. Bilingual-bicultural programs indicate the school's willingness to accept the child with his unique needs and capabilities and adapt the educational program so as to capitalize upon them. These programs may, in fact, provide models for all school districts that wish to develop bilingual citizens.

At any rate, the family and its influence upon student achievement must be looked upon from a broad perspective as having provided the structure from which to build the student's potential. Where the family provides a second language and cultural background, the school must build upon this background to enrich the total society.

MEASURING THE INFLUENCE OF FAMILY LIFE ON STUDENT ACHIEVEMENT    A functional summary of the major characteristics of family life which affect student achievement is provided in an analysis model developed in the Henderson study quoted earlier. It can easily be adapted to assess the background of students when planning a suitable educational program.

1. Socioeconomic status as determined by the Warner Scale (source of income, house type, dwelling area).

2. Achievement Press;
   Parental aspirations for the education of the child;
   Parents' own aspirations;
   Parents' interest in academic achievement, participation in educational activities.

3. Social Press for Academic Achievement;
   Educational attainment of close friends, relatives;
   Existence of academically successful models.

4. Standards of reward for educational attainment.

5. Parental knowledge of the educational progress of the child.

6. Parental planning and preparation for the attainment of educational goals;
   Financial preparation;
   Social preparation—selection of friends.

7. Parents' perceptions of vocational alternatives for the major wage earner.

8. Parents' perceptions of vocational alternatives for the child.

9. Parents' language habits;
   Quality of language usage;
   Opportunities for enlargement and use of vocabulary and sentence patterns;
   Proportion of Spanish to English spoken in the home;

Quality of Spanish spoken in the home;
Degree of verbal interaction in the home.

10. Parents' guidance on matters relating to school work;
Availability of guidance;
Quality of guidance;
Availability and use of materials and facilities related to school learning.

11. Frequency of family participation in community groups or sodalities.

12. Parents' perception of the importance of school for a successful life.[24]

The use of such an instrument of analysis necessitates communication with the parents. In order to use the model, the school must move out into the community. When this occurs, educators will be brought into contact with other perceptions and attitudes about school and society which may be new and controversial.

The Chicano attitude emerging in school and community should be considered when developing curriculum and teaching methodology because the Chicano student activist can be a motivating force to stimulate formal education or be a potent force to halt education. For most teachers and other members of the "establishment," the Chicano perspective is difficult to accept. He quotes Fidel Castro, spouts slogans about reclaiming the Southwest, has a whole new set of revolutionary heroes, and is active in student strikes and walk outs. To many educators, he is a problem. Nevertheless he is deeply involved and concerned about education, and his numbers grow in all age brackets.

# A Chicano Attitude Emerges

There is little doubt that Mexican Americans throughout the United States have found their voice, individually and collectively. Much of the impetus can be attributed to outspoken Chicano activists on college campuses and their political associates in the larger community. Together, they have succeeded in publicizing the plight of the Mexican American and have mobilized what might prove to be an effective force in furthering their cause, the betterment of living conditions for disadvantaged Mexican Americans.

To say that there is one Chicano attitude would be naive. There are as many attitudes as there are student movements, Mexican-American communities, leaders, etc. The movement is dynamic and sensitive to local needs. Yet there are common themes, just as there are common goals. Some of the Chicano themes and attitudes are disconcerting, at the very least, and frightening to many non-Chicanos.

Nevertheless, those attitudes which most significantly affect the school will be summarized as the final perspective of Mexican-American students to be considered for planning curriculum and teaching strategies.

A CHICANO DEMAND: CHANGES IN THE BASIC GOALS OF EDUCATION    *Chicanos feel the school has not helped them; they feel excluded and hindered.* Even during the initial stages of the Chicano Movement, Chicanos were quick to state what they felt were the major causes of their predicament and the conditions they felt were needed for remedying the situation.*

> "We had always seen ourselves as Americans in the modern school. We had no group consciousness; consequently, we blamed ourselves for our condition. We had to realize that individuals are created by society and place the blame upon the social system that had put us on the bottom of the economic scale and on the lowest levels of achievement in the schools. We had to develop group consciousness, a pride of belonging."†

The school as an instrument of society received the initial attack and continues to be a forum for confrontation. Chicano demands include changes in curriculum and staffing:

> "We want to have the school curriculum include the Mexican American historically and socially. We want the Anglo student to be aware of the presence of the Mexican American and his problems. Everywhere we have been excluded . . . literature, history, philosophy, folklore. Everything is geared to the Anglo or the English-European school of thought. We know little about South American playwrights, philosophers and even less of the Mexican intellectual. We want to know these people, and we want all students to know them."

> "We want Mexican Americans in administrative positions; we want to identify with these models starting in elementary school through junior high school and all the way through college."

Chicanos ask for changes in the basic objectives of education. They want the school to develop ideals of cultural pluralism or social individuality rather than social unity or conformity. At the same time they ask for economic uniformity in the larger community

---

* Major organization of Chicano students occurred in Southern California in September, 1967, with the help of two existing Mexican American organizations, La Causa and the Mexican American Student Confederation (MASC).

† Quotes are taken from taped interviews with Chicano student organizers at San Fernando Valley State College. The author is particularly indebted to Mr. Miguel Verdugo.

or a form of socialism; but they are careful to distinguish it from communism. At any rate, they do not express great loyalty to democracy as an ideology. This has great implications for the school, both in terms of how well it has educated students to participate in a democracy and what the task ahead is if democracy is to survive.

> "We can see the contradictions in our society, the way democratic ideals have been implemented. We can see how we have been excluded and we can't embrace something that has discriminated against us. Maybe we don't understand democracy or recognize its basic worth. We have to explore other ideologies."

CHICANO ATTITUDES ABOUT EDUCATORS    *Chicanos feel educators do not understand nor condone their concept of revolution and social change.* Chicano students identify with revolutionaries because they are concerned with social injustices and change. They project into their movement the idea of a revolutionary spirit fighting for the cause of a downtrodden people. Their heroes include Che Gueverra, Fidel Castro, Mao Tse Tung, as well as Emiliano Zapata and Pancho Villa.

> "Because they are revolutionaries in the true sense, they didn't tolerate the injustices of the system. They defy the stereotypes of Latins as being humble, docile. Many of them never contradicted themselves, they devoted their lives to the betterment of their people. Some even died as a result of a revolutionary act, assassination."

Chicano students are quick to add, however, that their concept of revolution does not include open warfare against the system.

> "Most people are afraid a revolutionary is going to pick up arms and fight. Other groups like the Minute Men are more able to fight, but they're not considered revolutionary!"

> "The students want change, but they don't want to die as martyrs. To arm and fight in the revolutionary sense means to fight in self-defense, or possibly as guerilla warfare."

The identification with revolutionaries and with the poor often takes symbolic form such as posters, slogans, terms, and dress. In a sense, the identification is more emotional than intellectual for many students who are experimenting and searching for answers to their problems. Nevertheless, they are quick to initiate action in the name of social justice.

To think that Chicano students believe only in using established channels or rational means to bring about change would be a mistake; they have seen, used, and achieved change more successfully through other means.

"For thirty years, organizations like the G.I. Forum and MAPA have been trying to make changes in the general society for the betterment of Mexican Americans. They have not done so because they tried to do it through "channels." They were tolerant, respectful; they believed the politicians and administrators. They learned something from the student movement; if you scream a little louder, intimidate, and demonstrate, you get more results. Now *they* are questioning a system that respond to violence and not to social problems."

Most important, Chicano students see the school as only one aspect of a system which has discriminated against them. Real reform, they feel, must be initiated and occur in the Mexican-American community because the school is a relatively ineffective means for bringing about social change.

"We have been mistaken in attempting to reform the school. It is an almost powerless institution. We are beginning to realize that not only are students powerless, but so are the teachers. They can't implement change; the authority lies elsewhere. It has to be general community reform."

A CHICANO PHILOSOPHY OF LIFE—GROUP COHESIVENESS  *Chicanos feel a sense of community.* Group cohesiveness is not only a means for survival and mobility to the Chicano student, it is a philosophy of life. To the Chicano student, community infers mutual needs, goals, communication, and support. Furthermore, during the time of struggle, the welfare of the group is placed somewhat above individual concerns.

"Do we force or intimidate an individual to keep him in the group? No, you can't achieve humanistic goals by being fascistic, but we are in a group struggle. People who want to be a part of the movement must do something for the group; they cannot be parasites. We don't want ('overnight Chicanos'). They don't understand the problems, they just want the benefits."

To Chicanos, community refers largely to the Mexican-American barrio where people have a common heritage as well as common problems. Even though students identify with the poor, they have increased their attempts to relate to and enlist the support of middle class Mexican Americans.

"We must close the generation gap by bringing families, older people, all Mexican Americans of the community into the movement. We create a little prick on the middle class ass to get it moving because they have the resources to get things done. And it's working!"

The sense of community, therefore, includes all members who wish to join the movement. Even the old separation of roles between the sexes disappears. The "chicana" is an active partner. She is a co-worker and often a leader within the group who shows every indication of becoming a knowledgeable, aggressive adult.

Most basic is the Chicanos' sense of debt to the community. Social consciousness means continuing to be involved in community affairs even when professional or economic security is attained.

> "Our people live in pain and sorrow. We must stay close to our people so that we can feel their pain; so that we do not forget when we, ourselves, stop hurting."

ONE CHICANO GOAL: RECOGNITION AS A CULTURAL ETHNIC ENTITY   *Chicanos feel educators do not recognize and understand their unique qualities.* Chicanos constantly ask for recognition as a cultural ethnic entity. Their search for self-identity, recognition, and respect from society in general and the school in particular takes many forms of action. One of the most obvious reactions has been the rejection of Anglo traditions and the promotion of Mexican culture.

> "It's 'Viva Mexico!' Viva the values, traditions, and customs that are no longer useful to us. It's blind, idealistic identification with Mexico when many Mexicans would reject us just like the Anglos. We're really somewhere in between Anglo and Mexican, but we're too bitter to be Anglo."

Another reaction has been the struggle to maintain identity as a minority group separate and apart from the Black Civil Rights Movement. In drawing distinctions between themselves and Black Americans, Chicanos point out a different history, cultural rather than racial differences, greater economic and educational deprivation. Most important, they accuse the general society of being more sensitive to the disadvantages suffered by Black Americans. Chicanos feel that they are caught in the Black-White syndrome in which they feel all the problems of discrimination and minority status but fewer of the advantages of special recognition.

> "Chicanos will not tolerate being the scapegoat for hostilities that Whites feel against Blacks; nor will Chicanos be left out or be secondary when their needs are greater . . ."

As the Chicano student expresses his feelings, it becomes apparent that he is not an "easy" student to manage or manipulate. He is complex, blunt, candid, suspicious, and defensive. However, he is articulate, informed, intelligent, and above all, motivated. What direction his social consciousness, his emotional commitments, and his energy take will depend largely upon his experiences in school and society. He is a challenge. Can the school accept the potent force of the Chicano student, thereby utilizing his potential to foster learning and improve society? It seems that this might be the most critical question schools will be called upon to answer in the decades ahead.

Stupid America

*stupid america, see that chicano*
*with a big knife*
*in his steady hand*
*he doesn't want to knife you*
*he wants to sit on a bench*
*and carve christfigures*
*but you won't let him.*
*stupid america, hear that chicano*
*shouting curses on the street*
*he is a poet*

*without paper and pencil*
*and since he cannot write*
*he will explode.*
*stupid america, remember that chicanito*
*flunking math and english*
*he is the picasso*
*of your western states*
*but he will die*
*with one thousand masterpieces*
*hanging only from his mind.*

Abelardo
CHICANO—25 pieces of a chicano mind*

---

*Used by permission of the author.

# 5

# PLANNING TEACHING STRATEGIES:
## Meeting the Needs of Mexican-American Students

If you can show me how I can cling to that which is real to me, while teaching me a way into the larger society, then I will not only drop my defenses and my hostility, but I will sing your praises, and I will help you to make the desert bear fruit.

Ralph Ellison

The quotation above asks educators to do what we have verbalized as a basic principle of education for decades—to educate each individual to his highest potential in order to enrich and improve the general society. In 1960, the Report of the President's Commission on National Goals in *Goals for Americans* reiterated the importance of the individual to the welfare of the nation:

The status of the individual must remain our primary concern. All our institutions—political, social, and economic—must further enhance the dignity of the citizen, promote the maximum development of his capabilities, stimulate their responsible exercise, and widen the range and effectiveness of opportunities for individual choice.[1]

That this goal has not been realized for the majority of Mexican Americans is obvious from statistics indicating low economic status, low educational attainment, and from the concerned statements of Mexican Americans themselves. Educational institutions so vital to the implementation of this goal have either ignored the needs of Mexican-American students and expected them to adapt to a set curriculum and standard teaching procedures or have considered Mexican Americans as "problem" groups of students whose handicaps are to be alleviated in the most expedient manner possible.

As late as 1966, a California State Department of Education survey revealed that out of 896 districts having large numbers of Mexican-American students in attendance 89 percent had no district-wide program specifically for them: 57 percent of the teachers did not have any special training in working with non-English speaking students; and 68 percent of the districts had no regularly scheduled conferences with parents. The report went on to say that 77 percent of the districts had no specially prepared curricular materials, nor had they engaged in any project to prepare such materials.[2]

# Special Programs for Mexican-American Students

Though today the picture throughout the nation is somewhat improved in that there are more special programs for Mexican-American students, the critical question becomes: What type and quality of educational programs have been instituted? Are the programs more than remedial or compensatory in nature? Do they recognize the dignity of the student and his heritage by reflecting his culture, history, values? Do the programs result in needed competencies and attitudes which facilitate further independent learning? Do the programs motivate the students to be participating members of the school or larger society? Do the teaching strategies challenge the student to develop his intellect, express his feelings, work through his emotional and social problems? Do the programs utilize the best professional knowledge, teaching strategies, technology, and resources available? Do they utilize what we know about Mexican-American students from a historical, cultural, socioeconomic and empirical perspective? Are the programs implemented at the classroom level? Does the behavior of teachers and students reflect the goals and purposes of these programs?

These criteria infer basic philosophic positions about the function and purposes of education as well as the nature of the learner. However, it is the last criterion that is most critical because intended objectives are unimportant unless they actually affect the individuals involved.

THE TEACHER: KEY TO PROGRAM IMPLEMENTATION    Since it is the teacher who plans learning activities, initiates action, and stimulates or retards student behavior, the teacher is the key to program implementation. In order for educational programs to become reality, teachers must consider the suggested program practical and its underlying assumptions consistent with their beliefs, which are by no means uniform as the following quotations indicate:

"Here are the pages, read them, and answer the questions. You cannot have an oral discussion with them. The only thing they function with is structure."

"I have a 5th grade. Not more than a third of my class can read the 3rd grade book. They read a chapter and do a little seat work. They fill in one word or they read a sentence and fill in the word above that belongs in the right place. Or they mark five little sentences true or false according to the book. I find that this is what they need because they will do it, and they enjoy doing it because they understand what they are doing."

"Our children are not far enough advanced to profit from projects, activities, or construction. They don't have the intellectual resources to sit and work quietly or independently. Besides, I can't see why we have to sneak up on children, and hit them over the head with a little bit of learning when they're not suspecting it. I don't see why they can't learn, knowing that they are supposed to be learning."

"If it doesn't move or you can't eat it, who needs it? Most of the things that I do are experience related. We make butter; we taste different kinds of meat. Then we talk about it, and they understand. We need more work with real things. We need to make the room exciting."

"Games! Do anything that can make learning a game! We started a math lab once a week on Fridays. Can you imagine Fridays—1:15-2:00, the hardest part of the week? We couldn't get them to clean up this week, they were so excited. They were doing math strictly by playing games. I think the whole key to teaching is a little gimmick or game, if you think of it."

PLANNING TEACHING STRATEGIES   To establish an educational program that would satisfy all the teachers quoted above would be impossible and serve little purpose. Therefore, a series of teaching strategies based upon explicit assumptions and objectives has been constructed to illustrate the type of educational program needed by Mexican-American students who live in an urban setting. A complete teaching unit is presented with objectives sensitive to the needs of Mexican-American students, curriculum content which is relevant, and teaching strategies which not only are consistent with educational objectives important for these students, but also consistent with current professional developments in curriculum design and teaching methodology. Every attempt has been made to keep suggestions practical by utilizing ideas and learning activities which have been tried in classrooms. The sources of information for teachers and students include multimedia teaching resources suitable for students who are likely to have English language handicaps.

For teachers who are bilingual (Spanish/English) the teaching unit is presented in Spanish, as well, to facilitate presenting the content or conducting the strategies in both languages. Either the concurrent bilingual approach or the separate language approach may be used. Appropriate teaching resources produced in Spanish are included. Most important, both the content and the teaching strategies encourage bicultural activities and learning. The strategies are often open-ended, explore different value structures, and encourage a discussion of differing viewpoints.

Generally, the unit emphasizes two curriculum areas which are most important to Mexican-American students, language and the social sciences. The social sciences logically provide curriculum content sensitive to the Mexican-American students' concerns about self and society. Within the social sciences, studies can be devised which capitalize upon the Chicano students' concern for community, cultural heritage, and his commitment to social change. Taught effectively, these studies can stimulate the learning of a variety of intellectual skills.

In the suggested teaching strategies, the social sciences are used as a vehicle to motivate language learning and as a base for meaningful application of language skills. However, it is assumed that systematic instruction in language is being conducted concurrently, and possibilities for utilizing the unit to motivate functional language lessons will be explored in the next chapter along with sources of appropriate language programs. In this chapter the unit is written so that it retains a content structure conducive to the orderly development of social science concepts which are essential to Mexican-American students. Furthermore, since the teaching strategies employed determine the extent to which the social sciences can perform a vital function in the education of any student, the role of the teacher and the role of the student are carefully drawn in the strategies so as to encourage students to establish relevant goals, habits of rationality, feelings of self confidence and personal control over a portion of their environment.

The teaching strategies emphasize development of the tools of inquiry to the extent that controversial issues and value differences may be approached rationally and in a manner that promotes continued and independent learning. Generally, the strategies are somewhat different in order to motivate students who may not like school. Throughout, activities are designed with concern for students' attitudes about self and school.

The unit is written for upper elementary grades or junior high school students. Similar content, objectives, and inquiry strategies can be adapted for different age levels. For example, many of the lessons could be simplified for primary children. The basic structure of the upper grade unit also is appropriate for high school students if art and manipulative activities (which seldom are possible in traditionally organized secondary schools) are eliminated and other texts or activities suitable to their maturity level are substituted. For example, lesson nine introduces concepts of leadership, government, and power through simulation. This would be an excellent motivational activity in civics, senior problems, or sociology courses. The content areas involved would be studied more in depth; and though the sequence of learning problems could remain the same, the conceptual outcomes for high school students would be of increased complexity.*

---

* The author wishes to acknowledge the assistance of Dr. Johanna K. Lemlech who contributed and field-tested parts of this unit.

# Community and Culture

*(A Unit of Study for Upper-Grade Mexican-American Students)*

### INTRODUCTION

"Community and Culture" is a unit that stresses communication and inquiry as the means of acquiring knowledge about important questions. It is written for a special group of students in grades five through eight who live either in the barrio or in the inner city of a large metropolis. Many of these students have changed their place of residence often and have transferred from school to school. Some are absent from school frequently and have never visited another part of the city. Many of these students lack English language skills and are shy or reticent to expose their language inadequacies in the classroom. Most of them are disenchanted with school and lack interest in schoolwork.

The unit is centered in the social sciences and attempts to implement three main goals of social science education, i.e., the goal of humanistic education, citizenship education, and intellectual education.[3] The first goal is directed toward assisting students to realize and satisfy their own ego needs and comprehend the elements involved in their own life style. The second goal, that of citizenship education, should help students interact effectively with their peers as well as prepare them for meaningful participation in adult society. The third goal, intellectual education, should help students develop thinking skills and the conceptual knowledge necessary for thinking.

Inherent in these goals and of notable importance in this unit are the levels of student thinking and feeling stimulated by the learning activities. Since both the affective and cognitive aspects of learning are important, many of the learning activities suggested are designed to move students from the simple cognitive and affective levels to the more complex through situations purposefully designed to stimulate student inquiry.

Inquiry has been selected as the major teaching strategy to be employed; therefore, it is necessary to define inquiry as it is intended for this unit and provide an overview of its essential elements and functions.

**What is an inquiry strategy?** An inquiry strategy is a teaching technique that stresses student output or production. It is designed to provoke student thinking. Although the teacher may set the stage and the conditions for learning, it is the student's responsibility to search, define, and theorize. Inquiry is process oriented.

Social scientists use modes of inquiry to study culture, society, or social problems. They may study *analytically* as they attempt to describe or examine evidence to discover why social phenomena occur in particular ways. They may study a culture or society *integratively* to discover holistic relationships. They may also study a culture or society's values in order to make future judgments *or policy-type decisions*.

How can an inquiry strategy be used to stimulate thinking and enrich the Mexican-American student's vocabulary? The perceptive teacher using this strategy plans his questions and activities to motivate a variety of thinking operations and verbal responses. Using Bloom's and Krathwohl's *Taxonomies of Educational Objectives,*[4, 5] "Community and Culture" provides examples of teacher questions and planned activities which encourage multi-levels of behavior in thought, response, feeling, and action. The following situation elicits cognitive and affective responses:

> Using a variety of media, students are seeking to discover the "ways of life" of one of the following early civilizations: Mayas, Toltecs, Aztecs, or Spanish during the conquest. In concluding their study, students will define culture and evaluate the influence and contributions of peoples to one another.

To elicit *knowledge* level of thinking and response, the teacher asks, "What happened in the daily life of the community?" Using media resources, the students will observe art, music, language, occupations, and learning in their chosen community. Students will share their knowledge by producing a picture or a mural, writing stories or plays, and discussing their community with other students.

To elicit comprehension level of thinking and interpretation the teacher may ask: "What types of activities did the people pursue?" "What types of things did the people believe to be true?" "Why was their civilization conquered?" The teacher determines extent of comprehension by listening to the student discussion and by observation of the group's project.

At the *application* level of thought, the teacher may ask: "In what ways did the activities of children differ from the activities of adults?" "How do your activities differ from the adults in *your* community?" As students perform in short plays, create scrapbooks or murals, the teacher will observe whether or not they have applied their knowledge and differentiated between the roles of adults and children.

To encourage higher level thinking, students will be asked to *analyze* their civilization in relationship to others: "What contributions did the community make to later civilizations?" "In what ways did conquest contribute to the Mexican heritage?"

To motivate *synthesis,* the teacher poses the following questions: "In what ways did the (Mayas) contribute to life in the barrio?" "If each civilization was more advanced than the one before it, what will life in the barrio be like in a hundred years from now?"

* Through discussion students *evaluate* the contributions of cultures to one another, after they have pursued activities which lead them to categorize aspects of culture and draw inferences about the way cultures borrow, appropriate, and diffuse.

Examples of affective motivation and developmental activities may be taken from the same lesson:

---

* For complete list of questions and activities refer to Lesson Six, "Community and Culture," page 118.

The teacher plays the record "Mariachi Aguilas de Chapala" and asks the students: "How does this music make you feel?" Some of the students will merely smile, keep time, or nod. These students are registering *awareness* or the *receiving* level of affect. Other students will verbalize and indicate a *responding* level of feeling. A third group of students may argue or engage in debate about what they hear and how it makes them feel. These students are engaging in *valuing*.

The teacher should ask: "Why do you associate these songs with the Mexican people or with life in the barrio?" The question will force students to organize their thoughts and feelings, and they will then be involved at a higher level of affective response. This level is called *organization*. The highest level of affective response, *characterization,* may be achieved by asking the students: "What can we learn about people by listening to the music that they enjoy?" "Why do we associate certain songs with certain people?" Finally, the students are asked to create or perform some music which they would associate with the barrio.

Actual classroom activities seldom separate the affective from the cognitive. When students cut, paste, list, and discuss items typically found in the barrio home and items typically found in the Anglo home, they are developing intellectual skills of comparing, contrasting, and organizing aspects of culture. At the same time, they are experiencing feelings about self-identity, minority-majority status, and about people who are alike or different from themselves. As students engage in evaluative discussions focusing upon their tasks and inquiries, controversy occurs and students learn to examine value statements, to define problems, and to question the relevancy of their information. The use of open-ended questions which allow a variety of conclusions stimulates cognitive and affective freedom. The learner may delve into a question deeply or superficially depending upon his ability and restrictions imposed by time and materials available.

Student responses and behavior as they engage in problem solving, decision making, the production of projects or materials provide the teacher with opportunities for both objective and subjective evaluation.

By observing students in a variety of activities, the teacher can recognize, diagnose, and prescribe in the areas of language and social studies according to the students' cognitive and affective needs.

**What are the elements of inquiry strategy in terms of teacher and student behaviors?** The elements of inquiry strategy are best described in terms of teacher and student tasks or responsibilities during the process. Examples of teacher tasks during inquiry:

1. Creates an environment that is rich in resources;
2. Creates situations, problems, and settings that are intrinsically motivating and relevant;
3. Creates open-ended questions so that the learner sets his own goals and works at his own cognitive and affective level;

4. Creates questions and activities based upon assessment of students' cognitive and affective levels of behavior and designed to demand increasingly complex and accurate student responses;
5. Creates a variety of means by which the learner may respond through voice and action;
6. Creates a general climate for learning that is supportive so that the student feels free to explore and express ideas;
7. Demonstrates confidence and faith in the rational abilities of students.

Examples of student tasks during inquiry:

1. Searches for solutions to problems using a variety of resources;
2. Questions, focuses, or defines a problem;
3. Initiates a new inquiry, plans a task;
4. Responds to another's inquiry;
5. Defines, infers, generalizes, concludes;
6. Makes decisions and choices on the basis of pertinent information and evidence;
7. Receives data attentively, responds through facial expression, gesture or words;
8. Acclaims, refutes, denies, confirms;
9. Creates—stories, articles, films, slides, pictures, scrapbooks, maps, time-lines, charades, scripts, plays, skits, records, paintings, crafts, songs, and dances.

During the unit activities, it is suggested that the students often be divided into small inquiry groups to pursue the problems listed. The optimum number of students for an inquiry group seems to be five to seven students, and the length of time needed for profitable work depends upon the social and verbal maturity of the group, as well as their familiarity with the procedure. Groups need to be small enough so that each student participates in the decisions to be made. It is also advantageous to have five or six different inquiry groups in the classroom working simultaneously to allow the teacher to observe and evaluate the interaction and to allow students freedom to think and debate.

**How does inquiry as a teaching strategy benefit students?** Some of the major benefits are as follows:

1. Small inquiry groups allow each student the opportunity to be both a contributor and a listener. If groups are heterogeneous, interaction is facilitated.
2. Small inquiry groups allow a certain anonymity which releases student inhibition when many groups are pursuing problems in different areas of the classroom and the teacher is "circulating."

3. During evaluation, students can discover that it is rare for two groups to interpret similar evidence in the same way. Controversy stimulates value conflict, debate, clarification, and organization.
4. Personal involvement in inquiry groups pursuing a problem revelant to the learner, hopefully results in increased motivation and learning.
5. If students are encouraged to communicate in their dominant language, inquiry groups provide vital practice and reinforcement to native language and second language teaching.

**What kinds of resources are needed for inquiry strategies?** Since inquiry is an output technique, students need many different sources of information which may or may not require fluency in English. Many multimedia resources can be used by the teacher to determine and depict currently significant conflict situations suitable to motivate student inquiry. Resources for inquiry activities, although not intended to be conclusive, include the following:

| | |
|---|---|
| texts; | posters, pictures, records; |
| atlas; | charts; |
| maps; | artifacts; |
| transparencies; | realia; |
| filmstrips; | slides; |
| recreational centers; | the community; |
| teacher-prepared materials; | industries; |
| 8 mm films; | businesses; |
| 16 mm films; | visitors, experts; |
| cultural centers; | situations, problems, stories; |
| role-plays; simulations; | experiences. |

**What kinds of situations or problems motivate inquiry?** Inquiry may be motivated by a story, a paragraph about a particular event, a picture, a film, filmstrip, an interview, a conflict situation, conflicting evidence, value conflict, discrepant information, ad infinitum. Inquiry *need not* be motivated through reading. Some examples of situations which have motivated inquiry are the following:

1. Six groups of students are each given a different menu to examine. The menu has no name, restaurant, date, or location on it. Students are asked to discuss or merely ask themselves questions about what the menu tells us about the people who ate these foods? The historical setting or time period for the menus might represent the following: A barrio restaurant today; Texas—in the 1800's; New England during the Colonial period; California during the Gold Rush mining period; any urban restaurant today; any ethnic restaurant today.

During an evaluative discussion, the teacher might focus upon:

   a. How does food reflect where we live?
   b. In what ways does our food reflect how we live?
   c. What are some things we can learn about people by observing the foods they eat?
   d. In what ways does the food we eat reflect our cultural heritage?

2. Students listen to three records. The records are not identified for them. They are asked to think about and discuss:

   a. In what ways are the records similar, dissimilar?
   b. What activities are reflected by the music?
   c. Who are the people involved?
   d. In what ways does music reflect cultural characteristics?

Suggested records might include childrens' songs of Mexico, California Indian songs, English folk songs.

3. A small group of students was given a paragraph to read concerning the need to fence in portions of the Southwest for farming purposes. Another group of students was given a paragraph to read concerning the need for ranchers to have open grazing lands for their cattle. Both groups of students were given plausible reasons stating the farmers' and ranchers' viewpoints. Then the students were asked to role-play what happened when these two groups came into contact. Students then inquired into the actual settlement.

**What kinds of questions motivate inquiry?** The questions teachers ask determine the quality of thinking that students will do. Questions which are open-ended allow the student more freedom to work at his own cognitive and affective level. For example, questions asking, "What happened?" affords each student the opportunity to describe what occurred in terms of his own observation. When the teacher next asks, "Why did it happen?" each student may interpret to the best of his ability, develop a theory, draw inferences, make a generalization, or come to a conclusion. In an inquiry situation, when students are asked to communicate their interpretations in some manner, they are forced to organize their ideas. When controversy occurs, students' judgments are questioned and tested; peers and teachers examine value statements, define new problems, and bring in pertinent information. The teacher's questioning techniques need to allow a variety of student responses growing out of different types of research.

**How can teachers help students organize the results of their inquiry and thereby evaluate pupil's cognitive and affective learnings?** As students organize or intellectualize the results of their inquiry their behavior and their products provide the teacher with the means for evaluating learnings. Teacher observation and judgment become important aspects of the evaluation process. Equally important, the students are provided with opportunities for self and peer evaluation. Some of the activities that can be used to help students organize and intellectualize the results of their research are the following:

1. Dramatizing the ways in which the Mexican settler modified and adapted the environment of the Southwest as he mined, farmed, or ranched;
2. Participating in simulations which demonstrate conceptual understanding of leadership and government;
3. Identifying changes in the Southwest resulting from immigration, technology, and government;
4. Choosing appropriate pictures in the barrio to film and paint;
5. Debating about problems which affect community life.

<table>
<tr><td>

## Synopsis of the Content and Conceptual Structure of "Community and Culture"

*(In order of development and complexity)*

</td><td>

## Una sinopsis del contenido y de la estructura conceptual de « comunidad y cultura »

*(Siguiendo el orden de desarrollo y complejidad)*

</td></tr>
<tr><td>

9. Decision-making reflects the creative power and leadership of a community.

8. People respond to change. Leaders ascend.

7. Technological change affects the community. Problems arise.

6. Our adaptation is reflected in our cultural expressions.

5. We modify and adapt to our environment.

4. Our community environment affects our behavior.

3. Groups migrate and join new communities to satisfy human needs.

2. I am important. My family and I are

</td><td>

9. La habilidad de hacer decisiones refleja el poder creativo y la iniciativa de la comunidad.

8. La gente reacciona ante el cambio. La iniciativa para dirigir asciende.

7. El cambio tecnológico afecta la comunidad. Surgen los problemas.

6. Nuestra adaptación se refleja en nuestras expresiones culturales.

5. Nos modificamos y nos adaptamos a nuestro ambiente.

4. El ambiente de nuestra comunidad afecta nuestra forma de comportarnos.

3. Los grupos migran y se unen a comunidades nuevas para satisfacer necesidades humanas.

2. Soy importante. Mi familia y yo somos

</td></tr>
</table>

contributing members of our community.

1. I live in a community. A community is people.

## Goals For Student Learning

1. Development of communicative skills in the student's dominant language and in his second language:

    a. by providing a variety of learning experiences to stimulate varied levels of language—comprehending, speaking, reading, writing;

    b. by providing opportunities to speak to small and large groups of peers and adults, to read, to organize and express ideas through physical movement, art, drama, writing;

    c. by providing a climate for learning that is "safe" so that the learner is motivated and free to express himself and communicate through a variety of media.

2. Enhancement of the self-concept:

    a. by providing opportunities to discuss self and family in a manner that enhances the unique contributions of individuals to society, of minority cultures to dominant cultures;

miembros que contribuyen a nuestra comunidad.

1. Vivo en una comunidad. Una comunidad está compuesta de gente.

## Metas de aprendizaje para el estudiante

1. Desarrollo de la destreza del estudiante en su idioma dominante y su segundo idioma. Este objetivo se realiza:

    a. dándose una variedad de experiencias en el aprendizaje para desarrollar varios nipeles en el idioma: comprender, hablar, leer, escribir.

    b. dándose oportunidades de hablar con grupos pequeños, o grandes, de jóvenes de la misma edad y de adultos; de leer; de organizar; y de expresar ideas por medio de movimiento físico, de arte, de drama, y de escritura.

    c. dándose una atmósfera de aprendizaje que sea "familiar", de modo que el estudiante sea motivado a expresarse libremente y a comunicarse a través de una variedad de medios.

2. Engrandecimiento del concepto de sí mismo. Este objetivo se realiza:

    a. dándose oportunidades de discutirse a sí mismo y a la familia de una manera que demuestre las contribuciones únicas de los individuos a la sociedad y las de las culturas de minorías a las culturas dominantes.

b. by providing a climate for learning which motivates student involvement, contribution, and choice.

3. Development of decision-making skills:

a. by providing conflict experiences and situations wherein the individual must value, gather data, define, test ideas, and commit himself to action in order to solve the problem or plan a task;

b. by providing a variety of activities which motivate student choice.

4. Development of research skills:

a. by providing a variety of resources including media for students to explore and use as they gather data;

b. by providing issues, problems, and focus questions to force problem solving and task planning.

b. dándose una atmósfera de aprendizaje en la cual el estudiante sea motivado a participar, a contribuir y a escoger.

3. Desarrollo de la destreza para hacer decisiones. Este objetivo se realiza:

a. dándose experiencias y situaciones de conflicto donde el individuo debe evaluar, colectar datos, definir, examinar ideas, y donde él debe comprometerse a actuar para resolver un problema o planear una tarea.

b. dándose una variedad de actividades las cuales motivarán las preferencias del estudiante.

4. Desarrollo de la destreza en la investigación. Este objetivo se realiza:

a. dándose una variedad de recursos incluyendo medios que los estudiantes pueden explorar y usar mientras recogen datos.

b. dándose discusiones, problemas, y fijando preguntas que refuercen la habilidad de resolver problemas y de planear tareas.

## Unit Objectives

## Objetivos de la unidad

At the end of the unit, competence will be demonstrated in the following ways:

1. Using a camera and/or a paint brush, the student will characterize his own community.
2. Students will identify with their own community by writing sto-

Al final de la unidad, la competencia será demostrada en las formas siguientes:

1. Usando una cámara fotográfica o un pincel, el estudiante representará a su propia comunidad.
2. Los estudiantes se identificarán con su propia comunidad, escri-

ries, articles, and sharing information about their community.

3. Students will define the concept of community.
4. During a discussion, students will identify, differentiate, and contrast a migrant community, a rural farm community, and an urban community.

5. Students will identify recent changes in the migrant, rural farm, and urban communities.

6. To his peers, the student will identify himself as a member of the community.

7. The student will state preferences concerning work and recreational activities.

8. The student will share information about his family.
9. The student will define the concept of "role." Students will interview community members and specify their roles.

10. Students will list, as a part of an evaluative summary, three reasons for migration: to improve life style, to escape political unrest, to search for natural resources.

11. Students will define the concept "migration."
12. Students will define the concepts "environment" and "behavior."

biendo historias y artículos y compartiendo información sobre la comunidad.

3. Los estudiantes definirán el concepto de "comunidad".
4. Durante una discusión, los estudiantes identificarán, diferenciarán y contrastarán una comunidad migrante, una comunidad rural-granjera, y una comunidad urbana.

5. Los estudiantes identificarán cambios recientes en las comunidades migrantes, rural-granjeras y urbanas.

6. El estudiante se identificará a sí mismo como un miembro de la comunidad, entre los jóvenes de su misma edad.

7. El estudiante declarará sus preferencias personales respecto al trabajo y actividades de recreación.

8. El estudiante compartirá información sobre su familia.
9. El estudiante definirá el concepto de "desempeñar un papel". Los estudiantes entrevistarán a miembros de la comunidad y especificarán el papel que éstos desempeñan en la comunidad.

10. Como parte de un sumario de evaluación, los estudiantes harán una lista de tres razones que impulsan la migración: para mejorar el estilo de vida, para escapar desasosiegos políticos, para buscar mejores recursos naturales.

11. Los estudiantes definirán el concepto de "migración".
12. Los estudiantes definirán los conceptos de "ambiente" y "conducta" (o comportamiento).

13. Students will use a topographic map of the United States to make decisions relating to human behavior. They will demonstrate their map-reading skills, knowledge, and comprehension of geographic concepts.

14. Students will "act out" ways in which the Mexican settler modified and adapted the environment of the Southwest as he mined, farmed, or ranched.

15. Students will identify changes in the American Southwest resulting from immigration, technology, and government.

16. Students will list contributions of the Mexican culture to the Anglo culture and the contributions of the Anglo culture to the Mexican culture.

17. Students will name individuals who contributed to the development of the Southwest.

18. Students will define the concepts of "modification" and "adaptation."

19. Students will categorize, define, and generalize about art, music, food, architecture, clothing, and speech as ways of expressing cultural orientation.

20. Students will engage in debate about future societal changes and the effect of them.

21. Students will define "urban-

13. Los estudiantes usarán un mapa topográfico de los EE.UU. para hacer decisiones relacionadas con la conducta humana. Demonstrarán su destreza en la lectura del mapa, su conocimiento, y su compresión de los conceptos geográficos.

14. Los estudiantes "actuarán" formas en las cuales se demostrará cómo el colono mexicano, modificó y adaptó el ambiente del Suroeste ya sea como minero, como granjero o como ranchero.

15. Los estudiantes identificarán los cambios efectuados en el Suroeste norteamericano, debidos a la migración, a la tecnología y al gobierno.

16. Los estudiantes harán una lista de las contribuciones aportadas por la cultura mexicana a la cultura angloamericana, y viceversa.

17. Los estudiantes nombrarán a individuos que han contribuido al desarrollo de la cultura del Suroeste norteamericano.

18. Los estudiantes definirán los conceptos de "modificación" y "adaptación".

19. Los estudiantes categorizarán, definirán y generalizarán sobre el arte, la música, la comida, la arquitectura, la ropa y la forma de hablar de la gente como medios de expresar la orientación cultural.

20. Los estudiantes entrarán en debate sobre los futuros cambios sociales y el efecto de éstos.

21. Los estudiantes definirán "ur-

ization," "technology," and "change."

22. Students will compare the functions, obligations, and privileges of leadership by participation in a skit, play, or charade; by writing an article or story; and by drawing a cartoon, mural, or map.

23. Students will set a plan to solve or alleviate a problem through participation in a game situation.

24. Students will express verbally values and alternatives in the decision-making process.

25. Students will make a verbal commitment to action, inaction, or postponement of action as they participate in the game situation.

26. Students will demonstrate use of the concepts of "power," "leadership," and "government," as they participate in the game of People Power.

banización", "tecnología", y "cambio".

22. Los estudiantes compararán las funciones, obligaciones y privilegios de la iniciativa (o mando) por medio de la participación en una composición dramática, representación o charada; escribiendo un artículo o cuento; dibujando una caricatura, un mural, o un mapa.

23. Los estudiantes fijarán un plan para resolver o aliviar un problema a través de la participación en un juego.

24. Los estudiantes expresarán oralmente los valores y las alternativas que existen en el proceso de hacer decisiones.

25. Los estudiantes se comprometerán a actuar, a no acutar, o a posponer la acción, cuando participan en el juego.

26. Los estudiantes demostrarán el uso de los conceptos de "poder", "liderazgo", y "gobierno", mientras participan en el juego "El poder popular".

## LESSON ONE

### QUESTION FOCUS

What is a community? Who lives in a community? In which ways are communities similar? Dissimilar?

### COGNITIVE LEVELS

Knowledge • Comprehension • Application • Evaluation

## LECCIÓN PRIMERA

### PREGUNTA DE ENFOQUE

¿Qué es una comunidad? ¿Quién vive en una comunidad? ¿En qué formas se parecen las comunidades? ¿En qué formas se difieren?

### NIVELES DE CONOCIMIENTO

Conocimiento • Comprensión • Aplicación • Evaluación.

## AFFECTIVE LEVELS

Responding • Evaluation • Organizing • Characterizing

## CONCEPT

Community

## OVERALL OBJECTIVE

Students will verbally identify three distinct communities and identify with their own.

## SPECIFIC OBJECTIVES

The learner will differentiate and contrast, during a group discussion: a migrant community, a rural farm community, and an urban community (barrio).

## CONTENT

Pictorial presentation of three communities: migrant, rural farm, and urban.

## SETTING

Present time (A); Historical (B)

## PROCEDURE

### Inquiry Experience A-1—Contemporary Setting

On a walking tour through the neighborhood community, students use cameras or make sketches of people, businesses, industry, home, work and play activities, and the natural environment.

In the classroom, students observe and examine a pictorial display of these three distinct communities. Each community (migrant, rural farm, and urban) is labeled and depicts people at work or in recreational activities.

## NIVELES AFECTIVOS

Reacción • Evaluación • Organización • Representación.

## CONCEPTO

Comunidad

## OBJETIVO GENERAL

Los estudiantes identificarán oralmente tres comunidades distintas y se identificarán con la suya.

## OBJETIVOS ESPECÍFICOS

Durante una discusión en grupo, el estudiante diferenciará y contrastará una comunidad de inmigrantes, una comunidad rural-granjera, y una comunidad urbana (barrio).

## CONTENIDO

Representación pictórica de tres comunidades: migrante, urbana, y rural-granjera.

## ESCENARIO

Tiempo presente (A); Histórico (B)

## PROCEDIMIENTO

### Experiencia de indagación A-1—Escenario contemporáneo

Dando un paseo en la vecindad de una comunidad, los estudiantes harán uso de cámaras fotográficas o harán dibujos de la gente, de los negocios, de la industria, de las casas, de las actividades de trabajo y de juego, y del ambiente natural.

En clase, los estudiantes observarán y examinarán una exhibición pictórica de tres comunidades distintas. A cada comunidad (migrante, urbana o rural-granjera) se le pondrá un rótulo, y éstas mostrarán gente trabajando o ejecutando actividades de recreación.

The migrant community will depict people at work in the fields; housing in cars, trailers, huts, and barracks; laundry facilities and day care centers (or lack of them); health care; sanitary conditions, etc.

Rural farm community depicts pastures, homes, work and play activities for children and adults.

The urban community depicts clinics, freeways, apartments, businesses, people in the low economic area of the city.

Evaluation: Teacher encourages students to talk about what they sketched, filmed, and examined in the classroom. The following question strategy may assist students in organizing their ideas:

1. Which community is most like the pictures we filmed/sketched?
2. What do we call the community in which we live?
3. In which way is our community different from the other two?

4. In which way is it similar?

At this time, the teacher may show a picture of an abandoned Western community and ask:

5. Is this a community?

Students are now in possession of enough information to analyze and define the concept of community—a group of people living and sharing together in a society—and to infer and generalize in terms of the conceptual definition.

## Inquiry Experience A-2

Students work in small inquiry groups of 5 to 7. They share their pictures and films

La comunidad de inmigrantes mostrará gente trabajando en el campo, viviendo en carros, en "trailers", en chozas, y en barracas; también mostrará lavanderías y centros diurnos para el cuidado de los niños—o la falta de éstos; mostrará centros de salubridad, las condiciones sanitarias, etc.

La comunidad rural-granjera mostrará pastizales, casas, actividades de trabajo y de juego para los adultos y para los niños.

La comunidad urbana mostrará clínicas, autopistas, apartamentos, negocios, y gente en la sección de la ciudad de bajos recursos económicos.

Evaluación: El maestro les dará ánimo a los estudiantes para que hablen sobre lo que ellos han dibujado, filmado, y examinado en clase. Las siguientes preguntas estratégicas pueden ayudar al estudiante a organizar sus ideas:

1. ¿Cuál comunidad se parece más a la que hemos filmado o dibujado?
2. ¿Cómo llamamos la comunidad en que vivimos?
3. ¿En qué formas difiere nuestra comunidad de las otras dos comunidades?
4. ¿En qué formas se parece?

En este momento, el maestro puede mostrar un grabado (foto o lámina) de una comunidad abandonada del Oeste y preguntar:

5. ¿Es ésta una comunidad?

Los estudiantes están ahora en posesión de suficiente información para analizar y definir el concepto de "comunidad", de inferir y de generalizar en términos de la definición conceptual. Comunidad: Una comunidad es un grupo de gente que convive y lo comparte todo en una sociedad.

## Experiencia de indagación A-2

Los estudiantes trabajan en grupos de indagación de 5 a 7 individuos. Comparten sus

from the previous experience (A-1). Each inquiry group is responsible for finding a means of presentation of their pictures to the other groups.

Suggestions:

1. Some groups may "map" their community by placing pictures or films in such a manner as to create a map of their neighborhood.

2. Groups may paint previously-sketched pictures or make a mural or collage of the community.

3. Groups may construct a puzzle map of the community by using parts or half pictures, thus devising a large puzzle for other inquiry groups to solve.

Evaluation: Who lives in our community? In what ways are we dependent upon each other? What types of things do we share in our community?

*Inquiry Experience B-1—Historical Setting*

Students study other communities in place and time. They work in inquiry groups. Each group is given a community to study. Groups use picture sets, film loops, film strips, or slides.

The focus for each group is:

1. What is happening in the community you are studying?
2. In what ways is that community different from our community?
3. In what ways do all communities seem to be alike?

dibujos y películas de la experiencia anterior (A-1). Cada grupo de indagación tiene la responsabilidad de encontrar medios para la presentación de sus dibujos o fotos a los otros grupos.

Sugerencias:

1. Algunos grupos pueden hacer un mapa de su comunidad usando los dibujos, fotos, o películas y arreglándolos en forma de un mapa del barrio.
2. Algunos grupos pueden pintar los dibujos comenzados previamente, o hacer un mural or *collage* de la comunidad.
3. Otros grupos pueden hacer mapas rompecabezas de su comunidad, cortando en varias partes las fotos o los dibujos, y creando con esto un rompecabezas grande para que los otros grupos de indagación lo resuelvan.

Evaluación: ¿Quién vive en nuestra comunidad? ¿En qué formas dependemos el uno del otro? ¿Qué tipo de cosas compartimos en nuestra comunidad?

*Experiencia de indagación B-1—Escenario histórico*

Los estudiantes estudian otras comunidades en el tiempo y el espacio. Los estudiantes trabajan en grupos de indagación. A cada grupo se le da una comunidad para estudiar. Los grupos usan series de fotos, películas, trozos de películas, o diapositivas.

Enfoque para cada indagación usando el concepto de *comunidad:*

1. ¿Qué está sucediendo en la comunidad que Ud. está estudiando?
2. ¿En qué forma es esa comunidad diferente de la nuestra?
3. ¿En qué formas parecen ser iguales todas las communidades?

4. In what other ways do people seem to be dependent upon each other?
5. In what ways are we dependent upon each other?
6. In what ways are all people interdependent?

Suggestions for communities to study:

1. A community in the American Southwest in the 1840's—mining, farming, ranching;
2. A mission or presidio;
3. A community in rural Mexico about 1910;
4. An African community.

Evaluation: Students describe the community they have studied and the conclusions they reach. Preparations may be made by one person from each group summarizing the group's inquiry or by the contribution of many students. When more than one group focuses upon the same community, there is an opportunity for students to contrast their findings and debate their inquiry.

4. ¿De qué forma parece interdepender la gente?
5. ¿De qué modo dependemos el uno del otro?
6. ¿De qué modo es todo el mundo interdependiente?

Sugerencias de comunidades para estudiar:

1. Una comunidad en el Suroeste norteamericano alrededor del año 1840: minera, granjera o ranchera.
2. Una misión o presidio.
3. Una comunidad rural en México alrededor del año 1910.
4. Una comunidad africana.

Evaluación: Los estudiantes describen la comunidad que han estudiado y las conclusiones a que han llegado. Las presentaciones pueden ser dadas por un representante de los miembros de cada grupo que resumirá la indagación ejecutada por el grupo, o por medio de la contribución de varios estudiantes. Si más de uno de los grupos fija su atención en la misma comunidad, se suscitará, entonces, la oportunidad para que los estudiantes contrasten sus hallazgos y debatan el resultado de su indagación.

## EXTENDED ACTIVITIES

1. Creative writing to accompany students' pictures and films of their own community.

2. Writing a play, radio or TV script about their own community or about an early community which they studied.

## EXTENSIÓN DE ACTIVIDADES

1. Composiciones creativas que acompañen las fotos y películas de la comunidad de los estudiantes.

2. Escribir una presentación o un guión para la televisión o radio que trate de la comunidad del estudiante, o de una de las antiguas comunidades que se han estudiado.

## MEDIA RESOURCES FOR INQUIRY EXPERIENCE USE

### 16 mm. Films

A-1 *Chicano from the Southwest,* 15 min., color, Encyclopaedia Britannica Educational Corporation.
B-1 *Mexican Village Life,* 17 min., color, Bailey Film Associates.
B-1 *Mexican Village Family,* 17 min., color, Bailey Film Associates.

B-1   *Boy of Central Africa,* 13½ min., color, Bailey Film Associates.
B-1   *Mission Life,* 20 min., color, Arthur Barr Productions.
B-1   *Rancho Life,* 20 min., color, Arthur Barr Productions.
B-1   *Missions of the Southwest,* 15 min., color, Arthur Barr Productions.

### Film Loops—Super 8

A     *City and Country Contrast,* Ealing Film Loops.
B     *Building a House: Africans of the River Niger,* Ealing Film Loops.
B     *Market Day in a Mexican Town,* Ealing Film Loops.

### Picture Sets

A     *Interaction of Man Series,* Rand McNally, 1969 Sound Filmstrips.
B     *Cuetzalán: A Small Town in Puebla,* Bailey Film Associates.


# LESSON TWO

# LECCIÓN SEGUNDA


## QUESTION FOCUS

Who am I? Who is my family? Who depends upon me?

## COGNITIVE AND AFFECTIVE LEVELS

All

## CONCEPTS

Self • Role • Interaction in the family

## OVERALL OBJECTIVE

To value self and family

## SPECIFIC OBJECTIVES

Students will identify themselves as members of the community to their peers; they will state preferences concerning work and recreational activities; they will share information about their families.

## PREGUNTA DE ENFOQUE

¿Quién soy yo? ¿Quién es mi familia? ¿Quién depende de mí?

## NIVELES DE CONOCIMIENTO Y NIVELES AFECTIVOS

Todos

## CONCEPTOS

El yo, el papel que se desempeña y la familia.

## OBJETIVO GENERAL

Evaluación de sí mismo y de la familia.

## OBJETIVOS ESPECÍFICOS

Entre los jóvenes de su misma edad, el estudiante se identificará a sí mismo como un miembro de la comunidad. El estudiante declarará sus preferencias en las actividades de trabajo y de recreación. El estudiante proveerá información sobre su familia.

## CONTENT

All members of the family and the community perform a role. Family members and community members depend upon each other.

## SETTING

The student's community: An historical community.

## PROCEDURE

### Inquiry Experience A-1—Contemporary Setting

Students work in small inquiry groups. Each group chooses a reporter to ask questions and a secretary to take notes. (Tape recorders may also be used.) Each member of the inquiry group, including the reporter and the secretary, respond to the following types of questions:

1. Who am I? (What does my family call me?)
2. Who are my parent(s)?

3. How do my parents earn a living?
4. Whom do I call my family?
5. How long have I lived in the Barrio? (Neighborhood)
6. Where else have I lived?
7. In what ways am I like other members of my family?
8. In what ways am I different from other members of my family?
9. Why am I important to my family?

10. What kinds of things am I expected to do?
11. What are some things that I expect other members of my family to do?
12. Who are some people who depend upon me?

## CONTENIDO

Todos los miembros de la familia y de la comunidad desempeñan un papel. Los miembros de una familia y de una comunidad dependen los unos de los otros.

## ESCENARIO

La comunidad del estudiante: Una comunidad histórica.

## PROCEDIMIENTO

### Experiencia de indagación A-1—Escenario contemporáneo

Los estudiantes trabajan en pequeños grupos de indagación. Cada grupo escoge un representante para que haga preguntas y una secretaria para que anote la información. (Se puede hacer uso de grabadoras). Cada miembro del grupo de indagación, incluyendo al representante y la secretaria, contestan a los siguientes tipos de preguntas:

1. ¿Quién soy? (¿Cómo me llama mi familia?)
2. ¿Quiénes son mis padres? (padre o madre)
3. ¿Cómo se ganan la vida mis padres?
4. ¿A quiénes llamo mi familia?
5. Cuánto tiempo hace que vivo en el barrio?
6. ¿En qué otro lugar he vivido?
7. ¿En qué me parezco a los otros miembros de mi familia?
8. ¿En qué me diferencio de los otros miembros de mi familia?
9. ¿Por qué soy importante para mi familia?
10. ¿Qué clase de cosas se espera que yo haga?
11. ¿Qué clase de cosas espero que los otros miembros de mi familia hagan?
12. ¿Cuáles son algunas de las personas que dependen de mí?

13. What are some things that I do well?
14. What are some things that I would like to do if I could?

Reporters may ask additional questions of their own choosing. When the groups are "talked out", reporters may be asked to share the story of their group.

Reporters may be encouraged to respond with the following types of stories:

1. How are the members of my group alike?
2. In what ways are the members of my group different?

Groups may desire to categorize and chart the information about each other. Chart categories may include the following:

Family Size • Responsibilities • Choices

*Inquiry Experience B-1—Historical Setting*

Each inquiry group uses the same community that it studied in the previous lesson (B-1)—a community in the American Southwest, a mission or presidio, a rural Mexican community or an African community.

Focusing upon the concepts of *role* and *interaction,* the following questions may assist students in their inquiry:

1. What are some jobs the community expects women to perform?

2. What are some things the community expects of its men?
3. What are some things that children are expected to do?

13. ¿Cuáles son algunas de las cosas que hago bien?
14. ¿Qué cosas me gustaría hacer si pudiera?

Los reporteros pueden hacer preguntas adicionales escogidas por ellos mismos. Después que los grupos han "hablado", se les puede preguntar a los informantes que relaten la historia de sus grupos.

Usando varios tipos de cuentos, se les puede dar ánimo a los reporteros para que contesten:

1. ¿En qué se parecen los miembros de mi grupo?
2. ¿En qué formas se diferencian entre sí los miembros de mi grupo?

Puede ser que los grupos deseen categorizar y apuntar la información sobre ellos mismos. Esto se puede hacer de la manera siguiente:

Número de individuos en la familia • Responsabilidades • Gustos

*Experienca de indigación B-1—Escenario histórico*

Cada grupo de indagación usará la misma comunidad que estudió en la lección anterior (Primera B-1)—una comunidad en el Suroeste norteamericano, una misión o presidio, una comunidad rural mexicana, o una comunidad africana.

Concentrándose en los conceptos de "papel" y de "interacción", las preguntas a continuación, puede que asistan a los estudiantes en su tarea de indagación:

1. ¿Cuáles son algunas de las faenas que la comunidad espera que las mujeres ejecuten?
2. ¿Cuáles son algunas de las cosas que la comunidad espera de sus hombres?
3. ¿Cuáles son algunas de las cosas que se esperan de los niños?

4. What are some ways that children prepare for adult life?
5. In what ways do people in the community work together?

Evaluation: After students share the focus of their inquiry, the teacher may assist students to contrast jobs and expectations of the historic communities with the students' own community. The concept of role may be defined at this time.

## EXTENDED ACTIVITIES

1. Students interview community members to find out—Who lives in our community? What role do they perform? In what ways do we depend upon the people in our community?

2. Students may write articles or stories about the members of the community, their family, or their inquiry group. Articles may be used for a class newspaper or bulletin board.

3. Students may draw or paint illustrations or use films from the previous lesson to accompany articles.

4. Students may paint self portraits.

5. Students may take pictures of each other using cameras.

6. Students may bring in family pictures or baby pictures of themselves to accompany articles or stories. A class photographic album may be compiled.

Students may listen to record "But I Am Somebody: Voice of the Poor," Steve Allen, narrator from Pete Records.

4. ¿En qué forma se preparan los niños para su vida adulta?
5. ¿En qué formas trabajan junto las gentes de la comunidad?

Evaluación: Luego que los estudiantes han compartido el enfoque de la indagación, el maestro los puede ayudar a contrastar los trabajos y las expectativas de las comunidades históricas con sus propias comunidades. El concepto de "papel" puede ser definido aquí.

## ACTIVIDADES DE EXTENSIÓN

1. Los estudiantes pueden entrevistar a miembros de la comunidad para averiguar lo siguiente: ¿Quién vive en nuestra comunidad? ¿Qué papel desempeñan los miembros en la comunidad? ¿De qué forma dependemos de la gente de la comunidad?

2. Los estudiantes pueden escribir artículos o cuentos ya sea sobre algunos de los miembros de la comunidad, de la familia del estudiante, o de los miembros del grupo de indagación. Los artículos pueden ser usados como material para un periódico de la clase o para un tablero de avisos.

3. Los estudiantes pueden dibujar o pintar ilustraciones, o usar las películas de la lección anterior para acompañar los artículos.

4. Los estudiantes pueden pintar sus autorretratos.

5. Usando cámaras fotográficas, los estudiantes pueden sacar fotos de sus compañeros.

6. Los estudiantes pueden traer fotos de su familia, y de ellos mismos cuando eran nenes, para acompañar los artículos o cuentos. Con esto se puede recopilar un álbum de fotografías para la clase.

Los estudiantes pueden escuchar el disco "But I Am Somebody: Voice of the Poor", Steve, Allen, Narrador de Pete Records.

## MEDIA RESOURCES FOR INQUIRY EXPERIENCE USE

Film Loops—Super 8

B  *Preparing a Meal: Africans of the River Niger,* Ealing Film Loops.
B  *River Bank Village: Africans of the River Niger,* Ealing Film Loops.
B  *Fishing: Africans of the River Niger,* Ealing Film Loops.
B  *Market Day in a Mexican Town,* Ealing Film Loops.

Filmstrips

B  *Family of Mexico,* Encyclopaedia Britannica Educational Corporation.
B  *Family of Jordan,* Encyclopaedia Britannica Educational Corporation.
B  *Mexican Children,* Encyclopaedia Britannica Educational Corporation.

| LESSON THREE | LECCIÓN TERCERA |
|---|---|

### QUESTION FOCUS

What makes people migrate from one community to another?

### COGNITIVE LEVELS

All

### AFFECTIVE LEVELS

Awareness • Responding • Evaluation • Organization

### CONCEPT

Migration

### OVERALL OBJECTIVE

Students will relate the migratory condition with the satisfaction of human needs.

### SPECIFIC OBJECTIVES

Students will define, verbally, the concept "migration"; they will list as part of an

### PREGUNTA DE ENFOQUE

¿Qué motiva a la gente a migrar de una comunidad a otra?

### NIVELES DE CONOCIMIENTO

Todos

### NIVELES AFECTIVOS

Realización • Reacción • Evaluación • Organización

### CONCEPTO

Migración

### OBJECTIVO GENERAL

Los estudiantes relacionarán la migración con la necesidad de satisfacer necesidades humanas.

### OBJETIVOS ESPECÍFICOS

Los estudiantes definirán, oralmente, el concepto de "migración". Los estudiantes

evaluative summary three reasons for migration: to improve life style, to escape political unrest, to search for natural resources.

## CONTENT

Migration of groups of people is influenced by sociological, economic, religious, and political factors. These factors were influential in the past and are relevant today.

## PROCEDURE

### Inquiry Experience A-1—Contemporary Setting

Teacher presents pictures of groups in motion: animal packs, herds, flocks of birds, school of fish.

Students are asked: What is happening? Why do you think it is happening? (As students observe, classify, and contrast the groups, they are gathering data.)

If students do not use the term "migration," the teacher may supply it.

Pictures are discussed in terms of *causes* for migration and possible location for future settlement.

Students may be asked to anticipate what might have happened if the group did not migrate.

Either in a large group discussion or in small groups, students are asked to define the concept of migration in terms of their observations and inferences:

1. Why do groups migrate?
2. What does the group hope to accomplish?

In order to come to a conclusion, students will be defining and generalizing about the concept.

harán una lista (como parte de un sumario de evaluación) de tres razones que motivan la migración: para mejorar el estilo de vida, para escapar desasosiegos políticos, y para buscar nuevos recursos naturales.

## CONTENIDO

La emigración de grupos de gente es influida por factores sociológicos, económicos, religiosos y políticos. Estos factores fueron influyentes en el pasado y lo son aún hoy.

## PROCEDIMIENTO

### Experiencia de indagación A-1—Escenario contemporáneo

El maestro presenta ilustraciones de grupos en movimiento: manadas de animales, rebaños de ganado, bandadas de aves, bancos de peces.

A continuación se les pregunta a los estudiantes: ¿Qué está sucediendo? ¿Por qué piensan Uds. que está sucediendo? (Los estudiantes recogen datos mientras observan, clasifican y contrastan los grupos).

Si los estudiantes no usan el término "migración", el maestro puede suplirlo.

Las ilustraciones deben ser discutidas en términos de las *causas* que motivan la emigración y los posibles lugares de estadía en el futuro para estos grupos emigrantes.

Se les puede preguntar a los estudiantes que anticipen lo que hubiera podido pasar si los grupos no hubieran emigrado.

Se les puede preguntar a los estudiantes—ya sea en grupos de discusión, pequeños o grandes—que definan el concepto de "migración" en términos de sus observactiones e inferencias:

1. ¿Por qué emigran los grupos?
2. ¿Qué espera lograr el grupo?

Los estudiantes definirán y generalizarán el concepto para llegar a una conclusión.

*Inquiry Experience B-1—Historical Setting*

Students are divided into small inquiry groups. Each group is given an inquiry problem to investigate. Inquiry problems may be in the form of a picture about a group, an incident about a group of people, a short paragraph, a record, or a film strip.

Inquiry Problem: In the past, different groups of people have migrated from one region to another. People migrate for many different reasons.

Try to discover:

1. The reason(s) or causes for the migration.
2. What did the group anticipate would happen in its new home?
3. Did the group intend to stay permanently in the new region?

4. How did the migration affect the group?
5. How did the migration affect others?

Inquiry Situations: Use pictures, stories, paragraphs, etc. (Note media suggestions.)

1. A migrant camp community (pictures used in Lesson One would be appropriate)

2. 17th century Spanish explorers, scouts—in the new world: de Vaca, Coronado, de Oñate, Father Kino, Father Serra
3. Forty-niners in California
4. Mexican and Chinese laborers building the railroads (Note: Wittenberg, *Patterns of the City.*)

5. American settlers after 1821 and before the Mexican war (1846) in Texas
6. Mexican citizens just prior to the

*Experiencia de indagación B-1—Escenario histórico*

Se divide a los estudiantes en pequeños grupos de indagación. A cada grupo se le da un problema para investigar. Los problemas pueden ser presentados en forma de ilustraciones: ya sea de un grupo, de un incidente entre un grupo de gente, de un párrafo corto, de un disco o de una película corta.

*Problema de indagación:* En el pasado, varios grupos de gente han migrado de una región a otra. La gente migra por muchas razones diferentes.

Trate de descubrir:

1. La razón o razones, y causas para la emigración.
2. ¿Anticipó el grupo lo que pasaría en su nueva localidad?
3. ¿Tuvo el grupo la intención de establecerse permanentemente en la nueva localidad?
4. ¿Cómo afectó la emigración al grupo?
5. Cómo afectó la emigración a otros?

Situaciones de indagación: usando fotos, cuentos, párrafos, etc. (Note las sugerencias de medios que se pueden usar).

1. Un campamento-comunidad de emigración (Las ilustraciones usadas en la lección primera pueden ser utilizadas).
2. Los exploradores del siglo XVII en el Nuevo Mundo, como: Cabeza de Vaca, Coronado, de Oñate, El padre Kino, el padre Serra.
3. Los hombres del' 49 en California.
4. Los trabajadores mexicanos y chinos que construyeron los ferrocarriles (Nota: Wittenberg, *Patterns of the City*).
5. Los colonos norteamericanos después de 1821 y antes de la guerra con México (1846), en Texas.
6. Ciudadanos mexicanos que emigraron

Mexican Revolution of 1910, emigrate to the U.S.

7. Any immigrant group between 1900 and 1930 entering the U.S. and living in an urban community

8. American pioneers after the Louisiana Purchase (1803)

9. Flood of immigrants after the Civil War

10. A Southern community—tenant farmers, Negro slaves.

Evaluation: Each group presents its inquiry. Presentations may be in the form of reports, dramatizations, stories, tape recordings, or a combination of pictures and reports. Groups may question and disagree with each other.

Greater involvement and interest are generated during the presentations when more than one inquiry group researches the same problem but discovers contradictory evidence.

Teacher may assist in the evaluation by asking:

1. What may have been the course of events if the migrating group had decided not to migrate?

2. What do you think is the effect of migrating close to your native land? Far from your native land?

3. What are some conclusions we can make concerning the reaons for migration?

## EXTENDED ACTIVITIES

1. Using each of the three basic reasons for migration, greater depth of understanding could be achieved through study of the contributions of the Mexicans in the Southwest.

---

a los EE.UU. un poco antes de la Revolución Mexicana en 1910.

7. Cualquier grupo de migrantes, entre 1900 y 1930, entrados en los EE.UU. y residentes en comunidades urbanas.

8. Colonos norteamericanos después de La Compra de Luisiana en 1803.

9. Masas de inmigrantes después de la Guerra Civil (en los EE.UU.).

10. Una communidad sureña—colonos, esclavos negros.

Evaluación: Cada grupo presenta su indagación respectiva. Las presentaciones pueden ser dadas en forma de reportes, de dramatizaciones, de cuentos, con grabadoras, o por medio de una combinación de láminas y de reportes. Los grupos pueden hacer preguntas y tener opiniones opuestas.

Se genera más entusiasmo e interés durante las presentaciones si más de uno de los grupos de indagación, al investigar el mismo problema, descubre evidencia contradictoria.

El maestro puede asistir en la evaluación preguntando:

1. ¿Cuál hubiera sido el curso de los eventos si el grupo emigratorio hubiera decidido no migrar?

2. ¿Cuál cree Ud. es el efecto que produce el migrar a una comarca vecina a la tierra natal? ¿Lejos de la tierra natal?

3. ¿Cuáles son algunas de las conclusiones a que podemos llegar con respecto a las razones que producen la emigración?

## EXTENSIÓN DE ACTIVIDADES

1. Se puede adquirir mayor profundidad de comprensión a través del estudio de las contribuciones de los mexicanos al Suroeste, mediante el uso de cada una de la tres razones básicas que causan la emigración.

a. Improvement of life style—Mexican contributions in art, architecture, music, language, food.

b. Search for natural resources—contributions to farming, ranching, mining.

c. Contributions to law and government—water laws, community property, mineral laws, family.

2. The study of Manifest Destiny.

3. Creation of a game board, researched by students, depicting the trials and tribulations of any minority group as they journey to the United States.

4. The Game of Caribou-Hunting—available through "Man—A Course of Study". Education Development Center, Inc., 15 Miffin Place, Cambridge, Mass. 02138.

5. Role-playing a minority group's problems in a new community.

a. Mejoramiento del estilo de vida—las contribuciones mexicanas en el arte, la arquitectura, la música, el idioma y la comida.

b. Búsqueda de recursos naturales—contribuciones a la siembra, a la ganadería y a la minería.

c. Contribuciones a la legislación y el gobierno—leyes de aguas, de bienes gananciales, de minas, de la familia.

2. El estudio del "Destino Manifiesto".

3. Creación de un juego de tablero, investigado por los estudiantes, que demuestre los problemas y tribulaciones de cualquier grupo de minoría, mientras viajan por los Estados Unidos.

4. El "Juego de cazar caribúes"—asequible por medio de "Man—A Course of Study". Education Development Center, Inc., 15 Miffin Place, Cambridge, Mass. 02138.

5. Dramatizar los problemas enfrentados por un grupo de minoría en una nueva comunidad.

## MEDIA RESOURCES FOR INQUIRY EXPERIENCE USE

### Film

B    *Missions of California,* 22 min., color, Bailey Film Associates.

### Study Prints

B-1    *California Story to 1870,* set of 12, Bailey Film Associates.

### Transparencies

B-1    *Settlement of the United States 1770-1890,* Hammond.
B-1    *Expansion of the United States 1783-1898,* Hammond.
B-1    *Conflicting Claims to the West,* Hammond.
B-1    *The Mexican War,* Hammond.
B-1    *Immigration,* Hammond.

### Filmstrips

B-1    *Spanish Explorers of the New World,* Encyclopaedia Britannica Educational Corporation.

**107**

B-1   *Colonial America,* Encyclopaedia Britannica Educational Corporation.
B-1   *Westward Expansion,* Encyclopaedia Britannica Educational Corporation.

### Sound Filmstrips

B-1   *Awakening: The Great Migration,* Multi-Media Productions, Inc.
B-1   *Mexican Revolution of 1910,* Multi-Media Productions, Inc.
B-1   *The Far Frontier,* Multi-Media Productions, Inc.
B-1   *Conflict of Culture: Conquest of the Borderlands,* Multi-Media Productions, Inc.

### Illustrated Books (in Addition to Student Bibliography)

B-1   *Under the Wide Sky* (B559). Children's Music Center.
B-1   *The Spanish-American West* (B591). Children's Music Center.
B-1   *Patterns of the City.* New York: Noble and Noble, 1969.

<table>
<tr><td>

# LESSON FOUR

## QUESTION FOCUS

In what ways does the physical environment affect human behavior?

## COGNITIVE LEVELS

Knowledge • Comprehension • Application • Analysis • Evaluation

## AFFECTIVE LEVELS

Responding • Valuing • Organization • Characterization

## CONCEPTS

Environment • Interdependence • Behavior

## OVERALL OBJECTIVE

To relate physical environment with human behavior.

## SPECIFIC OBJECTIVES

The learner will make decisions using a

</td><td>

# LECCIÓN CUARTA

## PREGUNTA DE ENFOQUE

¿En qué formas afecta el ambiente físico al comportamiento humano?

## NIVELES DE CONOCIMIENTO

Conocimiento • Comprensión • Aplicación • Análisis • Evaluación

## NIVELES AFECTIVOS

Reacción • Evaluación • Organización • Characterización

## CONCEPTOS

Ambiente • Interdependencia • Comportamiento

## OBJETIVO GENERAL

Relación del ambiente físico con el comportamiento humano.

## OBJECTIVOS ESPECÍFICOS

El estudiante hará decisiones usando un

</td></tr>
</table>

topographic map concerning his way of life which will be a result of time and place.

## PROCEDURE

### Inquiry Experience A-1—Contemporary Setting

Using a topographic map of the United States, the teacher elicits geographic concepts and map-reading skills from the students. Since this experience is preparatory to the actual inquiry experience of "B," it is important that the teacher assist students to apply map-reading skills to interpret environmental conditions. Map-reading skills may have to be taught as a separate lesson.

The following questions may be of assistance:

1. How can we tell where there are mountains, valleys, plateaus, rivers, lakes?
2. What does the map tell us about climatic conditions? What is the climate of a desert, semi-arid, subtropical, or humid continental region? What can we find out about wind direction? Why is it important to study weather?

3. Where do we live?
4. In what ways does our physical environment affect our way of life?

Using question 4, students should be encouraged to build large classes or categories such as: industry, agriculture, housing, clothing, recreation. Question 4 may be considered in either a whole class discussion or in small inquiry groups.

mapa topográfico que tenga que ver con su estilo de vida, el cual será el resultado de tiempo y espacio.

## PROCEDIMIENTO

### Experiencia de indagación A-1—Escenario contemporáneo

Usando un mapa topográfico de los EE.UU., el maestro saca de los estudiantes conceptos geográficos, y la capacidad de leer mapas. Ya que esta experiencia es preparatoria para la experiencia de indagación "B", es importante, entonces, que el maestro asista a los estudiantes a aplicar el conocimiento de la lectura de los mapas a las condiciones del ambiente. Tal vez sea necesario enseñar la capacidad de leer mapas en una lección separada.

Las preguntas siguientes pueden ser de asistencia:

1. ¿Cómo podemos saber dónde se encuentran las montañas, los valles, las mesetas, los ríos, y los lagos?
2. ¿Qué nos dice el mapa respecto a las condiciones climáticas?
   ¿Cómo es el clima de un desierto, de las regiones semiáridas, y subtropicales, o de las regiones húmedas continentales?
   ¿Qué podemos descubrir sobre la dirección del viento?
   ¿Por qué es importante que estudiemos el tiempo?
3. ¿Dónde vivimos?
4. ¿En qué formas afecta a nuestro estilo de vida el ambiente físico?

Usando la pregunta 4 se debe animar a los estudiantes a crear grandes clases o categorías tales como: industria, agricultura, alojamientos, ropa, recreación. La pregunta 4 puede ser considerada, ya sea en una discusión en la cual toda la clase participa, o en pequeños grupos de indagación.

To assist students to generalize about the relationship of environment and behavior, a demographic map may also be used.

At the conclusion of the activity, students should be assisted to define environment and behavior.

Environment: surrounding conditions which influence behavior.

Behavior: the ways in which the individual or group responds or reacts.

*Inquiry Experience B-1—Historical Setting*

Students work in small inquiry groups. Each group is given the following inquiry situation:

It is March 24, 1820. Your family has just arrived in the community which we know as _____. The present population of the community is 75 people. Study the map and decide in what ways the climate and environment of the community will influence your way of life. Following is a list of some of the decisions you must make. You may also make decisions concerning any other questions that you consider important to your way of life in the community.

1. Who are you?
2. How will you provide for your family?
3. What types of housing exist or will be built?
4. What types of clothing will you wear?
5. What kinds of food will you grow and eat?
6. What types of recreational activities might you enjoy?

Se puede hacer uso de un mapa demográfico para ayudar a los alumnos a generalizar sobre la relación entre el ambiente natural y el comportamiento humano.

Al final de la actividad, los estudiantes deben ser ayudados a definir ambiente y comportamiento.

Ambiente: las condiciones circundantes que tienen influencia en el comportamiento.

Comportamiento: las formas en que el individuo o grupo reacciona.

*Experiencia de indagación B-1—Escenario histórico*

Los estudiantes trabajan en pequeños grupos de indagación. A cada grupo se le da la siguiente situación de indagación:

Es el 24 marzo de 1820. Su familia acaba de llegar a la comunidad conocida como _____. La población de la comunidad consiste en 75 personas. Estudie el mapa y decida en qué formas el clima y el ambiente de la comunidad afectarán su estilo de vida. A continuación hay una lista de algunas de las decisiones que Ud. tendrá que hacer. Ud. también puede hacer otras decisiones que considere importantes para con su nueva vida como miembro de la comunidad.

1. ¿Quién es Ud.?
2. ¿Cómo mantendrá Ud. a su familia?
3. ¿Qué tipos de viviendas existen ya o serán contruidas en el futuro?
4. ¿Qué estilo de ropa usará Ud.?
5. ¿Qué cultivará y qué comerá Ud.?
6. ¿Qué tipos de actividades recreativas podrá disfrutar Ud.?

Choose your community

1. El Paso, Texas
2. San Antonio, Texas
3. Los Angeles, California
4. San Diego, California
5. Santa Fe, New Mexico
6. Tuscon, Arizona
7. Denver, Colorado

*OR*

8. Louisville, Kentucky
9. Charleston, South Carolina
10. Baltimore, Maryland
11. Boston, Massachusetts
12. New Orleans, Louisiana

Students should be reminded that the year is 1820 and that the Southwestern communities did not belong to the United States.

Evaluation: Groups present their inquiry decisions. Groups should verify their decisions (prove them) by collecting pictures, making their own illustrations, or reading excerpts from books which support their decisions. Groups may challenge each other.

The teacher may ask specific questions to direct the evaluation:

1. How did the region in which you settled influence your employment?

2. In what way did it influence your clothing, housing, and food?

3. In what ways may the physical environment influence recreation?
4. How did the state of technology influence the way in which you lived?
5. In what ways were settlers, in the 1820's, dependent upon each other?
6. In what ways was man dependent upon the physical environment?

Escoja su comunidad

1. El Paso, Texas
2. San Antonio, Texas
3. Los Angeles, California
4. San Diego, California
5. Santa Fe, Nuevo México
6. Tucson, Arizona
7. Denver, Colorado

*O*

8. Louisville, Kentucky
9. Charleston, Carolina del Sur
10. Baltimore, Maryland
11. Boston, Massachusetts
12. Nueva Orleans, Luisiana

Se les debe recordar a los estudiantes que es el año de 1820 y que las comunidades del Suroeste no pertenecían entonces a los EE.UU.

Evaluación: Los grupos presentan las decisiones a qué han llegado por media de la indagación. Los estudiantes deben verificar sus decisiones (probarlas) con una colección de grabados o láminas, haciendo sus propias ilustraciones, o leyendo trozos de libros que apoyen sus decisiones. Los grupos pueden retar los unos a los otros.

El maestro puede hacer preguntas especifícas para dirigir la evaluación:

1. ¿En qué modo influyó sobre su trabajo la región en que Ud. se estableció?

2. ¿En qué forma influyó ésta sobre su vestimenta, su tipo de alojamiento, y sus comidas?

3. ¿En qué formas puede el ambiente físico influir sobre la recreación?
4. ¿Cómo influyó el grado de tecnología sobre su modo de vivir?
5. ¿En qué formas dependían los hombres de 1820 los unos de los otros?
6. ¿En qué formas dependía el hombre del ambiente natural?

7. How did man's dependence upon the physical environment influence his behavior?

At this time, the teacher may introduce the concept of interdependence and ask students to generalize and relate the concept to their inquiry experience.

## EXTENDED ACTIVITIES

1. Role-play, using the concepts of environment, behavior, and interdependence, a conflict situation of what will happen when the settlers from the communities suggested in 8, 9, 10, 11, and 12 move westward and impinge upon the settlers in the communities of 1 through 7.

2. Groups may be assigned to study particular industries and their contribution to the American way of life.

3. Create a situation, related to a specific time period, concerning misuse of the physical environment, overpopulation, a technological problem. Have students decide what they would do—if.

4. Create a game situation relating migration to urban growth and urban problems.

5. Use the game of Neighborhood, and/ or Pollution. Abt Associates for: Wellesley School System, Seawood Road, Wellesley, Mass. 02181 or 55 Wheeler St., Cambridge, Mass. 02138.

6. Use film: Santa Fe and The Trail—19 minutes, color, Encyclopaedia Britannica Films. Film depicts differences and similarities between the Spanish and American cultures.

7. Use film: Southwest: Land of Promise —13 minutes, color, McGraw Hill Text Films. Describes problems resulting from a rapid growth in population.

7. ¿Cómo influyó sobre el comportamiento del hombre su dependencia del ambiente natural?

En este momento, el maestro puede presentar el concepto do "interdependencia" y puede preguntarles a los alumnos que generalicen y relacionen este concepto con su experiencia de indagación.

## EXTENSIÓN DE ACTIVIDADES

1. Dramatizar, usando los conceptos de ambiente, comportamiento e interdependencia, en una situación conflictiva que trate de lo que sucederá cuando los colonizadores de las comunidades sugeridas en 8 a 12 se muevan hacia el oeste y se impongan sobre los de las comunidades 1 a 7.

2. Se les puede asignar a los grupos el estudio de industrias privadas y las contribuciones que éstas han aportado al modo de vivir norteamericano.

3. Produzca una situación relacionada con un período de tiempo específico, que trate del mal uso del ambiente natural, del excesivo crecimiento demográfico, o de un problema tecnológico. Haga que los estudiantes decidan lo que ellos harían, *si. . .*

4. Organice un juego en el que se relacione la migración con el crecimiento urbano y con los problemas urbanos.

5. Use el juego "Vecindario", y/o "Polución". Abt Associates para: Wellesley School System, Seawood Road, Wellesley, Mass. 02181.

6. Use la película: *Santa Fe and The Trail* —19 minutos, a colores, Encyclopedia Brittanica Films. La película muestra las diferencias y las semejanzas que existen entre las culturas española y norteamericana.

7. Use la película: *Southwest: Land of Promise*—13 minutos, a colores, McGraw Hill Text Films. Ésta describe los problemas que son el resultado del crecimiento rápido de la población.

8. Students may create a scrapbook of fruits, vegetables, and plants brought to the Southwest by the Spanish settlers.

8. Los estudiantes pueden empezar un álbum de recortes que muestren las clases de frutas, de vegetales y de plantas que fueron traídos por los colonos españoles al Suroeste norteamericano.

## MEDIA RESOURCES FOR INQUIRY EXPERIENCE USE

### 16 mm. Films

B-1   *Geography of the Five Pacific States,* 15 min., color, Arthur Barr Productions.
B-1   *Food, Clothing, Shelter in Three Environments,* 15 min., color, Bailey Film Associates.
B-1   *Rain Forest Family: Daily Life,* color, Baily Film Associates.
B-1   *Maps of Our World* (Available in Spanish), 11 min., color, Bailey Film Associates.

### Maps

A   *Transparencies—Southwesetrn United States,* Hammond.
A   *Transparencies—United States* (Geographic Relationships), Hammond.
B   *World Book Atlas,* Historical Maps.

### Transparencies

B   *Man's Basic Needs: Foods,* 23 Visuals, 3M.
B   *Man's Basic Needs: Shelter,* 23 Visuals, 3M.
B   *Man's Basic Needs: Clothing,* 23 Visuals, 3M.

### Picture Sets

A   *Interaction of Man Series,* Rand McNally, 1969.

## LESSON FIVE

## LECCIÓN QUINTA

### QUESTION FOCUS

In what ways do people change the physical environment?

### PREGUNTA DE ENFOQUE

¿En qué formas cambia la gente el ambiente natural?

### COGNITIVE LEVELS

Knowledge • Comprehension • Application • Organization

### NIVELES DE CONOCIMIENTO

Conocimiento • Comprensión • Aplicación • Organización

## AFFECTIVE LEVELS

Evaluation • Characterization

## OVERALL OBJECTIVE

Adaptation

## SPECIFIC OBJECTIVE

The learner will "act out" ways in which the Mexican settler modified and adapted the environment of the Southwest as he mined, farmed, or ranched.

## CONCEPT

Modification, Adaptation

## SETTING

The student's own community: Southwest United States

## PROCEDURE

*Inquiry Experience A-1—Contemporary Setting*

Use is made of students' common experiences. Students are asked to go on a walking or a "thinking" excursion around their school, neighborhood, or community. Students are to observe the physical environment.

When students return to the classroom, three inquiry groups are to prepare lists of things which they consider "natural" to their community environment. (Hills, trees, soil, wild flowers, moss, bodies of water, etc.)

Three inquiry groups are to prepare lists of things which they consider man-made which man has brought to his environment. (Freeways, pipes, buildings, a reservoir, telephone poles and lines, etc.)

## NIVELES AFECTIVOS

Evaluación • Caracterización

## OBJETIVO TOTAL

Adaptación

## OBJETIVO ESPECÍFICO

El estudiante "actuará" formas en las cuales se demostrará cómo el colono mexicano modificó y adaptó el ambiente del Suroeste mientras minaba, labraba la tierra y hacendaba.

## CONCEPTO

Modificación, Adaptación

## ESCENARIO

La comunidad del estudiante: El Suroeste de los EE.UU.

## PROCEDIMIENTO

*Experiencia de indagación A-1—Escenario contemporáneo*

Se hace uso de las experiencias comunes de los estudiantes. Por ejemplo: se les pide a los estudiantes que vayan a dar un paseo o que tomen una excursión "pensativa" alrededor de la escuela, de su vecindario, o de la comunidad. Los estudiantes deben observar el ambiente natural.

Cuando los estudiantes regresen a la clase, tres grupos de indagación prepararán listas de cosas que ellos consideran "naturales" en el ambiente de su comunidad. (Colinas, árboles, terreno, florecillas silvestres, musgos, agua, etc.).

Tres grupos de indagación preparan listas de cosas que ellos consideran manufacturadas por el hombre y que éste último ha introducido en el ambiente natural. (Autopistas, tuberías, edificios, tanques de agua, postes telefónicos, etc.).

Evaluation: Students share their lists. Teacher has students decide which items brought about a change in the natural environment. At this time the concept of modification is introduced and defined.

Teacher asks students to generalize concerning the cause for man's environmental modification through the following questions:

1. What are some reasons why man changed his physical environment?

2. In what ways are we changing our environment today?

Students are asked to analyze the effect of man's environmental modification.

1. What changes have occurred as a result of man's additions to his physical environment? (Buildings, pipelines, freeways)
2. What kinds of changes can we anticipate in the future?

The concept of *adaptation* is defined at this time.

### Inquiry Experience B-1—Historical Setting

Students use the concepts of modification and adaptation as they inquire into the ways in which the Mexican settler worked and traveled in the American Southwest.
Teacher discusses with students, using the research findings from Lesson Four, the physical environment of the American Southwest.
Inquiry Assignment:

Prepare a skit for radio or TV to share with the other inquiry groups. Sketch pictures to accompany your skit. Find

Evaluación: Los estudiantes comparten las listas. El maestro les pide a los alumnos que decidan cuáles de los objetos observados han contribuido a cambiar el ambiente natural. En este momento se debe presentar y definir el concepto de modificación.
El maestro les pide a los alumnos que generalicen sobre la causa de la modificación del ambiente natural por el hombre, usando las siguientes preguntas:

1. ¿Cuáles son las razones por las que el hombre ha cambiado el ambiente físico?
2. ¿En qué forma estamos cambiando el ambiente natural hoy?

Se les pide a los estudiantes que analicen los efectos producidos por la modificación, introducida por el hombre, en el ambiente natural.

1. ¿Cuáles cambios han ocurrido como resultado de las adiciones aportadas por el hombre al ambiente natural? (Edificios, tuberías, autopistas.)
2. ¿Qué clase de cambios podemos anticipar en el futuro?

El concepto de *adaptación* se puede definir en este momento.

### Experiencia de indagación B-1—Escenario histórico

Los estudiantes usan los conceptos de modificación y adaptación mientras investigan cómo el colonizador mexicano trabajó y viajó en el Suroeste.
El maestro discute con los alumnos, usando las conclusiones halladas en la "Lección cuarta", el ambiente físico del Suroeste.
Tarea:

Prepare un guión para una presentación corta, ya sea para el radio o la televisión, y que pueda compartir con los otros

out the ways in which the Mexican settler modified or adapted the environment of the Southwest. What contributions did he make to the natural environment?

Each group may choose one of the following: farmer, rancher, or miner.

If groups appear to need an inquiry focus, the teacher might assist the "farmer" group by asking:

1. What crops will you grow? Are these crops natural to the Southwest or were they natural to your native land?
2. What tools will you use? Were these tools already in use in the Southwest? Somewhere else? Will you invent them?
3. What problems will you encounter as you farm? What contributions will you make?

The teacher might assist the "rancher" group by asking:

1. What animals are you likely to have on your ranch?
2. Were these animals natural to the American Southwest or did you bring them from your native land?
3. What tools will you use? What tools will you invent?

4. What contributions will you make to the ranching industry?

The teacher might assist the "miner" group by asking:

1. What are some natural resources you will find in the American Southwest?

2. What techniques will you use as you mine?

grupos de indagación. Haga dibujos que acompañen su presentación. Investigue cómo el colono mexicano modificó o adaptó el ambiente del Suroeste. ¿Qué contribuciones aportó él al ambiente natural?

Cada grupo puede escoger uno de los siguientes oficios: agricultor, ranchero, o minero.

Si los grupos dan muestras de necesitar un enfoque para la indagación, el maestro puede ayudar al grupo "agricultor", preguntando lo siguiente:

1. ¿Qué clase de cosechas cultivará Ud.? ¿Son estas cosechas originarias del Suroeste o de su país natal?

2. ¿Qué clase de herramientas usará Ud.? ¿Estaban ya en uso estas herramientas en el Suroeste? ¿En otro lugar? ¿Las inventará Ud.?
3. ¿Qué clase de problemas enfrentará Ud. mientras cultive la tierra? ¿Qué contribuciones aportará Ud.?

Al grupo "ranchero":

1. ¿Qué clase de animales tendrá en su hacienda, posiblemente?
2. ¿Estos animales son nativos del Suroeste o los trajo Ud. de su país natal?

3. ¿Qué clase de herramientas usará Ud.? ¿Qué clase de herramientas inventará Ud.?
4. ¿Qué contribuciones aportará Ud. a la industria de haciendas?

Al grupo "minero":

1. ¿Cuáles serán algunos de los recursos naturales que encontrará Ud. en el Suroeste norteamericano?
2. ¿Qué técnicas usará Ud. al minar?

3. What unique contributions will you make?

Interest will be increased if more than one inquiry group researches the same occupation.
Evaluation: Groups present their skits.

## EXTENDED ACTIVITIES

1. Using the concepts of modification and adaptation, relevant problems in urban life may be studied: over-population, crowded freeways, urban renewal, pollution.

2. Communities along the East coast of the United States may be studied contrasting the farming of that region with the farming in the Southwest.

3. A study of different schools or even classrooms within a given school may be used using the conceptual focus of this lesson.

4. Studies of primitive communities or modern technological communities in other parts of the world may be studied.

3. ¿Qué contribuciones únicas aportará Ud.?

El interés será aumentado si más de uno de los grupos de indagación investiga el mismo oficio.
Evaluación: Los grupos presentan sus piezas dramáticas.

## EXTENSIÓN DE ACTIVIDADES

1. Usando los conceptos de modificación y adaptación, se pueden estudiar algunos de los problemas de la vida urbana, como por ejemplo: el crecimiento acelerado de la población, las congestiones del tráfico en las autopistas, las renovaciones urbanas, la polución.

2. Se pueden estudiar las comunidades a lo largo de la costa del Este de los EE.UU., contrastando la agricultura de esa región con la del Suroeste.

3. Un estudio de diferentes escuelas, o aún de las aulas de una escuela específica, se puede hacer usando el enfoque conceptual de esta lección.

4. Se puede hacer un estudio sobre estudios hechos de comunidades primitivas o de modernas comunidades tecnológicas en otras partes del mundo.

## MEDIA RESOURCES FOR INQUIRY EXPERIENCE USE

### 16 mm Films

A-1  *Man's Effect on the Environment,* Bailey Film Associates.
A-1  *An African Community: The Masai,* 16 min., color, Bailey Film Associates.

### Sound Filmstrips

B-1  *Conflict of Cultures: Conquest of the Borderlands,* Multi-Media Productions.

### Transparencies

B  *Man Learns to Control His Environment,* 23 Visuals, color, 3M.

### Filmstrips

B  *The United States Interior West: Growth of a Mining Town,* Encyclopaedia Britannica Educational Corporation.

# LESSON SIX

## QUESTION FOCUS

In what ways does cultural background influence behavior? In what ways did early civilizations contribute to our way of life today?

## COGNITIVE LEVELS

All

## AFFECTIVE LEVELS

Evaluation • Organization • Characterization

## CONCEPTS

Culture • Assimilation • Conflict

## OVERALL OBJECTIVE

Students will use the concepts to study about their heritage.

## SPECIFIC OBJECTIVES

Students will categorize, define, and generalize about art, music, food, architecture, clothing, and speech as ways of expressing cultural orientation.

Students will list contributions of the Mexican culture to the Anglo culture and the contributions of the Anglo culture to the Mexican culture.

## SETTING

The Barrio; Mexico; American Southwest

## PROCEDURE

*Inquiry Experience A-1—Contemporary Setting*

Students work in small inquiry groups.

# LECCIÓN SEXTA

## PREGUNTA DE ENFOQUE

¿Cómo afecta la herencia cultural al comportamiento? ¿En qué forma contribuyeron las civilizaciones antiguas a nuestro estilo de vida actual?

## NIVELES DE CONOCIMIENTO

Todos

## NIVELES AFECTIVOS

Evaluación • Organización • Presentación

## CONCEPTOS

Cultura • Asimilación • Conflicto

## OBJETIVO GENERAL

Los estudiantes usarán los conceptos anteriores para estudiar su herencia cultural.

## OBJETIVOS ESPECÍFICOS

Los estudiantes categorizarán, definirán y generalizarán sobre el arte, la música, la comida, la arquitectura, la vestimenta y el habla, como medios de expresar orientación cultural.

Los estudiantes harán una lista de las contribuciones aportadas por la cultura mexicana a la cultura norteamericana, y viceversa.

## ESCENARIO

El Barrio; México; El Suroeste norteamericano

## PROCEDIMIENTO

*Experiencia de indagación A-1—Escenario contemporáneo*

Los estudiantes trabajan en pequeños gru-

Each group has its own tape recorder or phonograph to listen to some familiar Mexican music. (If this is not possible, then a suitable record for all to listen to at the same time will be acceptable.) Suggested record: Mariachi Aguilas de Chapala: Ojos Tapatíos, Las Mañanitas, La Bamba, etc.

Each inquiry group is given a 3 x 5 card with the following questions:

1. What are some things this music tells us about the Mexican people?

2. How does the music make you feel?

3. Why do you associate these songs with the Mexican people?

4. In what ways do you associate these songs with the Barrio?

5. What are some other songs that you associate with the Barrio? Why?

6. What can we learn about people by listening to the music that they enjoy?

7. Why do we associate certain songs with certain people?

Groups may tape their responses or appoint one person to take notes. Discussion for this activity—10 minutes.

Evaluation: At least one member of each inquiry group summarizes his group's feelings for the evaluation. (Time should be allotted for groups to disagree with each other.)

Teacher may assist the evaluation by having available artifacts associated with the Barrio, Mexican history, or the early Southwest and asking many of the same questions as listed above.

Teacher may suggest that students bring

pos de indagación. Cada grupo tiene a su disposición una grabadora o un tocadiscos con que se puede escuchar música mexicana popular. (Si esto no es posible, entonces un disco apropiado se puede tocar para que el grupo entero lo escuche al mismo tiempo). Se sugiere el disco: Mariachi Aguilas de Chapala: Ojos Tapatíos, Las Mañanitas, La Bamba, etc.

Se le da a cada grupo de indagación una tarjeta (3 x 5) que contenga las siguientes preguntas:

1. ¿Cúales son algunas de las cosas que este disco nos indica respecto a la gente mexicana?

2. ¿Cómo lo afecta la música a Ud.?

3. ¿Por qué asocia estas canciones con la gente mexicana?

4. ¿De qué modo asocia estas canciones con el barrio?

5. ¿Cúales son algunas otras canciones que Ud. asocia con el barrio? ¿Por qué?

6. ¿Qué se puede aprender sobre la gente con sólo escuchar su música favorita?

7. ¿Por qué asociamos ciertas canciones con cierta gente?

Los grupos pueden grabar sus reacciones o pueden nombrar a un individuo que tome notas. La discusión para esta actividad debe durar 10 minutos.

Evaluación: Al menos un miembro de cada grupo de indagación debe resumir los sentimientos de su grupo en la evaluación. (Se debe dar un tiempo limitado para que los alumnos puedan expresar distintos puntos de vista).

El maestro puede ayudar la evaluación teniendo en su posesión: artifactos asociados con el barrio, la historia de México, el antiguo Suroeste norteamericano, y volviendo a hacer algunas de las preguntas anteriores.

El maestro puede sugerir que los estudian-

to class items which they associate as *belonging* to the Mexican community.

### Inquiry Experience A-2

Students work in small inquiry groups. Using books, magazines, pictures, personal experience—each group prepares a list of items typically found in the Barrio home.

Teacher assists students to evaluate the ways in which people in the community are similar.

Inquiry groups use resources and brainstorm to prepare a list of items *typically* found in the Anglo home.

Teacher assists students to contrast the two lists to discover the ways in which people differ.

### Inquiry Experience A-3

Three inquiry groups inquire into ways of life which although originating in the Mexican (Spanish) home will also be a part of life in the Anglo home.

Three inquiry groups research ways of life that although originating in the Anglo home will also be a part of the Barrio home life.

Evaluation: Teacher assists students to note that in all three inquiry activities their lists contained certain categories of items: art, music, food, architecture, clothing, speech.

The evaluation should direct attention to the contribution of peoples (cultures) to one another. If students are "ready", the definitions for culture and assimilation may be offered. Culture: the many ways of behaving which express a people's beliefs, habits, and traditions. Assimilation: the appropriation (taking on) of another's characteristics (ways of behaving).

tes traigan a clase objetos que ellos identifican como pertenecientes a la comunidad mexicana.

### Experiencia de indagación A-2

Los estudiantes trabajan en pequeños grupos de indagación. Usando libros, revistas, fotos, y experiencias personales—cada grupo prepara una lista de objetos típicamente hallados en un hogar de barrio.

El maestro puede ayudar a los alumnos a evaluar las formas en que la gente de la comunidad se parece entre sí.

Los grupos de indagación usan recursos y sesiones inquisitivas para preparar una lista de objetos típicamente hallados en un hogar angloamericano.

El maestro ayuda a los estudiantes a contrastar las dos listas para que decubran las maneras en que la gente difiere.

### Experiencia de indagación A-3

Tres grupos de indagación investigan estilos de vida, que aunque originados en el hogar mexicano (español), serán también parte del estilo de vida del angloamericano.

Tres grupos de indagación investigan estilos de vida que, aunque originados en el hogar angloamericano, son también parte de la vida del hogar del barrio.

Evaluación: El maestro ayuda a los estudiantes a notar que en *todas* las actividades de investigación, las listas contienen ciertas categorías de objetos: arte, música, comida, arquitectura, ropa, habla.

La evaluación debe dirigir la atención a las contribuciones de una cultura a la otra.

Las definiciones de cultura y asimilación pueden ser ofrecidas ahora, si los estudiantes están preparados.

Cultura: los diferentes modos en el comportamiento que expresan las creencias, las costumbres y las tradiciones de la gente.

Asimilación: La adoptación o integración de características ajenas en el comportamiento.

120

*Inquiry Experience B-1—Historical Setting*

Each inquiry group chooses an early community to study: Mayas, Toltecs, Aztecs, the Spanish during the conquest.

Inquiry groups may use the categories established in Inquiry Experience A-3 to study their community or they may use the following categories: art, language, learning, government, occupations.

If groups appear to need assistance, the teacher may guide them with the following types of questions:

1. What happened in the daily life of the community?
2. What types of activities did they pursue?
3. What types of things did the people believe to be true?
4. In what ways did the activities of children differ from those of men and women?
5. What contributions did the community make to later civilizations?

As students study their chosen community, they may use their information to produce a scrapbook, mural, short stories or a play to share with the other inquiry groups.

Evaluation: Students share their inquiry experience. Teacher directs attention to the activities of people which reflect cultural orientation and the relationship in historical time of each community to the next.

*Inquiry Experience B-2*

Students work in inquiry groups. Each group may continue its community study

*Experiencia de indagación B-1—Escenario histórico*

Cada grupo de indagación escoge una comunidad antigua para estudiar: los mayas, los toltecas, los aztecas, los españoles bajo Cortés.

Los grupos de indagación pueden usar las categorías establecidas en la Experiencia de indagación A-3 para estudiar su propia comunidad o, también, pueden hacer uso de las categorías siguientes: arte, idioma, aprendizaje, gobierno, oficios.

Si los grupos parecen necesitar ayuda, el maestro los puede guiar haciéndoles el siguiente tipo de preguntas:

1. ¿Qué pasaba en la vida diaria de la comunidad?
2. ¿Qué clase de actividades se practicaban?
3. ¿Qué creencias tenía por verdaderas la gente?
4. ¿En qué diferían las actividades de los niños de las de los adultos?
5. ¿Qué contribuciones aportó esta comunidad a futuras civilizaciones?

Mientras los estudiantes estudian la comunidad escogida respectivamente, pueden a la vez usar su información para producir un álbum de recortes, un mural, para escribir cuentos o dar una presentación que se pueda compartir con los otors grupos de indagación.

Evaluación: Los estudiantes comparten entre ellos su experiencia de indagación. El maestro dirige la atención del grupo a las actividades de la gente que reflejan la orientación cultural y la relación en tiempo histórico de cada comunidad con la que la sigue.

*Experiencia de indagación B-2*

Los estudiantes trabajan en grupos de indagación. Cada grupo puede continuar el estu-

from B-1 or choose a new civilization to study. Each group studies the following questions:

1. What happened to the civilization?
2. Why did it happen?
3. In what ways was there conflict?
4. What contributions did each civilization make to the next?
5. In what ways did the conquest of civilizations contribute to the Mexican heritage?
6. In what ways did the conquest of civilizations contribute to the development of the American Southwest?
7. Who are some individuals who contributed to that heritage?

As students study their chosen community, they will find that they also need to study the three other communities. Groups may wish to confer with each other or the teacher may desire to have a large group discussion for groups to share their information.

If a suggested list of individuals who contributed to the development of the Southwest is desired, the following may be used: Álvaro Núñez Cabeza de Vaca, Fray Marcos de Niza, Esteban, Juan de Oñate, Father Kino, Fray Junípero Serra, Juan Bautista de Anza.

Evaluation: Groups choose their own means of presentation. Teacher assists students to define the concepts of culture, assimilation, conflict.

## EXTENDED ACTIVITIES

1. Students use cameras to record Barrio characteristics and way of life.

2. Students inquiry into what happened

dio de la comunidad escogida en B-1, o puede, si quiere, escoger otra civilización diferente para estudiar. Cada grupo estudia las siguientes preguntas:

1. ¿Qué le pasó a la civilización?
2. ¿Por qué sucedió esto?
3. ¿Qué clase de conflictos existieron?
4. ¿Qué clase de contribuciones aportó cada civilización a la siguiente?
5. ¿Cómo contribuyó la conquista de estas civilizaciones a la herencia cultural del pueblo mexicano?
6. ¿Cómo contribuyó la conquista de estas civilizaciones al desarrollo del Suroeste norteamericano?
7. ¿Quiénes son algunos de los individuos que contribuyeron a esa herencia?

Mientras los estudiantes estudian la comunidad escogida, se darán cuenta que tendrán que estudiar también las otras tres comunidades. Los grupos quizás deseen intercambiar opiniones entre ellos, o el maestro, tal vez, desee que todos los grupos tengan una discusión en conjunto para que puedan compartir su información.

Si se desea una lista de los nombres de algunos individuos que contribuyeron al desarrollo del Suroeste, la siguiente puede ser utilizada: Álvaro Núñez Cabeza de Vaca, Fray Marcos de Niza, Esteban, Juan de Oñate, El Padre Kino, Fray Junípero Serra, Juan Bautista de Anza.

Evaluación: Cada grupo escoge sus propios medios para dar su presentación. El maestro ayuda a los alumnos a definir los conceptos de cultura, asimilación, conflicto.

## EXTENSIÓN DE ACTIVIDADES

1. Los estudiantes usan cámaras fotográficas para fotografiar las características y los estilos de vida en el barrio.

2. Los estudiantes investigan lo que suce-

to the Indian communities of the New World.

3. Students study the French-Indian War and the conflict of cultures in Canada today.

4. Students may role-play conflict situations in history:

    a. The Spanish arrival at the Palace of Moctezuma II.

    b. Forty-niners as they "claim-jump", pan for gold, and set up mining camps.

    c. Small farmers from the Eastern United States as they "fence in" grazing areas in the Southwest.

    d. Treaty of Guadalupe-Hidalgo.

    e. Using newspaper articles and magazines with conflicting points of view concerning peace marches or problems in the Barrio.

5. Students learn Mexican folkdances.

6. Students sing Mexican folksongs.

7. Students listen to poetry and write their own.

dió con las comunidades indígenas del Nuevo Mundo.

3. Los estudiantes estudian la guerra franco-india, y el conflicto entre culturas que existen aún hoy en el Canadá.

4. Los estudiantes pueden dramatizar situaciones de conflicto en la historia:

    a. La llegada de los españoles al palacio de Moctezuma II.

    b. La toma de los derechos de propiedad de los pioneros del '49, los lavaderos de oro, y el establecimiento de campamentos.

    c. Granjeros menores del Este de los EE.UU. "cercando" pastizales del Suroeste.

    d. El tratado Guadalupe-Hidalgo.

    e. Uso de artículos periodísticos y de revistas que contengan puntos de vista diferentes respecto a las protestas por la paz y a los problemas del barrio.

5. Los estudiantes aprenden danzas folklóricas mexicanas.

6. Los estudiantes cantan canciones folklóricas mexicanas.

7. Los estudiantes escuchan poesía y escriben versos.

## MEDIA RESOURCES FOR INQUIRY EXPERIENCE USE

### 16 mm. Films

A-3   *Mexican Ceramics,* 18 min., color, Bailey Film Associates.
A-3   *Comparative Geography: A Changing Culture,* 17 min., color, Bailey Film Associates.
A-3   *Mission Life,* 20 min., color, Arthur Barr Productions.
A-3   *Rancho Life,* 20 min., color, Arthur Barr Productions.
A-3   *Missions of the Southwest,* 15 min., Arthur Barr Productions.
A-3   *Chicano from the Southwest,* 15 min., Encyclopaedia Britannica Educational Corporation.
B-1   *Early American Civilizations,* 13½ min., Coronet Films.
B-1   *The Mayas,* 11 min., Coronet Films.

### Sound Filmstrips

B-1   *Mexico's Indian Heritage* (6), three 12″ L.P.'s, Bailey Film Associates.
A-1   *Children's Songs of Mexico* (2), one L.P., Bailey Film Associates.

A-1 *Masterworks of Mexican Art* (6), six L.P.'s, Bailey Film Associates.
B-2 *Conflict of Cultures: Invasion of the Borderlands,* Multi-Media Productions.
B-2 *Conflict of Cultures: Conquest of the Borderlands,* Multi-Media Productions.
B-1 *Mexico of the Indians,* Multi-Media Productions.
B-1 *Twilight of the Gods,* Multi-Media Productions.
B-1 *The Aztecs and Cortes,* color, 51 frames, Doubleday and Co., Inc.

### Filmstrips

B *Indian Cultures of the Americas,* (6) color, Encyclopaedia Britannica Educational Corporation.
B-2 *Spanish Explorers of the New World,* Encyclopaedia Britannica Educational Corporation.
B-1 *Ancient American Indian Civilizations,* Encyclopaedia Britannica Educational Corporation.

### Records

A *Traditional Songs of Mexico,* 12″ L.P., Folkways.
B *Indian Music of Mexico,* 12″ L.P., Folkways.
A *Mexico: Its Cultural Life in Music & Art,* 12″ L.P., Art Book Chavez.

### Transparencies

B *Great Indian Cultures of the Southwest:* I., II., III, Visual Material, Inc.
B-2 *Spanish Exploration in the 16th Century,* Visual Material, Inc.

### Illustrated Books (in addition to Student's Bibliography)

A-2 *My House in Your House* (paperback), Children's Music Center.
A-2 *Spanish Songs of Old California* (B849), Children's Music Center.
A-2 *Spanish-American Poetry* (B580), Children's Music Center.
B-1 *The Aztecs; The Mayas;* Pan American Union.

| LESSON SEVEN | LECCIÓN SÉPTIMA |
|---|---|
| **QUESTION FOCUS** | **PREGUNTA DE ENFOQUE** |
| In what ways have communities changed? | ¿En qué formas han cambiado las comunidades? |
| **COGNITIVE LEVELS** | **NIVELES DE CONOCIMIENTO** |
| All | Todos |

## AFFECTIVE LEVELS

All

## OVERALL OBJECTIVE

Students will observe, prepare for, and anticipate change in their daily living.

## SPECIFIC OBJECTIVES

Students will identify recent changes in the migrant, rural farm, and urban communities.

Students will debate about future societal changes and the effect of them.
Students will identify changes in the American Southwest resulting from immigration, technology, and government.

## CONCEPTS

Urbanization • Technology • Change

## SETTING

The Barrio (The Local Community); American Southwest

## PROCEDURE

*Inquiry Experience A-1—Contemporary Setting*

Teacher displays the following types of pictures:

1. Migrant workers in the fields;

2. Migrant workers on strike;
3. Farm mechanization;
4. The urban skyline;
5. Urban renewal;
6. Men and women in line to apply for a job;

## NIVELES AFECTIVOS

Todos

## OBJETIVO GENERAL

Los estudiantes observarán, se prepararán, y anticiparán los cambios en su vida diaria futura.

## OBJETIVOS ESPECÍFICOS

Los estudiantes identificarán los cambios recientes en las comunidades migrantes rural-granjeras y urbanas.
Los estudiantes tendrán debates sobre los futuros cambios sociales y el efecto de éstos.
Los estudiantes identificarán los cambios ocurridos en el Suroeste norteamericano a causa de la migración, de la tecnología, y del gobierno.

## CONCEPTOS

Urbanización • Tecnología • Cambio

## ESCENARIO

El Barrio (La comunidad local); El Suroeste norteamericano

## PROCEDIMIENTO

*Experiencia de indagación A-1—Escenario contemporáneo*

El maestro muestra el siguiente tipo de grabados o fotografías:

1. Trabajadores migrantes en los campos.
2. Trabajadores migrantes en huelga.
3. Mecanización de la granja.
4. El perfil de los rascacielos urbanos.
5. Renovación urbana.
6. Hombres y mujeres haciendo cola para solicitar trabajo.

7. Freeways and bridges under construction;
8. Prefabricated housing;
9. Health centers, clinics, child care centers;

10. A proposed rapid transit system;

11. Cultural, recreational centers;

12. Colleges, schools, vocational classrooms.

Students observe the picture display.

Teacher directs a large group discussion by asking:

1. What is happening?
2. Why do you think it is happening?

Teacher encourages students to describe, clarify, define, infer, generalize, debate, and value as they talk about each picture.

Evaluation: Students work in small inquiry groups to evaluate and summarize their previous responses. Each group focuses upon the migrant community, *or* the rural farm community, *or* the urban community.

The evaluation centers upon the following questions:

1. In what ways has the community changed?
2. What is the effect of these changes?
3. What do you anticipate will be the effect of these changes?
4. What are some things that brought about the changes?
5. What additional changes and problems can we expect in the future?

Groups share their evaluations. Teacher

7. Autopistas y puentes en construcción.
8. Casas prefabricadas.
9. Centros de asistencia médica, clínicas, o centros para el cuidado de los niños.

10. Una propuesta respecto al sistema de transporte público.

11. Centros culturales y centros recreativos.

12. Universidades, escuelas, clases de artes y oficios.

Los estudiantes observan los grabados o fotografías anteriores.

El maestro, haciendo las siguientes preguntas, inicia una discusión en el grupo:

1. ¿Qué está sucediendo?
2. ¿Qué piensa Ud. que está sucediendo?

El maestro les da ánimo a los estudiantes para que describan, clarifiquen, definan, infieran, generalicen, debatan, y evalúen mientras hablan de cada foto.

Evaluación: Los estudiantes trabajan en pequeños grupos de indagación para evaluar y resumir sus reacciones anteriores. Cada grupo fija su atención en la comunidad migrante, *o* en la comunidad rural-granjera, *o* en la comunidad urbana.

La evaluación se concentra en las preguntas siguientes:

1. ¿De qué modo ha cambiado la comunidad?
2. ¿Cuál es el efecto de estos cambios?
3. ¿Qué preve Ud. como efecto de estos cambios?
4. ¿Cuáles son algunas de las cosas que causaron los cambios?
5. ¿Qué cambios y problemas adicionales podremos esperar en el futuro?

Los grupos comparten sus evaluaciones. El

assists students to define urbanization, technology, change.

*Inquiry Experience B-1—Historical Setting*

Inquiry groups explore changes in the American Southwest attributable to the Spanish and Mexican settler.

The following inquiry-oriented situations are presented. Each group chooses one situation to study in depth.

In 1862, America produced 5 million pounds of wool. In 1880, wool production had increased to 20 million pounds. What are some things that happened in the sheep-raising industry which brought about this change? What was the effect of the Spanish and Mexican system of land grants? What were some advantages or disadvantages of a system of fixed grazing rights?

In 1830, in Texas, there was about 100,000 head of cattle, roaming wild. In 1846, the number of cattle had increased to 382,733. What are some things that the Spanish owners and the Mexican *vaqueros* did which brought about this change? How did Spanish range laws influence life in the Southwest?

The physical environment of the Southwest is semi-arid. Water was extremely precious to the early settlers. How did the Mexican law of waters influence life in the Southwest and our life today? What were some other land-use systems developed by the Spanish and Mexican settlers which are important today?

Evaluation: Groups share their inquiries

*Experiencia de indagación B-1—Escenario histórico*

Los grupos de indagación exploran los cambios en el Suroeste norteamericano atribuidos al colonizador español y mexicano.

Se presentan, a continuación, las siguientes situaciones. Cada grupo escoge una situación para estudiarla a fondo.

En 1862, América produjo 5 millones de libras de lana. En 1880, la producción de lana ascendió hasta los 20 millones de libras. ¿Cuáles fueron algunas de las cosas que sucedieron en la industria de la cría de ovejas que causaron este cambio en la producción? ¿Cúal fue el efecto causado por las concesiones de tierra de los sistemas español y mexicano? ¿Cúales fueron las ventajas y las desventajas de un sistema fijo de pastoreo?

En 1830, en Texas, había cerca de 100,000 cabezas de ganado cerril. En 1846, el número de cabezas de ganado había llegado a 382,733 reses. ¿Cuáles fueron algunas de las cosas que hicieron el terrateniente español y el vaquero mexicano para inducir este cambio? ¿Cómo influyeron sobre la vida en el Suroeste las leyes españolas de ejido?

El ambiente natural del Suroeste es semi-árido. El agua tenía gran valor para los primeros colonos. ¿Cómo influyeron la vida del Suroeste de entonces y nuestra vida actual las leyes de aguas? ¿Cúales son los otros sistemas de tierra desarrollados por los colonizadores españoles y mexicano que son importantes aún hoy?

Evaluación: Los grupos comparten sus in-

through pictures, stories, or summarization. Groups may debate varying points of view.

Teacher may assist the evaluation by asking the following:

1. In what ways did laws motivate change?
2. How did new knowledge or inventions affect change?
3. What was the effect of population increase upon change?

## EXTENDED ACTIVITIES

1. Students may study changes in the Barrio by interviewing community members, talking with grandparents, recording changes via camera pictures.

2. Students may study in depth changes in our ways of living that have resulted from unionism, compulsory education, Medicare, Social Security, labor laws.

vestigaciones por medio de grabados, de cuentos, o de resúmenes. Los grupos pueden debatir los diferentes puntos de vista.

El maestro puede ayudar en la evaluación preguntando lo siguiente:

1. ¿Cómo motivaron cambios estas leyes?
2. ¿Cómo afectaron el cambio los nuevos conocimientos o las invenciones?
3. ¿Cúal fue el efecto del aumento demográfico sobre el cambio?

## EXTENSIÓN DE ACTIVIDADES

1. Los estudiantes pueden estudiar cambios ocurridos en el barrio por medio de entrevistas con miembros de la comunidad, hablando con abuelos, o captando los cambios por medio de fotografías.

2. Los estudiantes pueden estudiar a fondo los cambios en nuestro modo de vivir que son el resultado de los gremios obreros, de la instrucción obligatoria, del "Medicare", del Seguro Social, de las leyes obreras.

## MEDIA RESOURCES FOR INQUIRY EXPERIENCE USE

### Pictures

A & B   *Portfolio of Outstanding Americans of Mexican Descent,* 37 black and white prints, Educational Consultant Associates.

### Text with Illustrations

A & B   Nava, Julian. *Mexican Americans: A Brief Look At Their History.* New York: Antidefamation League.

### Sound Filmstrips

A & B   *Mexican Americans, Minorities Have Made America Great:* Set II, Warren Schlout Productions, Inc.

# LESSON EIGHT

## QUESTION FOCUS

Who are some people who have brought about community change?

## COGNITIVE LEVELS

All

## AFFECTIVE LEVELS

All

## OVERALL OBJECTIVE

To assist students to evaluate the function of leadership in a democracy.

## SPECIFIC OBJECTIVES

Students will compare the functions, obligations, and privileges of leadership by participation in a skit, play or charade; by writing an article or a story; by drawing cartoons, murals or maps.

## CONCEPTS

Leadership • Power

## SETTING

Present time; Historical past

## PROCEDURE

### Inquiry Experiences A and B

Teacher has students recall societal changes from the previous lesson and asks: Who makes changes happen? With the response that people influence change, students are asked to suggest leaders in the Mexican community who have influenced change. The fol-

# LECCIÓN OCTAVA

## PREGUNTA DE ENFOQUE

¿Quiénes son algunas de las personas que han ayudado a traer cambios a la comunidad?

## NIVELES DE CONOCIMIENTO

Todos

## NIVELES AFECTIVOS

Todos

## OBJETIVO GENERAL

Asistir a los estudiantes en su evaluación de la función que tiene el liderazgo en una democracia.

## OBJETIVOS ESPECÍFICOS

Los estudiantes comparan las funciones, las obligaciones y los privilegios de los líderes participando en una obrita de teatro; escribiendo un artículo o un evento; dibujando tirillas cómicas, murales o mapas.

## CONCEPTOS

Liderazgo • Poder

## ESCENARIO

Tiempo presente; pasado histórico

## PROCEDIMIENTO

### Experiencias de indagación A y B

El maestro hace que los estudiantes recuerden los cambios sociales de la lección pasada y pregunta: ¿Quién o quiénes producen los cambios? Siendo la respuesta que la gente influye en los cambios, se les pide entonces a los alumnos que sugieran los nombres

lowing is a suggested list which cuts across time reflecting both the present and the past:

de algunos líderes de la comunidad mexicana que hayan influido en los cambios. A continuación se sugiere una lista de nombres. Nótese que esta lista refleja tanto el presente como el pasado.

1. George Sanchez—Educator;
2. Cesar Chavez—Labor Leader;
3. Reyes Tijerina;
4. Dolores Huerta;
5. Leopoldo G. Wanchez—Judge;
6. Edward Roybal—Congressman;
7. Father Henry J. Casso—Social Leader;
8. Vikki Carr—Singer;
9. Henry Lopez—Attorney;
10. Trini Lopez—Singer, Guitarist;
11. Ernesto Galarza—Author;
12. Julian Nava—Educator;
13. José Ontonio Carillo—Constitutional Delegate in Calif.;
14. Portola—Spanish Explorer;
15. Julian Samora—Educator;
16. Juan Cabrillo—Spanish Explorer;
17. Sebastian Vizcaino—Spanish Explorer;
18. Explorers from Lesson Six, Inquiry Experience B-2;

19. Any leader the students suggest;

20. Ruben Salazar—Writer, Columnist.

1. George Sánchez—Educador;
2. César Chávez—Líder gremial
3. Reyes Tijerina;
4. Dolores Huerta;
5. Leopoldo G. Sánchez—Juez;
6. Edward Roybal—Congresista;
7. El padre Henry J. Casso—Líder social;
8. Vikki Carr—Cantante;
9. Henry López—Abogado;
10. Trini López—Cantante y guitarrista;
11. Ernesto Galarza—Autor;
12. Julián Nava—Educador;
13. José Antonio Carillo—Delegado constitucional en California;
14. Portola—Explorador español;
15. Julián Samora—Educador;
16. Juan Cabrillo—Explorador español;
17. Sesbastián Vizcaíno—Explorador español;
18. Los Exploradores de la Lección sexta, Experiencia de indagación B-2;

19. Cualquier líder que los estudiantes sugieran;

20. Rubén Salazar—Escritor, Columnista.

Individually or in small groups, students research the contribution of one or more of the above-mentioned leaders. Group presentations may take the following form:

Individualmente, o en grupos pequeños, los estudiantes investigan la contribución de uno o más de los líderes mencionados arriba. Las presentaciones de los grupos pueden ser dadas en las siguientes formas:

1. Skits, plays, or charades (costumes may be used).
2. Newspaper articles in the form of short biographies.
3. Cartoons, murals, paintings.
4. Maps depicting explorer's route.

1. En obritas de teatro cortas, dramas o charadas (se pueden usar disfraces).
2. En artículos de periódico en forma de biografías cortas.
3. En tirillas cómicas, murales, pinturas.
4. En mapas que muestren la ruta de los exploradores.

Teacher may assist the investigation with the following types of questions:

1. How did this person become a leader?
2. What did he do to help others in the community?
3. What did he do that was different?
4. How is he like all other people? How is he different?
5. What did he try to accomplish? In what ways did he succeed? In what ways did he fail?
6. How are you like this person? How are you different?
7. Who assisted this person? Whom did this person depend upon?
8. How are we dependent upon this person?

Evaluation: Individuals and groups present their investigation, skit or charade. Teacher focuses upon the need for community leadership, the characteristics of leaders, the concept of power and the implication for group action.

## EXTENDED ACTIVITIES

1. Classroom visitations by community leaders with a panel of students acting as reporters to interview the visitor.

2. Trips to City Hall, cultural centers, sports events.
3. Hypothetical situations.—What would have happened if:

a. Cortés did not conquer the Aztecs?

b. An explorer did not explore?
c. There were no unions or union leaders?
d. There had been no Mexican war?
e. Moctezuma II had not ruled the Aztecs?
4. Study of famous Latin Americans.

El maestro puede ayudar en la investigación haciendo el siguiente tipo de preguntas:

1. ¿Cómo llegó esta persona a ser un líder?
2. ¿Qué hizo él (o ella) para ayudar a los otros en la comunidad?
3. ¿Qué hizo que fue diferente?
4. ¿En qué se parece a la otra gente? ¿En qué se diferencia?
5. ¿Qué trató de conseguir? ¿En qué tuvo éxito? ¿En que falló?

6. ¿En qué se parece Ud. a esa persona? ¿En qué se diferencia?
7. ¿Quién ayudó a esta persona? ¿De quién dependía esta persona?
8. ¿Cómo dependemos nosotros de esta persona?

Evaluación: Los individuos y los grupos presentan su investigación u obra de teatro. El maestro se concentra en la necesidad de liderazgo dentro de la comunidad, en las características de los líderes, en el concepto del poder, y en la implicación para que el grupo actúe.

## EXTENSIÓN DE ACTIVIDADES

1. Visitas de los líderes de la comunidad a la clase. Éstos son entrevistados por grupos pequeños de estudiantes que actúan como reporteros.
2. Viajes el ayuntamiento, a centros culturales, y a eventos deportivos.
3. Situaciones hipotéticas: ¿Qué hubiera pasado si:

a. Cortés no hubiera conquistado a los aztecas?
b. un explorador no hubiera explorado?
c. no hubiera gremios obreros ni líderes, para éstos?
d. no hubiera habido guerra en México?
e. Moctezuma II no hubiera regido a los aztecas?
4. Estudio de lationamericanos famosos.

## MEDIA RESOURCES FOR INQUIRY EXPERIENCE USE

### 16 mm. Films

A-1   *The Cities: To Build A Future,* 54 min., Bailey Film Associates.
A-1   *The Cities: A City Is to Live in,* 54 min., Bailey Film Associates.
A-1   *Urban Sprawl,* 15 min., color, Arthur Barr Productions, Inc.

### Film Loops—Super 8

A   *Movement in the City,* Ealing Film Loops.
A   *Renewing the City,* Ealing Film Loops.
A   *Problems in the City,* Ealing Film Loops.
A   *Taking Care of the City,* Ealing Film Loops.

### Filmstrips

B   *The United States Pacific West: The Water Problem,* Encyclopaedia Britannica Educational Corporation.
A   *Then and Now in the Southwest,* Encyclopaedia Britannica Educational Corporation.
A   *Then and Now in Texas,* Encyclopaedia Britannica Educational Corporation.
A   *Then and Now in California* Encyclopaedia Britannica Educational Corporation.

### Picture Sets

A-1   *Interaction of Man Series,* Rand McNally, 1969.

| LESSON NINE | LECCIÓN NOVENA |
|---|---|
| **QUESTION FOCUS** | **PREGUNTA DE ENFOQUE** |
| What are some community changes that we can anticipate in the future? In what ways can we facilitate change? | ¿Cuáles son algunos de los cambios en la comunidad que podemos anticipar en el futuro? ¿Cómo podemos facilitar estos cambios? |
| **COGNITIVE LEVELS** | **NIVELES DE CONOCIMIENTO** |
| All | Todos |
| **AFFECTIVE LEVELS** | **NIVELES AFECTIVOS** |
| All | Todos |

## OVERALL OBJECTIVES

To involve students in decision-making in a game situation.

To involve students in power politics and leadership.

## SPECIFIC OBJECTIVES

The learner will set a plan to solve or alleviate a problem.
Students will express verbally values and alternatives in the decision-making process.

Students will make a verbal committal to action, inaction, or postponement of action.

## CONCEPTS

Leadership • Power • Community • Government

## SETTING

Any large urban center

## PROCEDURE

### Inquiry Experience—People Power

#### (A Decision-making Game)

The goal for this game situation is to involve students in rational decision-making; therefore, it is important that students understand and follow the game rules. It is also vital that students comprehend the decision-making process and the choices that are involved. The evaluation of the game activity will be the most important part of the learning experience. The Game will take approximately three class periods.

The Game involves leadership, a problem,

## OBJETIVOS GENERALES

Hacer que los estudiantes participen en el proceso de hacer decisiones por medio de un juego.
Hacer que los estudiantes participen en la busca del poder y en el liderazgo.

## OBJETIVOS ESPECÍFICOS

El estudiante forjará un plan para resolver o para aliviar un problema.
Los estudiantes expresarán oralmente los valores y las alternativas en el proceso de hacer decisiones.
Los estudiantes harán una promesa oral de tomar acción, de no tomar accion, o de posponer la acción.

## CONCEPTOS

Liderazgo • Poder • Comunidad • Gobierno

## ESCENARIO

Cualquier centro urbano grande

## PROCEDIMIENTO

### Experiencia de indagación—El poder popular
#### (Un juego para hacer decisiones)

El propósito de este juego es el de hacer que los estudiantes participen en situaciones en las cuales tienen que hacer decisiones de forma racional; por consiguiente, es importante que los estudiantes entiendan y sigan las reglas del juego. Es también vital que los estudiantes comprendan los procesos de hacer decisiones y las alternativas que se presentan. La evaluación de las actividades de este juego será la parte más importante de esta experiencia en el aprendizaje. El juego tomará, aproximadamente, tres períodos de clase.

El juego comprende el liderazgo, un

a plan, and a legislative body to make decisions.

Rules for People Power:

1. The class votes to select 11 members
   of the city council. Each member of
   the city council should represent a
   special group in the city. (The
   blacks, suburbs, middle class, barrio, etc.) Some special-interest
   groups will have more than one
   representative.
2. Students work in small inquiry
   groups. Each inquiry group selects
   a leader from the list in Lesson
   Eight. The inquiry group must be
   familiar with or obtain information
   from another group, or research the
   leader's life. If an historical leader
   is selected, that leader would "act"
   in the context of today for the game
   situation.

3. Each inquiry group must now select
   a problem, issue, or change which
   they believe their leader would attempt to solve or alleviate. Each
   group must select a different problem or issue. Groups may suggest
   their own issues or problems or select one from the following list:

a. A proposed freeway through the
   barrio will eliminate housing and
   recreation areas.

b. Urban renewal.
c. Industries are locating in and dis-
   placing residential areas and creat-
   ing hazardous conditions.

d. Community schools are not integrated.
e. Earthquake damage to barrio
   schools.

problema, un plan, y un grupo legislativo
que haga las decisiones.

Reglas para "El poder popular":

1. Los votos de la clase para elegir 11
   miembros del concejo municipal.
   Cada miembro del concejo debe
   representar un grupo especial de la
   ciudad. (Los negros, los suburbios,
   la clase media, el barrio, etc.) Algunos grupos de intereses especiales
   tendrán más de un representante.
2. Los estudiantes trabajan en pequeños grupos de indagación. Cada
   grupo selecciona un líder de la lista
   dada en la Lección octava. El grupo
   de indagación debe conocer a este
   líder, o debe obtener información
   de otro grupo, o debe investigar la
   vida del líder escogido. Si se selecciona un líder histórico, el líder
   debe actuar en el contexto actual de
   este juego.
3. Cada grupo de indagación debe seleccionar un problema, un tópico, o
   un cambio que necesite ser resuelto
   o aliviado, según el caso, por el
   líder del grupo. Cada grupo de indagación debe escoger un problema
   diferente. Los grupos pueden sugerir sus propios problemas o deben
   seleccionar uno de la siguiente lista:

a. El proyecto para la construcción de
   una autopista que atraviesa el barrio, eliminaría caseríos y centros
   de recreación.
b. Renovación urbana.
c. Las industrias se están estableci-
   do y en el proceso están desplazan-
   do zonas residenciales. También
   están creando situaciones peli-
   grosas.
d. Las escuelas en la comunidad no
   están integradas.
e. Daños causados por el terremoto
   en las escuelas del barrio.

f.  Unemployment.
g.  Lack of recreational and cultural centers.
h.  Lack of transportation services.

i.  Need for a skills training center, vocational school.

j.  Need for street paving and street lights in the barrio.

k.  Lack of a hospital and emergency services.
l.  City employees are threatening to strike; sanitation will be affected.

m.  School drop-out rate—70%

4.  Each inquiry group plans "action" steps to solve or alleviate the problem. (Both the "action" steps and the chosen problem should be consistent with the group's chosen leader.) The following guidelines for "action" steps must be observed.

a.  Action must be legal—within the law.
b.  Action must consider the needs and well-being and rights of all members of the barrio.

c.  Action must improve conditions in the barrio (local community).

d.  Action must be feasible in terms of technology.
e.  If action steps require additional money to rectify the situation, there must be a logical method to raise the funds.

f.  Action must be reasonable; not "emotional."

f.  La desocupación.
g.  La falta de centros recreativos y culturales.
h.  La falta de servicios de transportación.

i.  La necesidad de un centro vocacional donde se enseñen labores manuales.

j.  La necesidad de que se pavimenten las calles y de que se instalen luces en las calles del barrio.

k.  I a falta de los servicios de un hospital de emergencia.
l.  Los empleados cívicos están amenazando con irse de huelga; la sanidad pública será afectada.

m.  Los chicos cesan de ir a la escuela. El 70% de los alumnos interrumpe sus estudios.

4.  Cada grupo planea diferentes modos de acción para resolver o aliviar el problema. (Tanto los modos de acción como el problema escogidos deben de coincidir con el líder escogido por el grupo). Deben seguirse las siguientes directivas:

a.  La acción debe ser legal—dentro de la ley.
b.  La acción debe considerar las necesidades, el bienestar, y los derechos de todos los miembros del barrio.

c.  La acción debe mejorar las condiciones en el barrio (la comunidad local).

d.  La acción debe ser posible en términos tecnológicos.
e.  Si los pasos que se toman para la acción requieren dinero adicional para rectificar la situación, un método lógico debe ser seguido para colectar el dinero que se necesita.

f.  La acción debe ser razonable; NO "emocional".

5. Inquiry groups plan their "action".

6. Inquiry groups choose one member as the leader to present their plan to the city council. Since council members are also inquiry group members, it is permissible for a council member to be a leader and present a plan, if the group so desires.

7. Each issue is presented separately and debated by the council before the next issue is considered. (Unless the council decides to table the issue.) The council president, chosen by the council members, decides which issue is to be considered and in what order.

8. As each issue is considered, all students may act as interested citizens and ask to speak before the council. It is possible for the plan of one group to interfere with the plans from another group thereby motivating controversy.

9. The council votes on each issue. If no agreement can be reached, the council may vote to table the issue. council members may change the "action" steps presented by a group or make deals among themselves to protect the rights of their constituents.

10. Parliamentary procedure is used throughout.

Evaluation: After the Game, students need to analyze what happened at the city council meeting. The following questions may guide the evaluation:

5. Los grupos de indagación planean su "acción".

6. Los grupos escogen uno de sus miembros como "Líder" para que presente su plan ante el concejo municipal. Como los miembros del concejo son también miembros del grupo de indagación, se permite que éstos sean líderes y que presenten un plan, si el grupo lo desea así.

7. Cada problema es presentado de forma separada y es debatido por el concejo antes de que se considere el próximo problema. (A no ser que el concejo decida aplazar la moción). El presidente del concejo, escogido por los miembros del mismo, debe decidir cuál problema será discutido y el orden que seguirá la discusión.

8. A medida que cada problema es considerado, todos los estudiantes pueden actuar como ciudadanos interesados y pueden pedir la palabra ante el concejo. Se permite que el plan de un grupo interfiera con el plan del otro grupo para que se suscite controversia.

9. El concejo vota en cada problema. Si no se puede alcanzar un acuerdo, el concejo puede votar para que se aplace la moción. Los miembros del concejo pueden cambiar los proyectos de "acción" presentados por un grupo, o pueden hacer tratos entre ellos para proteger los derechos de sus constituyentes.

10. Procedimientos parlamentarios se usan desde el principio hasta el fin.

Evaluación: Después del juego, los estudiantes necesitan analizar lo que sucedió en la sesión del concejo municipal. Las preguntas siguientes pueden ser de ayuda en la evaluación:

1. To what extent did council members have choices? How did the council members express their choices?
2. To what extent did the council members use information presented by the inquiry groups when they made a decision?

3. Did council members present alternative solutions? Did they change the "action" steps?

4. To what extent did they anticipate future problems as a result of their decision?
5. To what extent were decisions made in terms of action?
6. How did the needs and desires of the whole city affect the council decisions?
7. In what ways will a decision affect the whole city?
8. In what ways will a decision affect just one community?
9. Who will be pleased or displeased by a given decision?

10. How can all residents of the city participate more in the decision-making process?

As students conclude the game of People Power and the study of Community and Culture, they should be encouraged to reflect upon the following:

1. What is government? Who is the government?
2. In what way is leadership important?

3. Is representation on the city council important when you are presenting an issue?
4. Are some groups more powerful than others? What difference does it make?

1. ¿Hasta qué punto tuvieron alternativas los miembros del concejo? ¿Cómo expresaron sus alternativas los miembros del concejo?
2. ¿Hasta qué punto usaron los miembros del concejo la información presentada por los grupos de indagación cuando hicieron una decisión?
3. ¿Presentaron los miembros del concejo soluciones alternativas? ¿Hasta qué punto cambiaron los pasos de la "acción"?
4. ¿Hasta qué punto anticiparon los futuros problemas que traerían el resultado de su decisión?
5. ¿Hasta qué punto se tomaron las decisiones en términos de acción?
6. ¿Cómo afectaron a las necesidades y a los deseos de la ciudad entera las decisiones del concejo?
7. ¿En qué formas afectará una decisión a la ciudad entera?
8. ¿En qué formas afectará una decisión a una sola comunidad?
9. ¿Quién va a estar satisfecho o a no estar satisfecho, por motivo de la decisión adoptada?
10. ¿Cómo pueden todos los residentes de la ciudad participar más en el proceso de hacer decisiones?

En el momento en que los estudiantes concluyen el juego "El poder de la gente" y el estudio de la Comunidad y Cultura, debieran ser animados a reflexionar sobre lo siguiente:

1. ¿Qué es el gobierno? ¿Quiénes constituyen el gobierno?
2. ¿En qué consiste la importancia del liderazgo?
3. Cuando Ud. presenta una moción ante el concejo municipal, ¿es importante la representación?
4. ¿Existen grupos más poderosos que otros? ¿Qué importa esto?

5. How can citizens change unpopular laws?
6. In what way are all citizens members of a special group as well as a member of the total community?

7. Why must the needs, interests, rights of all citizens be considered when decisions are made?

## EXTENDED ACTIVITIES

1. View film "Changing the Law," Bailey Film Associates, color.
2. Play "Legislature" by James Coleman, ½ hour.
3. Study leadership and government in other communities—Africa, Cuba, Haiti.
4. Study leadership and government during specific historical periods: Mexican Revolution of 1910; French Revolution; Mexican War; Russian Revolution.

5. Play "Starpower", Western Behavioral Sciences Inst., ½ hour.
6. Play "Metropolitics", Western Behavioral Sciences Inst., ½ hr.

5. ¿Cómo pueden cambiar los ciudadanos las leyes que no son populares?
6. ¿De qué formas todos los ciudadanos son miembros de un grupo especial, y a su vez, miembros de la comunidad total?

7. ¿Por qué deben ser considerados las necesidades, los intereses, y los derechos de todos los ciudadanos cuando se hacen decisiones?

## EXTENSIÓN DE ACTIVIDADES

1. Película—"Changing the Law". Bailey Film Associates, a colores.
2. Drama—"Legislature", por James Coleman, ½ hora.
3. Estudio del liderazgo y del gobierno en otras comunidades—África, Cuba, Haití.
4. Estudio del liderazgo y del gobierno durante específicos períodos históricos: La Revolución Mexicana de 1910; La Revolución Francesa; La Guerra con México; La Revolución Rusa.

5. Drama—"Starpower", Western Behavioral Sciences Inst., ½ hora.
6. Drama—"Metropolitics", Western Behavioral Sciences Inst., ½ hora.

## MEDIA RESOURCES FOR INQUIRY EXPERIENCE USE

### 16 mm. Films

A & B    *Peace and Voices in the Wilderness,* 9½ mins., color, (A discussion of the effects of and solutions for some of society's major problems), Bailey Film Associates.

A & B    *United States Elections: How We Vote,* 13½ mins., color or black and white, Bailey Film Associates.

A & B    *Chicano From the Southwest,* 15 mins., Encyclopaedia Britannica Educational Corporation.

# BIBLIOGRAPHY FOR STUDENT USE

Acuña, Rudolph. *Cultures in Conflict.* New York: Charter School Books, Inc., 1970.
Acuña, Rudolph. *The Story of the Mexican Americans.* New York: American Book Co., 1969.

Bailey, Hen Miller and Grijalva, Maria Celia. *Fifteen Famous Latin Americans.* Englewood Cliffs, New Jersey: Prentice-Hall, Inc., 1971.

Bauer, Helen. *California Gold Days.* New York: Doubleday and Co., Inc., 1965.

————. *California Mission Days.* New York: Doubleday and Co., Inc., 1965.

————. *California Rancho Days.* New York: Doubleday and Co., Inc., 1965.

Ben-Jochannan, Yosef; Brooks, Hugh; and Webb, Kempton. *Africa—Lands, Peoples, and Cultures of the World.* New York: W. H. Sadlier Inc., 1970.

Chambers, Bradford. *Aztecs of Mexico—The Lost Civilization.* Columbus, Ohio: Charles E. Merrill Books, Inc., 1965.

Greenblatt, Edward L. and Mary Lee. *Ancient Peoples of Mexico.* Pasadena: Franklin Publications, Inc., 1964.

Nava, Julian. *Mexican Americans Past, Present, and Future.* New York: American Book Co., 1969.

Tebbel, John and Ruiz, Ramon E. *South by Southwest.* Garden City, New York: Zenith Books, Doubleday and Co., Inc., 1969.

Wittenberg, Eliot. *Patterns of the City.* New York: Noble and Noble, 1969.

Wynne, Patricia. *Urban America—Problems and Promises/A Student's Resource Book.* New York: W. H. Sadlier, Inc., 1971.

## SUPPLIERS OF MEDIA MATERIAL

Audio Visual Enterprises, 911 Laguna Rd., Pasadena, California, 91104.

Arthur Barr Productions, Inc., P. O. Box 7-C, Pasadena, California, 91104.

Bailey Film Associates, 2211 Michigan Ave., Santa Monica, California, 90404.

Bowmar Publishing Co., P. O. Box 375, Santa Monica, California, 90406.

Children's Music Center, 5373 West Pico Blvd., Los Angeles, California, 90019.

Coronet Films, Coronet Building, Chicago, Illinois, 60601.

Doubleday & Co., Inc., 277 Park Ave., New York, New York, 10017.

Ealing Film Loops, 2225 Massachusetts Ave., Cambridge Mass., 02140.

Education Consulting Associates, P. O. Box 1057, Menlo Park, Calif., 94025.

Encyclopaedia Britannica Corporation, 425 N. Michigan Ave., Chicago, Illinois, 60611.

Educational Horizons, 3015 Dolores St., Los Angeles, Calif., 90065.

Folkways/ Scholastic Records, 906 Sylvan Ave., Englewood Cliffs, New Jersey, 07632.

Hammond Education Sales Department, 330 W. 42nd St., New York, New York, 10036.

Hi-Worth Pictures, P. O. Box 6, Altadena, California, 91001.

3M (Visual Products Division), Box 3344 St. Paul, Minnesota, 55101.

McGraw-Hill Text Films, 330 W. 42nd St., New York, N. Y., 10036.

Multi Media Productions, P. O. Box 5097, Stanford, California, 94305.

Rand McNally, Box 7600, Chicago, Illinois, 60680.

Warren Schloat Productions, Inc., Pleasantville, New York, 10570.

Silver-Burdett Co., Park Ave. and Columbia Rd., Morristown, New Jersey, 07960.

Social Science Service Center, 10000 Culver Blvd., Culver City, California, 90230 (Most of the media used in "Community and Culture" may be obtained through this service center.)

Society for Visual Education, Inc., 1345 Diversey Pkwy., Chicago, Illinois, 60614.

Visual Materials, Inc., 2549 Middlefield Rd., Redwood City, California, 94063.

# 6

# BILINGUAL-BICULTURAL EDUCATION
## The Chicano Challenge of the Future

"Impossible! To develop bilingual-bicultural individuals within a monolingual, dominant culture is impossible," say many educators. "Impractical," say critics. "Unamerican," say some. "A fad," say skeptics. Yet, most recent innovative educational programs for Mexican Americans include in their titles the terms, bilingual and bicultural.

Even though the label, bilingual-bicultural, is popular, there is no reason to assume that it is uniformly defined; nor are the concepts involved in this type of education uniformly implemented. Though the term implies an educational program which employs two languages for instruction, emphasizes the development of both languages, and includes culture study, many bilingual-bicultural programs in existence are varied in terms of their major focus, objectives, and teaching strategies.

In the previous chapter, lesson plans for the unit on "Community and Culture" were written in Spanish and English to encourage the use of both languages in presenting its content and guiding classroom activities. Though the activities emphasized the use of language, it would be naive to assume that the language needs of Mexican-American students could be met entirely through social studies units. This chapter proposes to look at the language instruction within the context of bilingual-bicultural programs of education. The focus will be:

1. The common assumptions underlying bilingual-bicultural education, and their importance to Mexican American students;
2. Illustrations of some common components and strategies employed in

bilingual-bicultural education, and some major problems in the implementation of these components.

# Basic Assumptions Underlying Bilingual-Bicultural Education

The concept of bilingual-bicultural education includes several basic ideas which could provide the stimulus for some of the most exciting educational innovations in recent years. Presently, bilingual education programs within the United States are found largely in elite private schools, parochial schools, or as special programs for linguistically-disadvantaged students. Illustrating the last category, Mexican-American students are being exposed to bilingual education in an attempt to reverse the statistics of academic failure which characterize them. In the broadest context, however, experiments in bilingual education may provide teaching models which could enrich the education of all American youth.

THE ASSETS OF BILINGUALISM    The first assumption fundamental to bilingual education is that an individual who can communicate through speaking, reading, and writing more than one language possesses an intellectual advantage and is an asset to society. He can, for example, enjoy a richer personal life because of his ability to enter more fully into the literary, philosophic, or social community of two cultures. At the same time, the bilingual individual possesses practical competencies needed in a variety of jobs and professions.

Related to this assumption is the idea that the more than six million Spanish-speaking persons within the United States provide a valuable source of existing and potential bilinguals. Rather than being considered a national liability with large numbers unemployed and undereducated, they might become a national asset, if their potential were developed.

THE CONTROVERSY OVER BILINGUAL-BILCULTURAL EDUCATION    Though the advantages of bilingualism have long been recognized, the question as to whether the development of bilinguals should be a *major* goal of public education has not been resolved. Whether the public schools should encourage cultural pluralism is even more controversial. Arguments against a comprehensive bilingual-bicultural program of instruction vary from concerns about practicality and learning interference to those involving the effect of bilingualism upon national security.

Bilingualism is potentially at once a powerful disruptive force and a source of enrichment for mankind. The danger is that a nation may attempt to control this force by destroying it . . . Aware principally of the disruptive power of language, the United States set about making of its people, drawn from all over the world, a monolingual nation. Now, at last, somewhat aghast at its success, the United States is becoming aware of the riches it has sacrificed to national unity and appreciative of the cultural groups that resisted its conscious, and unconscious, policies of homogenization. The new tendency is seen in educational programs which aim at preserving and fostering what remains of those treasures and at promoting the learning of foreign languages. Certainly the United States is now sufficiently influential to give the world an important example of linguistic tolerance. . . .[1]

In spite of growing acceptance of the concept of bilingual programs of instruction in public schools, the issues surrounding bilingual-bicultural education will draw supporters and opponents within any given community.

Some of the most complex and relevant questions about bilingual-bicultural education are raised by educators, themselves. Does bilingual instruction impede the development of creativity and higher thought processes? Does bilingual instruction hinder the acquisition of English language skills? Could instructional time be better spent teaching English since most Mexican Americans lack fluency in Spanish, as well as English?

The complete answer to these questions, and others, will depend upon continued and thoughtful research; however, there is currently some indication that bilingualism *per se* does not produce learning handicaps.

The evidence seems to be that the problems of bilingual children arise not from the fact of their speaking two languages, but from educational policy affecting the two languages, and from other factors, sociological and economic outside of the school. The fact is that bilingualism is eagerly sought world wide, both by the elite and by the middle and lower classes, for the intellectual and economic advantages it can bring . . .[2]

The same report goes on to state that review of "scores of studies of bilingualism reveal that where bilingualism has been found to be a problem is commonly in situations where child-speakers of a home language which is different from the school language are given no formal education in and through their home language."[3]

The point of view that instruction in Spanish is time wasted because the children speak inferior Spanish can be challenged from a variety of sources.

The derogatory remarks about the quality of the Spanish spoken in the American southwest are usually uninformed and should usually be discounted. It is true that there are regional variations from the standard Spanish of Mexico, notable the archaistic remnants in northern New Mexico and the 'pachuco' argots of some cities, and there is widespread recourse to lexical borrowing from English. What matters in determining school procedures is the extent to which the 'deep grammar' (the complex interrelated systems of sound, form, and vocabulary) varies from the standard . . . The minimum requirement for participation in the mother tongue development program is the ability to understand readily ordinary conversation and simple explanations given in the language by a native speaker.[4]

Making a value judgment upon the type of Spanish spoken by Mexican-American students is intellectually unsound. Linguistic scholars place the language characteristics of any group within a theoretical framework without attaching positive or negative connotations. The Spanish spoken by Mexican Americans can be considered a dialect of Spanish, and in some localities almost a Creole language drawn from both Spanish and English.*

Theories which attempt to classify types of bilingualism also do so without value judgments. For example, a common classification system distinguishes the "compound bilingual" from the "coordinate bilingual." The coordinate bilingual develops two sets of language systems which are culturally, temporally separated in time, or functionally separate. The compound bilingual develops a bilingual language system within a single context in which the symbols of two languages are interchangeable alternatives with the same meaning. The Mexican American often falls into the latter category; he uses the linguistic symbols of both languages mixed in a single utterance regardless of whether English or Spanish syntax is used.[5] Though this classification system may have significant implications for teaching and learning, it does *not* imply that either type of bilingual is superior culturally or intellectually.

In the classroom situation it is difficult to make an accurate assessment of the amount of Spanish spoken by the student, much less make a judgment about the quality spoken. Many Mexican-American students hide their Spanish linguistic ability in the schoolroom. For example, in one bilingual education program observed by the author, investigators attempting to determine the students' dominant language complained that many students systematically tried to "cover-up" their Spanish language abilities.

A similar situation occurred in a kindergarten room visited regularly. English speakers were matched with Spanish speakers to give each practice in hearing the second language. A child from each group was placed in the play corner for forty-five minutes and observed. After the first few minutes, the dialogue continued completely in Spanish in spite of the fact that *none* of the supposedly English speakers previously demonstrated any facility in

---

* Note: George Carpenter Barker, *Pachuco, An American-Spanish Argot and its Social Functions in Tucson.* 1970. Univ. of Arizona Press, Tucson.

Spanish. Serious questions should be raised about a learning environment in which children so quickly learn to hide their abilities.

Perhaps the research most significant to bilingual programs of education will deal with areas involving student attitudes about language and the culture it represents. Pedagogically, investigation is needed to clarify questions concerning the timing of introducing the second language, the sequence and pacing of teaching both the native* language and second language, the effects of culture and poverty in relation to teaching techniques, and the effects of bilingualism upon thought processes and creativity.

A majority of studies, to date, encourage the development of the native language until the learner is able to engage in abstract thinking. However, there is also adequate indication that the second language is best introduced between the ages of six and eleven years before the native language is completely developed and the learner develops self-consciousness about a "foreign" language. This evidence places great responsibility upon the elementary school for not only maintaining the native language, but also for effectively introducing the second language.

In the case of the Mexican-American student, the school must reevaluate the importance of the Spanish language not only as a medium of instruction, but as a foundation for learning English. It is reasonable to assume that when we curtail native language development, at its beginning levels (oral language with limited vocabulary and syntax), we may be violating developmental thought processes.

> In the area of ideation and expression, the Mexican-American child may encounter interference in the formation and communication of ideas. The Mexican-American child on the whole has become accustomed to hearing ideas expressed in Spanish . . . The child who is vocal and confident in his use of the Spanish language has only to acquire the English vocabulary in order that he might express himself in English and prepare himself to receive instructions in English.[6]

The curtailment of native language development, combined with the school's insistence that non-English speaking students learn a "foreign language" (English) before concepts are taught in science, social science, mathematics, literature, etc., could well account for much of the academic retardation experienced by a high percentage of Mexican-American students. It is not unusual for students who are recent arrivals from Mexico and who have well developed Spanish language skills to learn English quickly and to achieve academically more rapidly than Mexican Americans born in the United States.

---

* The term "native" as used in this chapter is synonmous with "first" language, but is to be distinguished from dominant language. Dominant language is defined as the language *most* used by the individual.

THE NEED FOR REFORM   Bilingual-bicultural instruction arises out of the need for reform in the education of Mexican-American students. Regardless of the doubts and controversies surrounding bilingual-bicultural education, many educators feel that the failure of overwhelming numbers of Spanish speaking students in traditional programs of education demand experimentation with school organization and instructional procedures. Proponents of bilingual education look to bilingual instruction in other countries and during other eras as proof that bilingual education can and does work. As a final argument, they propose that bilingual education offers a likely solution to the academic failure of Mexican Americans, and they feel certain that it could do no worse than existing instructional programs. In any case, most educators involved in bilingual-bicultural education exhibit a willingness to evaluate the results of their programs.

EXPERIMENTAL PROGRAMS   Bilingual-bicultural education is still experimental and embraces many programs at various stages of development. While some bilingual-bicultural programs are currently being developed and implemented, others are already entering a period of rigorous evaluation. Therefore, any discussion of the area must assume that continued experiments and validation will result in the expansion of certain practices and the discontinuation of others. Furthermore, there is every indication that the development of substantive bilingual-bicultural programs of instruction will involve experts from many disciplines because of the complexity of bilingualism and the widespread interest such programs arouse. Interdisciplinary development and evaluation may prove to be one of the most valuable aspects of present and forthcoming experiments in bilingual-bicultural education.

> Bilingualism is so complicated a phenomenon that one has the giddy feeling that in speaking of it one speaks of all things at once. It has been studied by psychologists because it raises problems about the use of two sets of language skills by a single individual and problems about the sometimes conflicting emotions and attitudes associated by the individual with his two languages. It has been studied by educators because of the basic relationship of language to all learning, because of the access which bilingualism allows two cultures, and because of the administrative problems to which it gives rise. It has been studied by linguists because of its effects on language usage. It has been studied by sociologists and anthropologists because associated with language are attitudes and norms which have an effect on social and cultural institutions. Finally, it has been studied by political scientists who see in it a challenge to political institutions.
>
> It is impossible for any one man to master all the disciplines required for the adequate description and study of bilingualism; so progress depends on the collaboration of representatives of these disciplines.[7]

The above reference to the political implications of bilingual education must be emphasized as a vital issue. It is central to the final and perhaps the most important assumption underlying bilingual-bicultural education.

EMPHASIS ON THE IMPORTANCE OF MINORITY CULTURE   Bilingual-bicultural education recognizes the importance of the minority student's culture. As the name implies, these programs assume that language is an important aspect of culture. Language is considered more than a tool for learning, a medium of instruction or communication. Language is seen as an intricate part of personality, an expression of culture significant to the self-image, an essential part of ethnic identification and cultural preservation. Hence, the term bilingual-bicultural emerges; it signifies a conscious effort to retain the cultural milieu from which language develops. To many members of the Mexican American-community, the Spanish language is symbolic of their culture, and bilingual-bicultural education programs are tangible evidence of the majority's willingness to legitimatize that culture.

There is concern, however, that bilingual-bicultural programs of education proliferate because of political expediency rather than because of educational value. For that reason, it is essential that educators interested in Mexican-American students become acquainted with the problems, teaching strategies, and contributions of promising bilingual-bicultural education programs.

# Major Elements of Functional Bilingual-Bicultural Education

Bilingual-bicultural education programs have been stimulated largely through the appropriation of federal funds with the greatest impetus coming from the Bilingual Education Act of 1968, Title VII, an amendment to the Elementary and Secondary Education Act of 1965.* In 1970 there were more than seventy-six ongoing projects in bilingual education. Subsequently, 66 more were funded, bringing the total number of projects to 142. Together, they operated a budget of over ten million dollars.**

---

* The following legislation has provisions for aid to bilingual education: National Defense Education Act of 1958; Adult Education Act of 1963; Vocational Education Act of 1963; Economic Opportunity Act of 1964; Higher Education Act of 1965; Elementary and Secondary Education Act of 1965, Title I Programs for the Disadvantaged, Title II School Libraries, Resources, and Instructional Materials, Title III Supplementary Centers, Title VII Programs for Bilingual Students.
** For a directory of Title VII, Bilingual Projects write to Mr. Walter Steidle, Bilingual Education Projects, U.S. Office of Education, Washington, D.C. 20202.

These projects extend throughout the United States from the urban centers in the east, midwest, and southern seaboard to the western and southwestern states with the largest number in California and Texas. Though each is distinct because of local differences in needs, resources, objectives and leadership, some common components emerge as essential to a sound bilingual-bicultural program. These components include: (1) utilization of the native language in the educational process to teach basic concepts and skills necessary for future learning; (2) continued language development in the native language; (3) the development of subject matter in the native language; (4) the development of subject matter in the second language; (5) the development of a positive self-image and cultural identity; (6) continued language development in the second language.[8]

It is apparent that these six components characterize an enriched curriculum in which the students receive and experience the full spectrum of subjects and educational activities. Language development is the central but not the sole element. Developing a curriculum which includes all of the above components is the task of educators committed to the concept of bilingual education, and various attempts to implement these components have been made within the many experimental programs.

UTILIZING NATIVE LANGUAGE    One of the foremost components of bilingual-bicultural education programs is utilization of the native language to teach basic concepts, attitudes, and skills which will facilitate later learning. Today, more and more educators are in agreement that children whose native language is Spanish should not have to wait until they can speak English before they are taught basic concepts in mathematics, science, social science, humanities, and the arts. From the time they enter kindergarten, they can explore, inquire, and express themselves creatively through art, music, rhythms, and language. As all young children do, Spanish-speaking children can explore their world and their role in it. That they use Spanish as the means of communication makes little difference, if the teacher speaks the language.

For example, in the Los Angeles Bilingual Schools Program, Spanish-speaking children in the primary grades are taught largely in Spanish the basic vocabulary and number concepts normally taught at this level. A look into the classroom will reveal children busily learning the beginning concepts dealing with numbers and number sets, place value, addition, subtraction, multiplication, division, fractions, decimals, geometry, and measurement.

Teachers are provided with a basic mathematics curriculum guide which includes appropriate terminology in Spanish. Basic concepts and vocabulary to be taught are isolated and translated into Spanish along with a core of questions relating to the concepts and utilizing the vocabulary. The teachers then create their own strategies for presenting the concepts to children. The following section is taken from the bilingual curriculum guide dealing with numbers and number sets.

# NUMBER AND NUMBER SETS*

1. **Vocabulary**

## Ordinal Numbers

| | Notation | Number | Nombre† |
|---|---|---|---|
| a. | 30th | thirtieth | treinta |
| b. | 40th | fourtieth | cuarenta |
| c. | 50th | fiftieth | cincuenta |
| d. | 60th | sixtieth | sesenta |
| e. | 70th | seventieth | setenta |
| f. | 80th | eightieth | ochenta |
| g. | 90th | ninetieth | noventa |
| h. | 100th | one hundredth | cien |

## General Terms

| | | |
|---|---|---|
| a. | even numbers, pairs | pares |
| b. | uneven numbers, odd numbers | nones |
| c. | number symbols | cifras |
| d. | set, group | conjunto, juego |
| e. | digits | dígitos |
| f. | numerals | numerales |
| g. | equivalent | equivalente |
| h. | equals, is the same | igual, es igual a |
| i. | equals sign | signo de igualdad ($=$) |
| j. | solve | resolver |
| k. | estimate | estimar, calcular |
| l. | column | columna, fila |
| m. | basic computational symbols | signos operacionales ($+ - \times \div$) |
| n. | mathematical statement | enunciado |
| o. | number line | recta numérica |

---

* Developed by Mrs. Naomi S. Harrison, Curriculum Consultant Title VII. Mr. Leo Aparicio, Project Director. † Used after the noun: *el muchacho treinta*/the thirtieth boy.

## 2. Concepts

a. Numerals are names for numbers.

Los numerales son nombres para los números.

b. The cardinal number symbols and the number names tell how many there are.

Los números cardinales y las palabras numéricas indican cuántos hay.

c. Zero is a number.

El cero es un número.

d. Zero is the cardinal number of the empty set. It stands for nothing.

El cero es el número de conjunto vacío. Es igual a nada.

e. unequal sets

conjuntos desiguales

f. equal sets

conjuntos equivalentes

g. Two or more sets that have the same number of objects in each set are called equal sets.

A dos o más grupos que contienen cada uno el mismo número de objetos se les llama "grupos de igual tamaño."

h. One-to-one relationship

correspondencia uno a uno (aparear)

i. 8 is greater than 5. (8 > 5)

8 es más que 5. (8 > 5)

j. 5 is less than 8. (5 < 8)

5 es menos que 8. (5 < 8)

k. When you take something away from a set to find out how many are left, you subtract.

Cuando se descompone un conjunto para hallar cuántos elementos quedan, se resta.

l. When comparing two sets to find how much bigger one set is than the other, you must subtract.

Cuando se comparan dos grupos o conjuntos para hallar en cuánto un conjunto es mayor que el otro, se resta.

m. Zero is the symbol that is used to represent the absence of elements in a set.

El cero es el símbolo que se usa para representar la ausencia de elementos de un conjunto.

## 3. Questions

a. What number is before __?

¿Qué número está antes de __?

b. What number is after __?

¿Qué número sigue después de __?

| | |
|---|---|
| c. What number is between __ and __? | ¿Qué número queda entre __ y __? |
| d. What is meant by the term one-to-one relationship? | ¿Qué se entiende por la correspondencia uno a uno? |
| e. What is the number of this set? | ¿Cuál es el número de este conjunto? |
| f. What does zero tell us? | ¿Qué nos dice el cero? |
| g. What does this sign tell us? | ¿Qué representa este signo? |
| h. What does this __ mean? | ¿Qué se entiende por __? |
| i. What symbols are used to write a mathematical statement? | ¿Qué símbolos se utilizan para escribir un enunciado matemático? |

Various bilingual projects tend to emphasize different curriculum areas within which to develop basic concepts and skills needed for further school success. The areas then serve as a core to stimulate and reinforce native and second language development. Typical combinations are mathematics and social sciences, mathematics and science, or mathematics and literature. Art and music are usually considered enrichment, while physical education is included in all programs.

Several daily schedules, again taken from the Los Angeles Title VII Bilingual Program, illustrate the manner in which major curriculum areas can be interrelated:

### Suggested Three-Hour Kindergarten

9:00- 9:20: Room Business
9:20- 9:40: Teacher directs reading (group or individual)
9:40-10:00: Group activities:
        viewing, listening, handwriting, spelling
        follow-up
        manipulative activities
        exploratory activities (math, science)
        art, illustrations for stories, experience charts
        library browsing
        learning games
        individual writing, typewriter
        speaking and recording center, dictate or tell stories into a tape
        second language with an aide, Spanish as a Second Language (reading readiness or reading)
10:00-10:20: Recess
10:20-10:40: Math Instruction
10:40-11:20: Native Language reading period

11:20-11:40: Peabody Language Kit* Magic Circle,** AAAS***
11:40-12:00: Music, P.E., Rhythms

## Divided Day Kindergarten

8:30- 8:45: One half of the group in attendance
         —Language activities, stories, puppets, poems
8:45- 9:30: One fourth of class reading English; one fourth of class reading Spanish
         (teacher directs lesson and individual activities)
9:30- 9:45: Room business
9:45-10:00: Magic Circle or AAAS
10:00-10:20: Recess
10:20-10:40: Math Instruction
10:40-11:00: Music, Physical Education, Rhythms
11:00-11:15: ½ class using Peabody Language Kit directed by teacher.
         ½ class studying English Second Language—aide.
11:15-11:30: ½ class using Peabody Language Kit directed by teacher.
         ½ class studying Spanish Second Language—aide.
11:30-11:40: Dismissal and Transition (½ of class is dismissed)
11:40-12:25: Second reading period
12:25-12:30: Dismissal

## First and Second Grades
## Non-divided Day
### *(9:00-2:00) Bilingual Teacher*

9:00- 9:10: Room business
9:10- 9:55: Reading in native language and related activities
10:00-10:20: Recess
10:20-11:00: Math (2-3 groups taught in Spanish and English concurrently)
11:00-11:55: Reading in the second language
12:00- 1:00: Lunch
1:00- 1:30: Oral Language: Peabody, AAAS, Magic Circle, Enrichment

---

* Sources of Curriculum Materials:
  Peabody Language Kit—American Guidance Service Inc., Publishers Bldg., Circle Pines, Minnesota
         55014.
** Magic Circle—Institute for Personal Effectiveness in Children, Dr. J. K. Southard, Exec. Director,
         P.O. Box 20233, San Diego, Calif. 92120.
*** AAAS—American Assoc. for the Advancement of Science, 1515 Mass. Ave., N.W. Washington,
         D.C. 20005.

1:30- 1:50: Physical Education, Rhythms, Music
1:55- 2:00: Evaluation and Dismissal

### Second Grade—Team Teaching
### Regular Day
### *(9:00-2:00 p.m.)*

9:00- 9:10: Room business
9:10-10:00: Reading (each teacher teaches own class)
              BL—Spanish (Bilingual Teacher)
              ML—English (Monolingual Teacher)
10:00-10:20: AAAS or Magic Circle
10:20-10:40: Recess
10:40-11:00: Math
11:00-11:20: Peabody—Oral Language
11:20-11:40: Physical Education, Music, Rhythms
11:40-12:00: Magic Circle or AAAS
12:00- 1:00: Lunch
 1:00- 1:50: Reading—teachers meet each other's children and take them to their room
           for reading
 1:50- 2:00: Reading groups return to room for evaluation and dismissal

These schedules not only indicate subject matter emphasis and organization, but also reflect instructional groupings. It is the philosophy of the program directors in the Los Angeles Bilingual Schools Program to utilize heterogeneous language grouping procedures, so that in each classroom at least four linguistic groups are distinguishable, i.e., predominantly Spanish-speaking students, predominantly English-speaking students, bilingual students, and those who do not possess a dominant language but use a mixture of Spanish-English to communicate.

Because of this linguistic mixture, the preferred teaching strategy involves the concurrent method in which both Spanish and English are used to present a given concept within a single lesson. The pattern of teacher-pupil dialogue may proceed as follows:

### Language Pattern—Lesson Procedure

| *Language* | *Interaction Between Pupil and Teacher* |
|---|---|
| English | Teacher questions |
| English | Pupils answer |
| English | Teacher confirms, summarizes |
| Spanish | Teacher confirms, summarizes *the same information,* Teacher questions |
| Spanish | Pupils answer, ask question |

Spanish . . . . . . . . . . . . . . . . Teacher redirects question, asks related questions
Spanish . . . . . . . . . . . . . . . . Pupils answer, elaborate upon question
Spanish . . . . . . . . . . . . . . . . Pupils interact
Spanish . . . . . . . . . . . . . . . . Teacher confirms, summarizes, redirects
English . . . . . . . . . . . . . . . . Teacher confirms, summarizes, redirects
English . . . . . . . . . . . . . . . . Pupils respond

Proponents of the concurrent method theorize that this approach assures each child an opportunity to hear instructions, information, and questions in his own language. Furthermore, he will hear the second language in a meaningful context.

However, more study is needed to determine the advantages and disadvantages of the *concurrent* method as compared to the *single* language approach in which one language is used predominantly during the presentation of a given concept. The same concept is then presented again in the second language during another period. In the separate language approach, the second lesson may be given by the same teacher or by another person, whereas the concurrent approach demands a bilingual teacher.

It should be emphasized, however, that the concurrent method is used in the Los Angeles program largely when instruction is being given in content areas: science, social science, mathematics, etc. When language development is the major objective (oral language, reading, composition), the pupils are grouped according to language dominance, and one language is used as the medium of instruction with the second language brought in only to clarify directions, encourage pupils, or clarify meaning.

At the upper grades or secondary level the subject areas are more formally delineated. Teaching strategies generally are less varied and the separate language method of instruction is more common. However, even at the secondary level, most bilingual projects utilize the concept of a core curriculum, and there is conscious effort to make the curriculum relevant to the interests and needs of students.

In Michigan, for example, the Lansing Bilingual Program utilizes teaching teams composed of an English teacher, a social studies teacher, and a bilingual teacher who teaches Hispano-American cultures and language courses. The students explore such topics as bilingualism in the United States; the Treaty of Guadalupe Hidalgo of 1848; agriculture and Cesar Chavez; the unity of the family; Mexican American music and dances; Hispano-American architecture, sports and customs; Hispano-American social and educational movements; Hispano-American writers, athletes, and leaders.

The manner in which language study emanates from some of these topics can be seen at the end of this chapter (page 164) in excerpts from two lessons prepared for Spanish-speaking high school students.

Additional lessons aimed solely upon language development in Spanish (reading, vocabulary building, comprehension, pronunciation) follow this excerpt. Second language exercises (English oral expression, pattern practice, reading, structured compositions) also are built around this and similar stories which become more complex as student abilities increase.

In the examples of the Lansing curriculum, as in most bilingual-bicultural education projects, the educators involved have had to create curriculum to fit their needs. Particularly in the social sciences, the guides, texts, and strategies used in Latin America, Mexico, Spain or other Spanish-speaking countries can seldom be used without considerable adaptation or supplementary exercises. At times, existing curriculum materials such as the Peabody Language Kit or the AAAS (American Association for the Advancement of Science) materials have been translated into Spanish.

Both types of materials, those taken from other countries and those produced here and translated, have become the target of persons interested in the cultural ramifications of curriculum and teaching techniques. Educators, psychologists, and many Mexican-American intellectuals raise serious questions about the suitability of many materials and teaching strategies used with Mexican-American students.

In spite of inherent problems, however, bilingual-bicultural projects are producing curriculum and patterns of school organization which bear watching. Besides those already mentioned, the San Diego City Schools Bilingual-Bicultural Project, the San Antonio Unified School District Bilingual Project, and the Michigan Department of Education's Bilingual Curriculum Development Project have developed complete curriculum guides which outline the concepts and skills to be taught in the major content areas as well as the sequence for teaching language skills. (See Chart 1, page 160.)

Probably one of the oldest and most continuous experiments in bilingual education is the Dade County Public Schools Bilingual Program. Initiated in 1961 in response to the large numbers of Cuban refugees, this project has produced a model for a bilingual school (see Chart 2, page 162.) and numerous materials, including the well-known *Miami Linguistic Readers*. Recently, this project has been awarded a $500,000 federal grant to produce a national core curriculum for Spanish-speaking children.

The bilingual programs discussed are but a few worthy of attention. A brief description of twenty innovative bilingual-bicultural projects appears in Appendix C. They were selected not as a result of extensive evaluation, but rather because they represent a variety of innovations.

Worth noting are their: (1) utilization of multimedia methods of instruction; (2) increased community involvement through such structures as Dad's Clubs and Dame Schools; (3) various means of grouping students for instruction (by interest, learning potential, or heterogeneous cultures and abilities as well as homogeneous grouping); (4) utilization of varied and highly motivating subjects as the core of the curriculum (dramatics, public speaking, community action); (5) use of tutors; (6) use of traveling teachers and teacher-aide teams; (7) attempts to isolate cognitive styles of bilinguals; (8) in-service teacher education programs which include sensitivity training. Generally, these twenty projects provide the reader with an overview of the experimentation occurring under the umbrella of bilingual education. Specifically, the projects illustrate the variety of ways educators have combined and implemented the six components of a functional bilingual-bicultural program.

CONTINUED LANGUAGE DEVELOPMENT  Continued language development in the native language is a second component found in most functional bilingual-bicultural programs. This component is reflected in a variety of categories and labels in the schedules and curriculum materials presented in the previous section. For the native Spanish speaker, Spanish for Spanish Speakers (SSS) or Spanish Language Arts (SLA) often designate recognition of this component.

A major problem has arisen in the detection of the native language of many Mexican-American students who speak a mixture of both Spanish and English. As brought out earlier, Mexican-American students often tend to hide their Spanish abilities; nevertheless, teacher judgment is often the means for grouping children for instruction in their dominant language. As tests and other reliable techniques for language assessment are perfected, these groupings should become more valid.

The most critical and controversial element, however, is the philosophy regarding the worth and function of the Spanish language. Many bilingual-bicultural programs view Spanish as a bridge to learning English. Instruction in Spanish is seen as a stopgap measure to be used only until the student is able to receive instruction in English. In these programs, Spanish language instruction is concentrated in the primary grades. Children may be taught to read Spanish, but little provision is made to develop higher levels of the language, such as composition or literature.

Other bilingual-bicultural programs emphasize the Spanish language in its own right. Native Spanish speakers are taught to read and write Spanish while native English speakers study Spanish as a second language (SSL). Though an increasing number of bilingual-bicultural programs profess this philosophy, few, if any, are well enough established to present a completely articulated strand of Spanish language study from kindergarten through high school or junior college.

However, most bilingual-bicultural programs do include a well-developed kindergarten-primary model in which students are taught to read Spanish. If reading is assumed to be essentially a decoding of written symbols which represent meaningful speech sounds, then the process is relatively simple for pupils who already speak Spanish. Spanish is phonetically consistent, and spelling patterns are quite constant. Once the student masters the vowel and consonant phonemes when they are represented by written symbols (graphemes), the student can decode words quite successfully, when given sufficient practice.

> . . . The process of learning to read is the process of transfer from the auditory signs for language signals which the child has already learned, to the new visual signs for the same signals . . . Learning to read, therefore, means developing a considerable range of high-speed recognition responses to specific sets of patterns of graphic shapes.[9]

An illustration from a Spanish language beginning reading program illustrates the phonetic regularity of the language. The vowel sounds /a/, /e/, /i/, /o/, and

155

/u/ are consistent. When they are combined with similarly regular consonant sounds, they form meaningful words and sentences.

| | |
|---|---|
| Esa es su mamá. | (That is your (her) mother. |
| Su mamá ama a Ema. | Ema's mother loves her. |
| Ema ama a su mamá. | Ema loves her mother. |
| Mi mamá me ama. | My mother loves me. |
| Yo amo a mi mamá. | I love my mother.) |

A large number of charts and textbooks used in beginning Spanish reading programs are borrowed from Spanish-speaking countries. However, Spanish reading programs are beginning to appear in larger numbers from professional groups charged with curriculum preparation as well as from commercial publishing houses in the United States.*

Most innovative teachers helping students learn to read Spanish prepare their own materials. They create charts and stories based upon current interests. A favorite technique is an adaptation of the "experience approach" to reading in which students verbalize their experiences, the teacher or an aide writes the experience as dictated, the students read their stories and are given related language exercises to develop needed reading skills. The technique serves as a natural means for integrating and relating subject areas. The following story was dictated by a first grade child after hearing the story of the Three Bears (in Spanish and in English) and after painting her interpretation of the story.

Yo pinté una casita de la mamá y del papá y del hijito oso. La casa tiene una chimenea, una puerta amarilla y un árbol y una flor. La casita tiene una ventana, tiene un sol, y tiene el cielo.

Por Norma
(Grade 1, Haddon Elementary School,
Los Angeles)

(I painted Mama, Papa, and little bear's little house. The house has a chimney, a yellow door, a tree, and a flower. The little house has one window, the sun and the sky.)

Writing skills are taught immediately following reading skills, and in some cases simultaneously. Since most Latin American countries teach young children to write cursive

---

* See the Los Angeles Unified School District Developmental Reading Program-Reading Task Force, Bilingual-Bicultural Component and Title VII Bilingual-Bicultural Education Program, *Initial Reading Skills, An Adaptation of El Método Onomatopéyico.* Also, note Houghton Mifflin Program, *Preparándose Para Leer.*

style immediately, many bilingual projects are re-evaluating the tendency to begin primary writing experiences with manuscript writing.

Once the initial writing skills are developed, children engage in creative language experiences expressing themselves in Spanish prose and verse.

| | |
|---|---|
| Tenía una mesa<br>   redonda como una cabeza.<br>Y arriba tenía un mantel<br>   que hice de papel. | Y también tengo una gata<br>   color de plata.<br>Y me retrata<br>   pero un hombre<br>     la mata. |

      Luz Chacon
      (Grade 3, O'Melveny Elementary School, Los Angeles)

While some children experiment with the language by composing rhymes and ditties, others create functional compositions which can reflect feelings and culture. When a classmate fell on the playground and broke his arm, a second grade boy dictated this letter to his friend. The class liked the letter so much that they all read it and copied it into their own language books.

Querido José,
   Sentimos mucho que te quebraste el brazo, y tu juguete también. Ojalá que te mejores pronto, amigo de mi vida.
                 Tu amigo de sangre,
                 Alejandro


(Dear Jose,
   We're very sorry that you broke your arm and your toy, too. God grant that you're better soon, my dear friend.
                 Your bloodbrother,
                 Alejandro)


Considerable evaluation is needed to determine the extent to which Spanish literacy can be developed through bilingual programs, the extent to which creativity is subsequently increased or hindered, and the ease with which children learn English when they are taught to read their native language first. Nevertheless, teachers cannot ignore the changes that are evident in children participating in bilingual programs. Teachers working in bilingual programs provide many testimonials about the positive values of developing the native language. There comes to mind a personal experience which involves two children in the fourth grade who were classified as non-readers. After six weeks of instruction in reading Spanish, both children eagerly and flawlessly read a third level reader for visitors.

Literacy in Spanish cannot be underestimated if we are to realize the four remaining components of bilingual-bicultural education to be considered in this chapter—subject matter in the native language, subject matter in the second language, the development of a positive self-image, and cultural identity.

SUBJECT MATTER IN THE NATIVE LANGUAGE    Subject matter in the native language at the upper levels of education can be achieved only if the learner has sufficient literacy in the native language. For native Spanish speakers, this would demand a Spanish language program articulated from kindergarten through high school. Correlated subjects offered in Spanish would have to be available at all levels. Language courses would have to deal with the specialized vocabulary needed in subjects at the upper levels of instruction and teachers who have sufficient fluency in the language would have to be found. This type of comprehensive bilingual educational program is so demanding that it cannot possibly come into being unless bilingual education becomes a national goal for all children who can profit from it. Bilingual education in these dimensions cannot be considered merely as a compensatory measure for Mexican Americans.

SUBJECT MATTER IN THE SECOND LANGUAGE    Subject matter in the second language for native English speakers would involve the kind of educational program that foreign language teachers dream about. Again, it would be a comprehensive program in which the majority of our children receive instruction in a second language, and content courses taught in the second language would be available at all levels of elementary and secondary education.

For native Spanish-speaking Mexican-American students, subject matter in the second language is nothing new. They have always been expected to learn in the second language, English. The problem is that educators have not considered English the second language and have not given sufficient thought to teaching it as such. Realistically, teaching English as a second language so that Mexican-American students can compete effectively in an English-speaking society is one of the most important tasks for the educator.

Every functional bilingual program includes a strong component devoted to the second language development. Because this component is so essential and because traditional teacher education programs seldom devote much attention to it, teaching English as a second language is discussed in the next chapter. It is, however, an integral part of bilingual education, and a component conducive to reaching the goal of a positive self-image because it provides an important means for personal success.

DEVELOPMENT OF POSITIVE SELF-IMAGE    The development of a positive self-image and cultural identity is the crux of a bilingual-bicultural program. It is, however, one of the most complex and illusive components because individual feelings and attitudes are involved and because culture is too often viewed superficially. Nevertheless, there are some common sense elements in bilingual education that must be recognized as conducive to a positive self-image.

First, there is greater assurance of initial school success when students are allowed to continue learning in their native language, and these feelings can affect subsequent success. Certainly, at any level of education feelings of success are essential to a positive self-image.

Second, bilingual-bicultural programs for Mexican-American students recognize Spanish as a language worth learning and as an acceptable medium for instruction. Recognition and acceptance of this aspect of self and family should contribute to feelings of personal and cultural worth. Most important, true literacy in Spanish gives the student access to his intellectual heritage of the Spanish-speaking world.

Third, in the selection of curriculum content for bilingual programs, there usually is a conscious effort to include information about Mexican-American and Latin cultures. Knowledge of this heritage and the school's formal recognition of it should be conducive to the development of a positive self-image and cultural identity.

However, for all the above elements to be effective, certain more subtle factors must exist in the learning climate. A few of these factors are enumerated below. First, a positive teacher attitude and confidence in Mexican-American learners is essential. Second, if the teacher lacks fluency in Spanish, he may unconsciously use more English during instruction and indirectly award the majority's language and culture preferred status. Third, subjecting the Mexican-American learner to only rote memory and teacher directed lessons will exert a subtle, negative influence upon the student's concept of himself and his intellectual ability.

Somewhat more direct, but still difficult to control, is the negative effect of curriculum materials which have a built-in bias that favors the majority culture. Translating materials into Spanish does not negate the effect of attitudes and values reflected in many materials written for the majority culture, which may conflict with the values of Mexican-American culture.

Nevertheless, bilingual programs of education stand as tangible efforts to forestall the alienation felt by many Mexican-American students when they go to school and find the language foreign and the curriculum meaningless. Perhaps these programs are a partial answer to the feelings expressed by this Chicano student.

### The Immigrant's Experience

*I'm sitting in my history class*
*The instructor commences rapping,*
*I'm in my U.S. History class*
*And I'm on the verge of napping.*

*The Mayflower landed on Plymouth Rock,*
*Tell me more! Tell me more!*
*Thirteen colonies were settled,*
*I've heard it all before.*

*What did he say?*
*Dare I ask him to reiterate?*
*Oh, Why bother,*
*It sounded like he said*
*George Washington's my father.*

*I'm reluctant to believe it,*
*I suddenly raise my "mano,"*
*If George Washington's my father,*
*Why wasn't he Chicano?*

Richard Olivas
(Student at San Jose State College)

## CHART 1. AN OVERVIEW OF THE INTERDISCIPLINARY PROGRAM

| UNIT I—Lessons 1-10 | UNIT II—Lessons 11-20 |
|---|---|
| **LINGUISTIC:** Using formulae of personal identification; using the simple and *-s* form of verbs, affirmative and negative, in *Noun+Verb+Noun* and *Noun+Verb+to+Verb* and related questions. | **LINGUISTICS:** Using simple commands; using patterns of place, direction, manner; using the present and past of *Noun+Verb+Noun, Noun+ Verb+to+Verb* and related questions. |
| **CONCEPTUAL:** Distinguishing one-to-one correspondence, including identification of self and others with given names, school and home place names, and age number names. Distinguishing between objects; need for, their names, uses and symbols (toys, class and personal hygiene items). | **CONCEPTUAL:** Discriminating spatial relations, position and persons and objects, and their movement both individually and with help. Discriminating the effects of actions on objects and symbols; identifying use of objects and using them safely. |
| **SCIENCE INPUT:** Identifying and discriminating persons, objects and large motor actions. | **SCIENCE INPUT:** Discriminating spatial relations, position and movement of persons and objects; identifying and discriminating actions and symbols. |
| **MATH INPUT:** Counting pupils and objects using numbers one through ten; numbers as a measure of how many; matching one-to-one correspondence. | **MATH INPUT:** Matching objects to objects and people; developing concepts of sets and equivalency; written symbols 1, 2 and 3, pre-addition. |

CHART 1.   AN OVERVIEW OF THE INTERDISCIPLINARY PROGRAM (Continued)

| UNIT I—Lessons 1-10 | UNIT II—Lessons 11-20 |
|---|---|
| **SOCIAL STUDIES INPUT:**<br>Identifying self and others through name, age, school group, grade and class, and place of residence. Identifying classroom needs, wants and resources. | **SOCIAL STUDIES INPUT:**<br>Obtaining resources by knowing where they are, how to obtain them through individual and group means. Using up resources, combining them to satisfy wants and needs. |

| UNIT III—Lessons 21-30 | UNIT IV—Lessons 31-40 |
|---|---|
| **LINGUISTIC:**<br>Using *Noun+(is, are)+Noun* and *Noun+(is, are)+Adjective* and questions in singular and plural, affirmative and negative, to identify objects and to describe size, shape, color, quantity and grouping of objects. | **LINGUISTIC:**<br>Using *Noun+(is, are)+doing,* and *Noun+(is, are)+Verb+ing, Noun+(is, are)+Verb+ing+Noun* and questions in singular and plural, affirmative and negative, to describe grouping by utility, direction, location, and individual and group actions. |
| **CONCEPTUAL:**<br>Discriminating and classifying objects and sets of objects by their attributes of number, color, size, shape and use. | **CONCEPTUAL:**<br>Discriminating and classifying objects, sets and subsets of objects by attributes of utility, direction and position in space; discriminating and classifying individual and collective actions and the effects of those actions; making symbols which are identified. |
| **SCIENCE INPUT:**<br>Discriminating and classifying by attributes of number size, shape, utility and color. | **SCIENCE INPUT:**<br>Discriminating and classifying by attributes of utility, direction, position, form; effects of energy on objects; classifying by two attributes. |
| **MATH INPUT:**<br>Using the word "set" and investigating the formation of sets; using the attributes of size and shape for set formation. | **MATH INPUT:**<br>Grouping objects in sets by more than one attribute; recognizing shapes; counting sides of shapes; unique correspondence; developing concepts of subsets. |
| **SOCIAL STUDIES INPUT:**<br>Identifying uses of resources and means of obtaining them, investigating how the attributes of resources help to determine their use. | **SOCIAL STUDIES INPUT:**<br>Identifying persons in the school as resources; how each takes care of needs (teacher, bus-driver, cook, custodian). Satisfying classroom needs through collective use of classroom resources. |

Michigan Department of Education, *Interdisciplinary Oral Language Guide Primary One,*
Bilingual Curriculum Development, 1969

Chart 2.   ORGANIZATION OF A BILINGUAL SCHOOL IN DADE COUNTY,
FLORIDA

I.   CLASSIFICATION OF STUDENTS BASED upon command of English. No
facility in English = Non-Independents; some facility in English are Intermediates; good English facility are Independents; native English speakers. Students
are grouped, re-grouped, retained or promoted on the basis of progress within the
program, but are not penalized for speaking Spanish.

II.  ELEMENTARY SCHOOL ORGANIZATION

*Primary Grades*

The time allotted to each subject the same as other schools within the county, but
time is divided between instruction in two languages. Pupils work toward receiving
approximately half their instruction in each language. Pupils of all language classifications mixed for physical education, music, art, free plan, lunch.

*A.M.*   Pupils receive instruction in language, reading, arithmetic, science, social
studies in their *native language*.

*P.M.*   Pupils receive instruction in language, reading, arithmetic, science, social
studies in the *foreign language*. Instruction designed to reinforce concepts
and skills introduced in the native language.

*Non-independents* receive English as a Second Language (ESL) three hours daily:
Drill and pattern practice; reading and writing patterns orally introduced; factual
reading or transferring reading skills learned in native language.

*Intermediates* receive ESL two hours daily.

*Independents* received ESL one hour daily or take English with native English
speakers.

ESL instruction offered in contained classrooms or students are pulled out to form
instructional groups of similar ability.

*Native Spanish speakers* receive Spanish for Native speakers (Spanish-S) to achieve
literacy and appreciation of Spanish heritage.

*Native English speakers* receive Spanish as a Foreign Language (Spanish-FL).

*Intermediate Grades and Upper Grades*

Time allotted to subject areas continues to parallel county requirements but divided
between instruction in two languages. Pupils receive half their instruction in each
language. Pupils of all language classifications mixed in Physical education, art,
music, industrial arts, home economics, mathematics.

*A.M.*   Students receive instruction in their native language.

*P.M.* Students receive instruction in the foreign language. Students may study complimentary units of instruction, such as U.S. History in English and Latin American History in Spanish. Emphasis is placed upon ability to think and study in the foreign language.

Native Spanish-speaking students continue to receive instruction in ESL according to their classification and need.

Native Spanish-speaking students continue to receive instruction in Spanish-S and move to higher levels of language development, composition and literature.

Native English-speaking students continue to receive instruction in Spanish as a Foreign Language but move into higher levels of language development.

## III. SECONDARY SCHOOL ORGANIZATION

Students grouped according to language facility. Students receive the same subjects either in the foreign language or the native language depending on language classification. Where language is not a major handicap, students of all classifications mixed—Physical education, art, music, industrial arts, home economics, mathematics. Instruction in ESL continues.

Native Spanish-speaking students receive instruction in ESL from one to three hours depending upon classification; receive one unit of high school credit for ESL (not penalized for speaking Spanish); receive high school credit for courses taken in native language.

Native English-speaking students receive instruction in Spanish as a foreign language (Spanish-FL); receive instruction in major studies in Spanish and in English.

## IV. TEAM TEACHING

Native English and Native Spanish speakers form the teaching team. A team of three is assigned to 60 pupils. On each team there is a certified North American teacher and two former Cuban teachers. The Cuban teachers, as aides, contribute to the instructional program and serve as liaison between the school and the Spanish speaking community. Special in-service training is given to all teachers especially in teaching English as a Second Language and teaching Spanish as a vernacular.

## V. INSTRUCTIONAL MATERIALS

The Miami Linguistic Readers series was developed. Teaching English as a second language and beginning reading activities are reflected in the series which attempts to combine modern linguistic sciences and conventional developmental reading programs. Other materials published in Spanish and English are used in various subject areas.

# Excerpts from Lessons in Lansing Bilingual-Bicultural Education Program

## THE HISPANO-AMERICANS IN THE UNITED STATES

### *They Are Bilingual\**

Armando Rodriguez, Raymond L. Telles, George I. Sanchez, Ernesto Galarza, and Cesar Chavez are some of the many Americans of Hispanic origin who have given important services to the United States. These individuals have become famous and have earned great respect for their valuable contributions. All of them are bilingual. Their bilingual ability has had great importance in their lives and in the success they have achieved in their jobs.

Let us take a look at the jobs these men have performed:

Armando Rodriguez:
    Works at the Office of the Secretary of Education in Washington, D.C. and is head of the office which is dedicated to the problems encountered by the Spanish-speaking people.

Raymond L. Telles:
    Was the United States' ambassador to Costa Rica.

George I. Sanchez:
    Is a writer and a social investigator who has dedicated 40 years to the educational and social problems of the Hispano-Americans.

Ernesto Galarza:
    Is a well-known sociologist and writer.

Cesar Chavez:
    Is the champion of the field workers.

## LOS HISPANOAMERICANOS EN LOS ESTADOS UNIDOS

### *Son bilingües\**

Armando Rodríguez, Raymond L. Telles, George I. Sánchez, Ernesto Galarza y César Chávez son algunos de los muchos americanos de origen hispano que han prestado servicios[1] importantes a la nación de los Estados Unidos. Estas personas se han hecho famosas y han ganado un gran respeto por sus valiosas[2] contribuciones. Todos ellos son bilingües. Su bilingualismo ha tenido mucha importancia en su vida y en el éxito[3] que han logrado[4] en su trabajo.

Veamos el trabajo que han desempeñado[5] estos hombres:

Armando Rodríguez:
    trabaja en la Secretaría de Educación en Washington, D.C., y es jefe de la oficina que se dedica a los problemas de las personas de habla española.

Raymond L. Telles:
    fue embajador de los Estados Unidos en Costa Rica.

George I. Sánchez:
    es un escritor e investigador[6] social que ha dedicado 40 años a los problemas educacionales y sociales de los hispanoamericanos.

Ernesto Galarza:
    es un conocido sociólogo[7] y escritor.

César Chávez:
    es el campeón de los trabajadores del campo.

## Suggestions for the Professor

1. Show slides of bilingual people.
2. Play a record by Trini López or Vikki Carr with songs in Spanish and English.
3. Assign a project of the additional activities numbers 1, 2, and 3.

---

## Suggestions and Commentaries by the Professor

### Pre-evaluation

1. (a) More or less, how many Hispano-Americans live in the United States?
   (b) How many of them are bilingual?
2. How useful has their bilingualism been to them?
3. Which are the advantages of a bilingual person?
4. What types of jobs exist for bilingual persons in the United States?

* Gilberto Ibarra, Guillermo De Hoogh, Marcia Seidletz

1. that have rendered services: that have given services.
2. valuable: those things are valuable that are worth or cost a great deal, that have a high price.
3. Success: triumph.
4. that have attained: that have been obtained through their own effort.
5. work that they have accomplished; work that they have had; work that they have done.
6. researcher: a man who does research.
7. sociologist: a man who has studied the science that deals with human societies, sociology.

## Sugerencias para el profesor

1. Mostrar transparencias de personas bilingües.
2. Tocar un disco de Trini López o Vikki Carr con canciones en español y en inglés.
3. Asignar un proyecto de las actividades adicionales, números 1, 2 y 3.

---

## Sugerencias y comentarios por parte del profesor

### Pre-evaluación

1. (a) Más o menos, ¿cuántos hispanoamericanos viven en los Estados Unidos?
   (b) ¿Cuántos de ellos son bilingües?
2. ¿Qué tanto les ha servido su bilingüalismo?
3. ¿Cuáles son las ventajas de una persona bilingüe?
4. ¿Qué tipos de trabajo existen para personas bilingües en los Estados Unidos?

* Gilberto Ibarra, Guillermo De Hoogh, Marcia Seidletz

1. que han prestado servicios: que han dado servicios.
2. valiosas: son valiosas las cosas que valen o cuestan mucho, que tienen un precio alto.
3. éxito: triunfo.
4. que han logrado: que han obtenido por su esfuerzo.
5. trabajo que han desempeñado: trabajo que han tenido, trabajo que han hecho.
6. investigador: hombre que hace investigaciones.
7. sociólogo: hombre que ha estudiado la ciencia que trata de las sociedades humanas, la sociología.

# LA LENGUA DE NUESTROS PADRES

1. Cuando hablamos, ¿qué produce los sonidos que hacemos?
2. ¿Qué necesitamos saber para pronunciar bien los sonidos que no conocemos?
3. ¿Qué consonantes pronunciamos de una manera diferente en inglés y en español?
4. De las siguientes letras subrayadas, ¿cuál tiene una pronunciación diferente a las demás?

    a. *D*ame la mano.
    b. El es el *d*entista.
    c. ¿*Cuándo* fuiste?
    d. ¿Qué *d*ijo María?

5. En español, ¿qué diferencia hay en la pronunciación de la *b* y de la *v*?

## VII-A) LA PRONUNCIACIÓN DE LAS LETRAS *D, B, Y V*

VII-A-1) Al hablar producimos sonidos diferentes. Movemos la boca y la lengua para que el aire, que produce los sonidos, salga de diferentes maneras. Cada una de estas posiciones de la boca y de la lengua hace un sonido diferente. El español tiene sonidos que no tiene el inglés. El inglés también tiene sonidos que no tiene el español. Lo mismo ocurre con otras lenguas. Para aprender sonidos nuevos necesitamos saber cómo poner la boca y la lengua y cómo dejar salir el aire.

    (a) La letra *d* se pronuncia de una manera cuando va al principio de una frase después de una pausa.

    Ejemplos:  *D*ame la mano.
                *Di* tu nombre.
                *D*olores está enferma.

# OUR NATIVE LANGUAGE

1. When we speak, what produces the sounds we make?
2. What do we need to know in order to pronounce well the sounds that we do not know?
3. What consonants do we pronounce in a different way in English and Spanish?
4. Of the following underlined letters, which one has a different pronunciation than the others?

    a. *D*ame la mano.
    b. El es el *d*entista.
    c. ¿*Cuándo* fuiste?
    d. ¿Qué *d*ijo María?

5. In Spanish, what difference exists in the pronunciation between *b* and *v*?

## VII-A) THE PRONUNCIATION OF THE LETTERS *D, B,* and *V*

VII-A-1) When we speak we produce different sounds. We move our mouth and tongue so that the air which produces sounds comes out in different manners. Each one of these positions of the mouth and tongue makes a different sound. Spanish has sounds that English lacks. English also has sounds that Spanish lacks. The same thing occurs with other languages. In order to learn new sounds we need to know how to position the mouth and tongue and how to let the air come out.

    (a) The letter *d* is pronounced in one way when it is placed at the beginning of a sentence after a pause.

    Examples:  *D*ame la mano.
                *Di* tu nombre.
                *D*olores está enferma.

# 7

# DEVELOPING THE SECOND LANGUAGE, A SOCIAL NECESSITY

> Anyone who sees me knows I'm Mexican, but when I walk into an office and ask the secretary in rounded tones and clipped English, "Excuse me, Miss, could you tell me who is in charge?" She answers, "Yes Sir," and thinks, "Oh, he must be Spanish, probably the son of an aristocrat." But if I were to walk into the same office and say, "Ecuse mee Mees, koujew dell mee hoo ees een sharze?"—I'd be lucky to get an answer!
>
> Leonard Olguín

Development of the second language for many Mexican-American students means learning English. Because the acquisition of English language skills is of such importance, an active component of teaching English as a second language (ESL) is found in all bilingual-bicultural programs.

In order to serve its vital function, however, the program must be theoretically sound as well as practical. Several elements are essential. Teaching methodologies should be based upon the most knowledgeable source of information about language, the field of linguistics. Second, teaching methodologies must incorporate the finest techniques of foreign language instruction. Third, throughout this phase of language instruction, teachers must be highly conscious of the cultural implications of learning a second language, particularly when it is the dominant language in the country. Fourth, since bilingual-bicultural programs occur anywhere from kindergarten through the secondary levels of education, teaching techniques must take into consideration varied levels of student maturity and interest.

In practice, not all bilingual-bicultural ESL programs reflect the four elements listed above. One of the major reasons for not doing so is that it is difficult to find professionals who are prepared in all the areas enumerated. The elementary school classroom teacher seldom has training in teaching English as a second language, linguistics, or foreign language instruction. A typical result is that there is either no special program for children who do not speak English when they enter school, or there is over-reliance

167

upon prepared teaching materials. Pupils are put "through" the program whether they need it or not, and *all* students are forced to move at the same pace. On the other hand, the linguistic scholar who could analyze student language needs or prescribe and construct suitable material seldom has the desire to become involved in teaching at the elementary or secondary level. The teacher who is specifically trained in ESL often has secondary school experience and may, or may not, be sensitive to the needs of elementary students. Consequently, all of these factors can contribute to making an ESL program less than desirable.

At any rate, there is considerable reorganization and refinement occurring in the field as more specialists are being prepared and more classroom teachers become knowledgeable as a result of preservice and in-service education. From a substantial number of good ESL programs, it is possible to extract a core of information and principles which reflect the major trends and which have been found effective in teaching Mexican American students English as a second language. All teachers facing the challenge of teaching non-English speaking students must, at the very least: (1) become familiar with linguistic terminology and concepts commonly found in related literature; (2) become familiar with basic principles governing modern language instruction so as to make intelligent decisions regarding the use of new teaching materials; (3) become skilled in the use of foreign language teaching techniques.

# Terminology and Concepts from the Scientific Study of Language

Many of the techniques of contemporary language instruction derive directly from new knowledge about the nature of language acquired through scientific study. Linguistic scholarship does not provide *a method* for teaching language any more than biological scholarship prescribes a method for teaching biology. Linguistics does, however, seek to uncover the structure of language; and what linguists have discovered may suggest that some methods of presenting this structure are more effective than others.

Most important to the language instruction of Mexican-American students is a branch of applied linguistics known as Contrastive Analysis. Such analysis attempts to lay bare the precise points at which two languages are in conflict, or the ways in which their structures differ. The three layers of structure are the *Phonology* (the sound system of the language), *Morphology* (the system of word forms and units of meaning in the language), and *Syntax* (the system of rules which specify the well formed sentences of the language).

THE SOUND SYSTEM OF A LANGUAGE     *Phonology* is the name given by linguists to that layer of linguistic structure which characterizes the sound system of a language. Phonologists have analyzed languages in terms of the smallest functional units of sound, the phoneme, and in terms of pauses, variations in pitch (intonation), stress, and rhythm. All of these elements are important because they distinguish the meaning of one sentence from that of another. Familiarity with the phonological system of English allows teachers to help pupils pronounce the language correctly. Comparison between English and Spanish phonological systems provides valuable information which enables teachers to anticipate problems that probably will arise when Spanish speakers learn English.

Through a process of analysis, linguists have isolated some forty-odd distinguishable phonological units (called phonemes) which serve as segments of sound to differentiate one word from another in English. An example of phonemic difference can be seen in the two English words *zip* and *sip.* The environments *ip* remain the same with only the initial sound changing; these two words can be called "a minimal pair" since they are minimally differentiated in only one phonemic segment: *s/z.* The phonemic segment is significant because when the *z* is changed to *s,* a different meaning is conveyed to another English speaker. Therefore, *z* and *s* are considered two different *phonemes* and are written or transcribed between slanted lines /z/, /s/, to distinguish this usage of the symbols from the usage in ordinary English orthography.

Though languages contain a number of basic phonemes, speakers of the language vary from the "true" phoneme sound as they pronounce phonemes in different environments. As the English speaker pronounces the word *pill* the phoneme /p/ has a strong quality with considerable air being emitted or aspirated after the sound. In the word *whisper* the /p/ is softer or unaspirated. These subtle differences are called variants or allophones; they represent differences in pronunciation but not differences of basic sound units. Allophones are transcribed in brackets /p/ = [pʰ] (aspirated) or [p⁼] (unaspirated); these types of differences are important in analyzing dialects of non-standard English or Spanish.

The phonemes and their variants are produced or articulated by specialized use of the speech organs, the lips, tongue, mouth, throat, and vocal cords. Native speakers of a language use these organs to control the flow of air or vibration of the vocal cords in such a manner as to produce the desired sound. Consequently, phonologists have developed a system to describe the manner in which sounds are produced. They can classify a sound in terms of: (1) the speech organ used to make it; (2) the continuity of the stream of air, whether it is continuous as in /v/ or is stopped and then released as in /t/; (3) the use of the vocal cords, whether the sound is voiced as in /d/ or unvoiced as in /t/. Such a precise system of classification and description of production enables teachers to diagnose pronunciation problems and to prescribe procedures to overcome such problems.

There are available numerous charts, lists, and diagrams which compare Spanish and English phonemes. Usually the sounds are further subdivided into consonant and vowel phonemes. Methods of transcribing the phonemes may differ; however, with a minimal amount of practice the teacher can develop enough familiarity with the system to isolate the similarities and problem areas revealed by contrastive studies of Spanish and English.

Obviously, since the phonemic structure of each language differs, the native Spanish speaker will have difficulty pronouncing some English phonemes. He may not even hear an English phoneme because it does not exist in Spanish as a *distinguishing phoneme*. The sound may exist in Spanish as a variant of a basic phoneme; or even where it does exist as a phoneme, it may sound different because it is produced at a different point of articulation. Furthermore, Spanish speakers may have difficulty with certain English words because Spanish words do not use the phonemes in the order or sequence allowed in English words. Hence the Spanish accent is born; the Spanish sound system is imposed upon English words. Some examples of these difficulties can be found in the following situations:

| English Pronunciation | Spanish Pronunciation |
|:---:|:---:|
| dog | *thoug* |

The Spanish /d/ is articulated by touching the tongue to the front teeth, a dental position; while the English /d/ is articulated by placing the tongue upon the ridge behind the front teeth, the alveolar ridge. The final consonant /g/ will be difficult because Spanish seldom has a consonant at the end of a word. Common English words like *heard* or *world* are even more difficult because Spanish does not have consonant clusters at the end of words.

|  |  |
|:---:|:---:|
| study | *estuthy* |

Spanish does not place a consonant cluster *st* at the beginning of words; therefore, the Spanish speaker will carry over into English the Spanish system of preceding such a cluster with a vowel, i.e., *e*studiante (student), *e*studiar (study), *E*spaña (Spain)

ship                                            *cheep/sheep*

chip                                            *cheep/sheep*

> The Spanish speaker will inter-
> change the English phonemes /s/
> with /c/ because they are not sepa-
> rate phonemes in Spanish. The Span-
> ish vowel phoneme /i/ is produced
> higher in the oral cavity.*

From these few examples, it should be apparent that pronunciation "mistakes" made by many Mexican American students are the result of their carrying Spanish-language habits over into English. Contrastive analysis of the two language systems enables teachers to predict problem areas; and since the mistakes are systematic, materials and lessons can be devised to eradicate the problems.

Other concepts derived from study of the sound system of languages involve larger patterns during which the voice rises or falls, becomes loud or soft, assumes a rhythm with pauses, hesitations, and stops. This general lilt or melody of the language carries important connotations of meaning during communication. Linguists use the term *intonation* to describe these characteristics of language. "No utterance can be made in either language (Spanish-English) without its carrying an intonation pattern, the components of which are *stress* (relative prominence of syllables), *pitch* (highness or lowness of tone), and *terminal junctures* (certain features which signal the phrasing of speech).[1]

English characteristically possesses a primary stress in each phrase with accompanying secondary and weak stresses in between. The syllable or word receiving the heaviest stress also receives a longer duration of time, while those syllables in between which receive less stress are given a shorter but uniform duration of time. English has an even, phrased-timed rhythm.

> English . . . (makes use) of stress to provide a rhythmic unit greater than the
> syllable, somewhat analogous to the bar in music. This unit is called the 'foot'.
> In English phonology each foot consists of one strong syllable, either alone or
> followed by one or more weak syllables; rarely more than six. Since the strong
> syllables tend to occur at roughly regular intervals of time, whatever the num-
> ber . . . of weak syllables occurring in between, the language has a definite
> 'beat'.[2]

---

\* See Appendix E for a quick diagnostic test based upon contrastive analysis of English/Spanish phonemes.

English has three levels of stress: primary, secondary, and weak with a sentence stress pattern superimposed over the entire utterance.* Some examples of English word, phrase, and sentence stress will illustrate how the system functions and how meaning can be affected by changing the pattern.

## Word Stress:

*constitution*

| còn | stĭ | tú | tĭon |
|-----|-----|-----|------|
| (secondary) | (weak) | (primary) | (weak) |

| *pérmit* | (a noun) | *permít* | (a verb) |

## Phrase Stress:

*with the people*

| with | the | PEOPLE—(matter of fact) |
|------|-----|------------------------|
| (secondary) | (weak) | (strong) |

| WITH | the | people—(not against the |
|------|-----|-------------------------|
| (strong) | (weak) | (secondary)   people) |

## Sentence Stress:

I said NOW, not next YEAR.

I know what YOU said, but what did HE say.**

Spanish stress and rhythm patterns differ from English; Spanish has two degrees of stress, strong and weak, with a sentence stress that is not as clearly defined as it is in English. Furthermore, the Spanish weak stress is not as weak as the English weak stress so that some linguists classify it more like the English secondary stress. However, the important thing is that in comparison, the Spanish utterance is more controlled by syllable stress; and when this pattern is carried over into English, the results sound odd or may carry an unintended meaning to the English speaker.

Some examples of the Spanish system will illustrate the possible areas of confusion which may arise, particularly when students begin to read and write the new language. In the Spanish word *constitución,* the primary stress syllable is marked and the other sylla-

---

* Some linguists recognize two degrees of intermediate stress, secondary and tertiary, making a total of four levels.

** Examples are taken from Robert Lado, *Linguistics Across Cultures, Applied Linguistics for Language Teachers,* Ann Arbor: The University of Michigan Press, 1957, pp. 1-35. Used by permission.

bles receive a secondary (or weak) stress. The primary stressed syllable does not receive a longer duration of time, as is common in English.

In reading or speaking English sentences, the native Spanish speaker may carry over the Spanish sentence stress pattern. In the sentence, "¿Cómo está usTED?" (How are you?), the combination of word and sentence stress results in an even rhythm with the stress of usTED being much like those found on the stressed syllables of *Cómo* and *está*. Spanish speakers would impose this even, syllabic stress pattern upon English sentences and must be taught to lengthen the duration of English sentence and phrase stresses. Spanish speakers will also substitute secondary stress syllables for the weak stresses of English which results in a stacatto-like utterance with primary stresses not clearly marked: "HOW are YOU to DAY?" rather than "How ARE you today?" or "How are YOU today?" Again, it is obvious that the often stereotyped Spanish accent has a very systematic basis.

When stresses are combined with voice pitch and pauses or junctures, the melody of the language is complete. Voice pitches during speech are relative; they are not fixed points on a scale. However, allowing for variations within each classification, English pitch can be classified as extra-high (x or 4), high (h or 3), medium (m or 2) and low (1 or 1). Higher pitches often accompany the syllables or words receiving maximum stress and may occur at a terminal juncture. Spanish, however, has three discernable pitches which are not spaced as far apart as those of English.

Viewed musically, a comparison of the English and Spanish pitch contours might look like this:*

| | | |
|---|---|---|
| X | | |
| X | | |
| X | | X |
| X | | X |
| English | | Spanish |

When the Spanish pitch contour is imposed upon English, the result may seem dull or uninteresting to English speakers. The Spanish speaker may appear disinterested, unconcerned, or perhaps less intelligent. On the other hand, the sounds of English to a Spanish speaker may sound harsh, shrill, impolite, or frightening.

In summary, the native Spanish speaker learning English will have to listen for many language elements before he can distinguish the subtle meanings conveyed in English. Furthermore, all these elements occur simultaneously during normal speech and differ somewhat with the individual. Consider the following intonation patterns:

_____

* Taken from Robert P. Stockwell, and J. D. Bowen, *The Sounds of English and Spanish*, Chicago, University of Chicago Press, 1965, p. 25.

He's a STUdent.    (Stress indicates a normal matter-of-fact report)

m        h      l =    (Voice pitch, medium, high, low sequences)

He's a STUdent.    (Indicating that statement is not finished; or that the state-
m        h      m    ment is like an afterthought)

He's a STUdent.    (Indicating mild doubt as to his being a student, or as if
m        h      h    trying to remember if he is a student)

He's a STUdent.    (Indicating strong disbelief or surprise)[3]
m        h      x

It should be obvious that opportunities must be given for the students learning English to hear the language *in a meaningful context*. Furthermore, when we read statements declaring that non-English speaking students should be able to understand English or use English orally before they begin to read it, we are being asked to teach some very specific elements of language. Oral command of the language does not mean merely the ability to follow directions or the sequence of a story.

THE SCIENTIFIC STUDY OF WORD FORMS    *Morphology,* the systematic study of the words and word forms of a language, provides the teacher with principles involving word boundaries, meaningful word forms, word classifications, and functions. Whereas the basic unit of sound is called the *phoneme,* by analogy, the smallest unit of language carrying an identifiable meaning of its own within the structure of the language is called a *morpheme.* The relation between the two is that sequences of phonemes *represent* morphemes.

Most teachers are quite familiar with morphemes, but they refer to them in such terms as *word stems, roots, endings, prefixes,* and *suffixes.* For example, a morpheme can be "bound" to other morphemes as in *sub*way, *sub*terranean, *sub*standard. "Sub" is a morpheme that means something fairly specific in English; it means "below", "under", "beneath", or "lower". Morphemes can also stand alone, as in the word "house". "House" is a "free-form" morpheme which carries a *lexical* meaning (refers to a specific item within the language and culture).

Teachers may be less familiar with the terminology and precise grammatical function that linguists ascribe to words and word forms. A detailed analysis is not necessary; but it would be helpful for the teacher faced with the task of developing a student's English vocabulary to recognize some gross classifications of words. Some of the following classifications of words are easier to teach than others; however, it will be apparent that some classifications, though difficult, are essential to the students' command of the language.

1. function words—perform grammatical functions; relate one part of the utterance to another, as do prepositions and conjunctions; or express such grammatical concepts as mood, time or tense.

2. substitute words—substitute for other words or classes, i.e., *he, she, they,* can replace nouns.
3. grammatically distributed words—show unusual grammatical restrictions in distribution, i.e., *some, any, few, many, one.*
4. content words—carry a contexual, specifiable meaning: processes, qualities; the bulk of vocabulary of a language.[4]

Most teachers find themselves developing content words (4) through audio-visual aids and primary experiences. The other classifications must be taught through actual manipulation of the language; in fact, through sentences that utilize function words and substitute words in their normal way. It is important for teachers to know which exercises will best develop the needed vocabulary.

It is important for teachers to distinguish between a student's active and passive vocabularies. Furthermore, a student's command of a language must be distinguished from his written command. It is perhaps also useful to distinguish between the common or core vocabulary known to all members of the speech community and the specialized vocabularies known to certain groups, such as teachers, engineers, linguists. All these concepts point to a rather systematized view of vocabulary development; again, it is not just a matter of memorizing a list of words.

Comparative studies of Spanish/English morphology have been made which reveal some implications for teaching vocabulary. Some principles which can guide vocabulary instruction are presented with the caution that the comparisons involve standard Spanish/English words, not the language of the barrio.

1. Words that are similar in form and meaning are easier to teach. Cognate words like hospital-*hospital,* general-*general,* yard-*yarda* (barrio dialect) could occur early in the learning sequence.
2. Words that are similar in form but different in meaning post difficult learning problems because they sound and look similar but represent different realities, i.e., assist (English—to help), *asistir* (Spanish—to attend).
3. Words that are similar in meaning but different in form, i.e., house-*casa,* may carry subtle differences in meaning, but essentially the student need only to learn and practice a new form for a known reality.
4. Words that are different in form and in meaning may represent uncommon realities or a "strange" way of looking at reality. Cultural differences may be represented in these comparisons and make the new word difficult to learn. The "hands and face" of a clock are difficult for a Spanish speaker to conceive because in Spanish those terms are reserved for people not things. (The Spanish consider a clock a "dial" with "needles" to indicate the time.)
5. Words that differ in construction from the native language may combine to make one lexical meaning and may be difficult for the Spanish speaker. For

example, we say "call-up" Mary to mean telephone Mary. Spanish does not utilize two units to mean one lexical item; therefore, these phrases may be difficult to learn.

6. Words that are similar in meaning but with specific connotations in a geographic region may be difficult initially. The extent to which we teach a specialized vocabulary functional to the region or a general vocabulary may vary with the age group. However, for comparative studies any attempt to analyze existing language patterns in the barrios would find geographic influence of great importance.[5]*

THE SYNTAX OF A LANGUAGE    Only when sounds, intonation, words and word forms are used as an organized system to convey meaning do we have language. The system of relationships and formal devices which convey meaning and distinguish one sentence from another, taken as a whole including morphology and phonology, is the *grammar* of a language. The system by which words are combined to form clauses and sentences is its *syntax.*

Historically, grammar has meant a set of usage rules which carried a value judgment connoting social correctness or intellectual status. The contemporary view is that individuals use standard grammar or nonstandard grammar, as the case may be, but each grammar is characterized by a highly intricate language system.

When the teacher helps students speak meaningful English sentences, he is engaged in teaching grammar; however, for the teacher, the rules and devices which govern English are automatic and, perhaps, difficult to isolate for instruction. Furthermore, most teachers are familiar with traditional Latin grammar rules which have been applied to English. Latin grammar which attempts to systematize English in terms of Latin categories (not English ones) is no longer considered adequate.

A thorough discussion of the systems of English grammar is beyond the scope of this work; however, in order to use the new teaching materials for language instruction, teachers should be aware of some of the systems which underly the materials and suggested techniques. Generally, teaching materials reflect two basic types of grammatical organizations: (1) Signals grammar, formalistic grammar, taxonomic grammar, or slot and substitution grammar;[6] (2) Immediate constituent analysis or phrase structure grammar, or transformational grammar.[7]

*Signals grammar, formalistic grammar, taxonomic grammar, or slot and substitution grammar* recognize types of syntactical signals which carry meaning, i.e., word order, function words, inflection (endings) or affixation (prefixes and suffixes), correlation of forms (agreement), intonation, and juncture. Based upon comparative analysis, lessons

---

* See "Pachuco: The Birth of a Creole Language" by Rafael Jesus Gonzales in the Winter, 1967, issue of *Arizona Quarterly.*

and programs are developed around those elements of English Grammar which might be difficult for native Spanish speakers. Students are systematically exposed to the basic "signals" of English used by native English speakers and are given considerable practice and drill using these signals. They are then taught variations of the language patterns using appropriate substitutions of words of similar classes consistent with the rules.

*Immediate constituent analysis* or *phrase structure grammar,* and *transformational grammar* employ a system which utilizes the concept of noun clusters and verb clusters in their various forms and constructions. Lessons are built around the rules for expanding and transforming these clusters to convey intended meanings.

Transformational rules provide a systematic means for changing declarative sentences into those involving negation, interrogatives, imperatives, and passive voice. Essentially these rules modify the sentence by changing the order of the elements, introducing additional elements, deleting or replacing elements. Transformational grammar integrates other systems of grammar into a comprehensive system. Complex transformational rules involve the combining of simple, kernel sentences into ones containing complements and other complex constructions.

How the transformations differ for Spanish and English becomes the domain of the contrastive linguist. The classroom teacher becomes involved as he helps students learn basic English sentence patterns and the transformations which allow him to change meanings.

The order in which the grammatical elements of English is taught to non-English speaking students may vary according to the philosophy of those preparing the materials or the teacher selecting lessons from these materials. However, some generalizations concerning order can be suggested.

1. English patterns which are functional or needed by the students may receive top priority.
2. Those patterns of noun phrases and verb phrases which are similar in both languages may appear early in the learning sequence.
3. Related structures (transformations) can be taught together, i.e., "This book is mine. It's mine."
4. Related sets, days of the week, months of the year, etc., can be taught together.*

In summary, precise analysis, description, and contrast of the phonology, morphology, and syntax of Spanish and English can provide valuable insight for providing Mexican American-students with systematic instruction in English. To translate the insights into teaching techniques and materials remains a formidable task. Nevertheless, certain prin-

---

* Adapted from Robert P. Stockwell, and J. D. Bower, *The Sounds of English and Spanish.* Chicago University Press, Chicago, Ill. 1965, p. 25.

ciples, again derived from the scientific study of language may guide the classroom teacher.

# Some Basic Principles Governing Modern ESL Instruction

---

The major purpose of language is to communicate ideas and thoughts from one person to another. The basic form of communication is oral language; therefore, verbal communication is a *primary* language experience. Reading and writing are *secondary* language experiences and should follow an understanding of the oral language system.

*When should native Spanish speakers be taught to read and write English?*

Language habits are learned through imitation and practice within a meaningful context and in relation to the needs of the learner. After language becomes automatic, the learner concentrates upon intended meaning and personal satisfaction. The function of language, not its form, assumes major importance. Teaching language as a "habit" or "skill" implies imitation and practice.

> *How can we implement the concept of "meaningfulness" as well as the concept that language is an automatic habit? What role do other subjects in the curriculum play in making language exercises meaningful?*

Language patterns are learned at an early age; even language "mistakes" are generalizations about language structure that have been internalized.

> *How will internalization of the Spanish language structure affect Mexican-American students learning English?*

The development of language patterns depend upon the experiences of the learner, the amount of practice he has had in abstracting and verbalizing these experiences. Often the structures of the language reflects what is important in a culture.

> *What does this mean for Mexican-American students who come from economically disadvantaged environments? What does this mean for those students who come from a home that practices Mexican traditions? How is the barrio reflected in Pachuco language? How much of the barrio language should the teacher know?*

The manner in which a second language is learned differs from the manner in which the native language is learned because certain elements of the native language system may block or provide interference in learning the second language. On the other hand, if the student has developed language facility in his native language, he can abstract, generalize, and verbalize experience. Certain aspects of vocabulary, sound system, and syntax of the native language may facilitate learning the second language. The ESL teacher capitalizes upon the areas of similarities between languages for *facilitation* of learning; at the same time, he provides specific lessons and drills to overcome *interference*.

The major objective of teaching ESL is to provide language experiences for the student in a sequence which parallels native language development but proceeds at a systematic, accelerated pace.

*Which stages of language development are critical to learning the second language?*

# The Application of Foreign Language Teaching Techniques to ESL

Most characteristic of foreign language teaching is the structured and controlled use of the new language during oral communication, reading and writing. The presentation of specific language patterns and subsequent drills is the core of the program.

Basically the student is introduced to one new point or pattern at a time; he is drilled for control and exposed to periodic review for mastery of the new language habit. Similar classes, patterns, and structures of the new language are taught as a unit.

Any given language lesson might include: providing the student with a *model* of the language pattern to be learned; opportunity to *imitate* the model; opportunity to *practice* the model with attention and correction when needed; opportunity to *vary* and *manipulate* the model through substitution of words, classes, tenses, or other grammatical forms: and opportunity to *apply a variation* of the model during free communication.

The drills which follow the initial teaching of a new language skill reflect the unique structure of the language and are presented in a meaningful context, i.e., in a sentence, dialogue, story, etc. Pupil interest and enjoyment are sustained through games, variety and rapid pacing in procedure.*

---

\* See: Teaching Techniques During the Aural-Oral Phase: Devices for Presentation and Practice, Appendix D.

The problem areas revealed through contrastive language study generally provide the focus for drill and practice in the new language. Specific lessons would deal with the new sound system, vocabulary, or grammatical patterns. For example, native Spanish speakers would be helped with English grammatical structures involving:*

1. The inclusion and use of function words, e.g., <u>do</u>, <u>be</u>, <u>can</u>, <u>may</u>, <u>will</u> <u>have</u>, <u>a</u>, <u>the</u>, <u>an</u>, <u>this</u>, <u>that</u>. In Spanish similar situations are handled through inflection (endings) or intonation.

| English | Spanish |
| --- | --- |
| I'm <u>going</u> to sing. | Cantar<u>é.</u> |
| He <u>speaks</u> Spanish. | Habl<u>a</u> español. |
| <u>Does</u> he speak Spanish? | ¿Habl<u>a</u> español? |

2. Word order and stress in questions, statements, and commands. In Spanish function words may be used as well as word order.

| English | Spanish |
| --- | --- |
| A Spanish teacher (teacher of Spanish) | Un profesor <u>de</u> español |
| A Spanish teacher (of Spanish origin) | Un profesor español |

3. Inclusion of the subject pronoun. Spanish identifies the subject pronoun through inflection in the verb.

| English | Spanish |
| --- | --- |
| <u>I</u> write. | Escrib<u>o.</u> |
| <u>He</u> writes. | Escrib<u>e.</u> |

4. Correlation of forms, e.g., using the "s" inflection of the English verb with the singular form of subject; correlation of gender; agreement of modifiers and nouns in number and gender. Spanish structure has a highly developed system of gender and agreement of modifiers with nouns that may be imposed upon English by native Spanish speakers.

| English | Spanish |
| --- | --- |
| Mary writ<u>es</u>. | María escrib<u>e.</u> |
| Jack writ<u>es</u>. | Juan escrib<u>e.</u> |
| They writ<u>e</u>. | (Ellos) escrib<u>en.</u> |

---

* Adapted from: Robert Politzer, *Teaching Spanish, A Linguistic Orientation*, Boston: Ginn & Company, 1961, p. 96-99.

| | |
|---|---|
| The books (neuter) | Los libros (masculine) |
| I see her; I give her the book. | La veo; le doy el libro. |
| I see them; I give them the book. | Los veo; les doy el libro. |
| I see the white doves. | Veo las palomas blancas. |

5. Position of words to signal subject and indirect object. The Spanish structure may use function words or inflection.

| English | Spanish |
|---|---|
| I want to tell him the truth. | Quiero decircle la verdad. |
| I want him to tell the truth. | Quiero que (él) diga la verdad. |

6. The use of inflection to signal possession " 's ". Spanish uses a function word to signal possession.

| English | Spanish |
|---|---|
| My sister's house. | La casa de mi hermana. |

Though foreign language exercises and drills are structured, the teacher's role is important. The teacher must maintain pupil interest, select those lessons which are most functional, provide individualized instruction when needed, and maintain some balance in the language arts program between drill and creative language experiences.

Teaching students to read and write a foreign language also utilizes the concept of controlled language experience. One of the clearest examples of reading material prepared specifically for students learning English as a foreign language is the Miami Linguistic Readers series. The principles which underlie their construction are worth noting.

1. The content of beginning reading materials must deal with those things which time has shown are truly interesting to children.

2. The materials must reflect the natural language forms of children's speech.

3. The child must have aural-oral control of the material he is expected to read.

4. In developing beginning reading materials the focus must be on the decoding skills involved in the process of reading rather than on the uses to which reading is put after the process is mastered.

5. The presentation of sound-symbol correspondences in beginning reading should be in terms of spelling patterns rather than in terms of individual letter-sound correspondences.

6. Grammatical structure as well as vocabulary must be controlled.

7. The child must learn to read by structure (be taught the grammatical units) if he is to master the skills involved in the act of reading.

8. The learning load in linguistically oriented materials must be determined in terms of the special nature of the materials (in terms of sequences of letters and space as they form patterns—not discrete forms such as sight words).

9. Writing experiences reinforce listening, speaking, and reading.

10. The materials must be so selected and organized that they will enable the learner to achieve success as he progresses through the materials.[8]

Some of these elements can be found in most "traditional" reading programs. However, their order of importance and the emphasis upon certain premises differ significantly, i.e., decoding skills, controlled sound-symbol correspondence, natural speech patterns, controlled structure.

It might also be pointed out that *writing* skills (point 9) are developed along with reading skills and are used to reinforce reading. Generally, the "ESL" approach to writing restricts writing to language patterns that have been used orally and read often.

Initial compositions may be developed through questions which are designed to have students review vocabulary and patterns previously learned. An illustration of question/answer approach can be seen in the following instructional aid prepared for an in-service workshop in ESL for junior high school teachers. Sentence patterns, verb forms, and vocabulary are reviewed in the questions and models.[9]

| *Questions* | *Model* |
|---|---|
| How old are you? | I am fourteen years old. |
| When were you born? | My birthday was October 21, 1954. |
| Where were you born? | I was born in Guadalajara. |
| Where do you live? | I live at 1234 East Third Street. |
| How long have you lived there? | We have lived there for two months. |

Using the models students substitute information which describes them. The questions provided can cover a variety of topics which are interesting to the student. With more experience the students are expected to write on a topic without the use of specific models, and finally the students are allowed to bring in topics or writing assignments related to other classes.

The extremely structured approach to instruction imposed in ESL and foreign language teaching may be new and somewhat suspect to many elementary and secondary teachers involved in teaching language skills. The emphasis upon practice and drill may, in fact, depress the majority of teachers who view the language arts as creative thought processes and who receive personal satisfaction through designing creative teaching situations. Furthermore, separating the process of language from its function may run contrary to long standing principles of education.

These concerns have led some educators to consider ways to make systematic language instruction meaningful and functional. In addition to bilingual programs where instruction is given in both languages, other approaches to teaching English are tried, either alone or in combination with structured, linguistic approaches. Language instruction may be integrated with other content areas of the curriculum.

> . . . It is recommended that:
> the benefit of oral-aural techniques be combined with content drawn from science, social studies, mathematics and literature to produce a language instructional program based on meaningful experiences which would develop cognitive powers ahead of spoken language, spoken language ahead of formal reading skills, and reading skills ahead of writing and composition.[10]

Other educators would emphasize language development not as an end, in itself, but as a means for cognitive growth. These educators are most concerned about Mexican American students' seemingly limited ability to engage in critical thinking. Many feel the cause is directly related to school programs which may be overly structured, teacher-directed, or limited in scope without concern for application of skills.

> The Mexican-American student needs help in the application of language skills to the content areas. . . The error can be made here in believing that the Mexican-American student will automatically apply his English knowledge to the content areas.
> The thesis advanced here is that, among other factors, one of the principal ones that is involved in the school performance phenomena is the lack of sufficient attention to the cognitive development of the Spanish speaking pupil. . . Since concept development and language are so intimately related, the English as a second language programs need to pay much more attention to cognitive learning than is true of current practice. . . In the typical school curriculum the more abstract and difficult processes begin to be emphasized about the fourth grade. It does not appear desirable, however, to wait until the fourth grade to give direct instruction in thinking; such preparatory work for the higher level of thought processes must begin with the first grade.[11]

When English as a second language is viewed as part of a total curriculum, criticisms like those above can be avoided. As one component of a good bilingual program, English as a second language can be a vital link to social success.

# 8

# EDUCATING TEACHERS TO MEET THE CHALLENGE

It seems appropriate to end the discussion with some consideration of teacher preparation in the light of what we know about Mexican-American students and their community. Reiterated throughout this work has been the concept that the teacher is the critical element in developing the student's personal and academic competencies. Equally fundamental has been the theme that schools and teachers, to date, have failed to help the majority of Mexican-American students achieve academic success and all the social benefits that accrue from it. A third recurring concept has been the emerging role of the Chicano minority community and the student, himself, as vital forces in bringing about institutional and social change. A fourth theme has been a plea for improved instruments and techniques of evaluation with which to assess the Mexican-American student's potential, as well as the effectiveness of instruction. Of final and related interest have been innovative school reorganization, curriculum design, and teaching strategies which focus upon the needs of Mexican-American students.

## An Urgent Need: Reform in Teacher Training

In all of these strands are implications and assumptions about the type of teacher and needed teaching competencies. To make these competencies a reality demands reform at all levels of teacher education. Though there are numerous experimental programs throughout the country, more are needed which are especially designed for teachers who wish to accept the challenge of teaching students who are culturally different, who face language barriers or come from impoverished homes.

The author does not endorse the concept that good education and effective teaching are the same everywhere. There may be some common elements in all good educational

184

programs, but the competencies needed to work effectively with Mexican-American students warrant special training.

COMPETENCIES TEACHERS NEED   Teachers of Mexican-American students need competencies in several key areas in order to be prepared for the realities which face them.
First, and most obviously, teachers must have the language competencies needed to communicate with students and parents. Fluency in the Spanish language and some knowledge of dialects used in the barrio should be a prerequisite for teachers who work in schools where Mexican-American students comprise a sizable part of the student population.

Second, teachers must be helped to develop knowledge in critical content areas so that they can create, adapt, or make intelligent decisions about teaching materials. This implies an interdisciplinary approach to teacher preparation and possible realignments of college faculties and facilities.

Third, teachers who work with Mexican-American students need professional training in techniques of counseling and guidance because their students are likely to experience social and emotional problems related to minority status. Teachers need to be able to help students cope with the feelings that accompany academic failure, identity problems, cultural conflict, acculturation, or alienation.

Fourth, a teacher characteristic most difficult to develop, but essential to the success of both teacher and student, is acceptance of and sensitivity to the Mexican-Amercan individual and his culture. One of the most promising means for developing his competency is the utilization of personnel and resources provided by ethnic studies departments within universities and colleges, i.e., Chicano Studies, Mexican-American Studies, Latin-Hispanic-Mexican-American Studies Departments. The recency of the organization of these departments and their commitment to the improvement of education for Mexican-Americans provides a structure that is flexible and relevant to the needs of Mexican Americans.

HOW ETHNIC STUDIES DEPARTMENTS CAN HELP   Ethnic studies departments can provide teachers with subject-matter background in anthropology, art, music, literature, and history of the Mexican American in the southwest and Mexico. Equally important, these departments deal directly with the problems of minority group members and their community. Often, special courses which examine conflicts between cultures, problems associated with acculturation and minority status, problems of the barrio, etc. take prospective teachers into the community and help them become sensitive to the feelings, needs, and problems of Mexican Americans. Most important, ethnic studies departments provide teachers with opportunities to interact with Mexican Americans in professional and social relationships. Through this contact, individuals from both cultures can be helped to understand their feelings and reactions to those who are different.

Through channels provided by ethnic studies departments or through those developed by schools of education or school districts, the final element of an effective teacher education program provides teachers ample opportunity to evaluate their own attitudes, values, and reactions to Mexican Americans.

Concurrently, there must be more valid teacher selection procedures and provision for self-selection utilizing criteria involving personality characteristics, emotional stability, and flexibility in stress situations which are inevitable when persons of different cultural and value orientations come in contact.

These elements of an effective teacher education program imply early contact with Mexican-American students and parents; therefore, laboratory experiences must be an integral part of teacher education in its earliest stages. Field work in the barrio, "live-in" experiences, on-site methods classes, and service within community organizations are vehicles which can be used to bring prospective and practicing teachers together with Mexican Americans as they work for constructive goals.

A COMMON GOAL OF EDUCATORS AND BARRIO RESIDENTS    To achieve better education for Mexican-American students is an illustration of a constructive goal held in common by both the majority of people in the barrio and those in the teaching profession. Working together to meet this goal could help both dispel the stereotypes they hold about one another. For example, the Chicano community has little confidence in professional educators and will, at times, refuse help which could be provided by professional expertise. Educators, on the other hand, often are unaware of what the community has to offer. They fail to realize that each barrio is different with unique needs and character. Sometimes educators do not recognize the barrio as a community, at all, because its structure is foreign to them. When each group becomes aware that it needs the other in order to successfully work out their problems, they are forced to reassess one another's worth.

Where a formal vehicle is established for reciprocal involvement the results of school-community cooperation have been encouraging. For example, in the Los Angeles Unified School District, community advisory boards have been established at the local level. In most cases, these advisory boards have acted as the school-community liaison and as a stimulus to educational innovation.

In response to pressure exerted by the Chicano community, a Mexican American Education Commission* was established in 1969 to act as a special advisory body to the Los Angeles City Board of Education. The commission was free to define its role, gather data from target schools, initiate programs of education, monitor pupil performance, and generally play a key role in board decisions which affect Mexican Americans. Composed largely of community people from East Los Angeles, the Commission has dealt with such matters as retraining teachers, promoting better relationships between schools and parents, coordinating and stimulating programs designed to stop the excessive dropout rate of Mexican-American students, stimulating innovative programs in language teaching,

---

* The author is indebted to Mr. Edward Moreno, Administrative Secretary, Mexican American Education Commission, for interviews and access to the minutes of the commission.

improving vocational education and increasing counseling and guidance services for Mexican-American students. Generally, the commission has assumed a unique communicative role as it provides ombudsman service for students, parents, and teachers who have grievances or who wish to change the institution.

The long-range effects of the commission, advisory boards, and other bodies similar in purpose remain a matter of speculation. However, one fact comes through loud and clear; the Mexican-American community *does* know what kind of teacher it needs. The barrio is telling us:

> *Send us a teacher who knows how to teach and one who knows us.*
>
> *Send us a teacher who knows how to teach our children to speak, read, and write English, but who does not make them ashamed of their Spanish.*
>
> *Send us a teacher who can speak to us, or at least try to communicate with us in our language.*
>
> *Send us a teacher who is sensitive to us, who knows our culture, our traditions, our values, and our history.*
>
> *Send us some teachers who are Mexican American.*
>
> *Send us a teacher who understands our children and knows how to teach them to think, to be secure in their abilities, and to be proud of their heritage.*
>
> *Send us a teacher who respects us, one who doesn't feel he is better than we are, or believes his values are better than ours.*
>
> *Send us a teacher who respects our barrio, who does not see it as a slum or as something foreign.*
>
> *Send us a teacher who respects* me. *I am different from other Chicanos, even though I am one!*
>
> *Send us a teacher who cares—before it is too late!*

# APPENDIX A

## Selected Readings and Resources

### BIBLIOGRAPHIES

Beauchamp, Martha. *Bilingualism with Reference to American Minority Groups (Especially Spanish-Americans)*. LB 15 USD. ED 248, 1967. The Library of Congress Legislative Reference Service. Education and Public Welfare Division, Washington, D.C.

Gomez, Q. *Selected Materials on the Chicano*. Mexican American Cultural Center, U.C.L.A., 405 Hilgard Street, Los Angeles, Calif.

*Mexican-American Education, A Bibliography Prepared for the National Conference on Educational Opportunities for Mexican-Americans, 1968*. Commodore Perry Hotel, Austin, Texas.

*Mexico and the Mexican Americans*. Center on Mexican American Studies, Whittier College, 13406 East Philadelphia, Whittier, California.

Revelle, Keith. *Chicano! A Selected Bibliography of Materials By and About Mexico and Mexican Americans*. The Latin American Library, 1457 Fruitvale Avenue, Oakland, California. 94601.

Sheridan, George. *An Annotated Bibliography of Mexican American Education. First Papers on Migrancy and Rural Poverty, An Introduction to the Education of Mexican Americans in Rural Areas*. Teacher Corps Rural Migran, University of Southern California, School of Education, Los Angeles, California.

### BOOKS

#### New World Beginning of Mexican Americans

Bolton, Eugene (Ed.). *Spanish Explorations in the Southwest 1542–1706*. New York: Barnes and Noble, Inc., 1952.

Coe, Michael D. *Mexico, Ancient Peoples and Places*. New York: Frederick A. Praeger, 1962.

Coe, Michael D. *The Maya, Ancient Peoples and Places*. New York: Frederick A. Praeger, 1967.

Ellis, Havelock. *Soul of Spain*. Boston: Houghton Mifflin Co., 1924.

Leon Portilla, Miguel. *Aztec Thought and Culture: A Study of the Ancient Nahauatl Mind*. Norman: University of Oklahoma Press, 1963.

Prescott, William. *The Conquest of Mexico*. New York: Heritage Press, 1957.

Soustelle, Jacques. *The Daily Life of the Aztecs on the Eve of the Spanish Conquest*. New York: Macmillan Co., 1962.

Vaillant, G. C. *Aztecs of Mexico*. Baltimore: Penguin Books, 1966.

Wolf, Eric. *Sons of the Shaking Earth*. Chicago: Phoenix Press, 1959.

#### The Modern Mexican Heritage of Mexican Americans

Alba, Victor. *The Mexicans: The Making of a Nation*. New York: Frederick A. Praeger, 1967.

Azuela, Mariano. *The Underdogs.* New York: A Signet Classic, 1962.

Brandenburg, Frank R. *The Making of Modern Mexico.* Englewood Cliffs, N.J.: Prentice-Hall, 1967.

Crockcroft, James. *Intellectual Precursors of the Mexican Revolution.* Austin: University of Texas Press, 1968.

Diaz, Bernal. *The Conquest of New Spain.* Baltimore: Penguin Classics, 1963.

Fernandez-Florez, Dario. *The Spanish Heritage in the United States.* Madrid: Publicaciones Espanolas, 1965.

Johnson, William Weber. *Heroic Mexico.* Garden City: Doubleday & Co., 1968.

McWilliams, Carey. *North from Mexico, the Spanish Speaking People of the United States.* New York: Greenwood Press, 1968.

Nava, Julian. *Mexican Americans Past, Present and Future.* New York: American Book Company, 1969.

Parkes, Henry Bamfor. *A History of Mexico.* Third Edition. Boston: Houghton Mifflin Company, 1960.

Paz, Octavio (Ed.). *An Anthology of Mexican Poetry.* Bloomington: Indiana University Press, 1965.

Paz, Octavio. *The Labyrinth of Solitude.* New York: Grove Press, Inc., 1961.

Romanell, Patrick. *Making of the Mexican Mind: A Study of Recent Mexican Thought.* South Bend, Ind.: University of Notre Dame Press, 1967.

Ramos, Samuel. *Profile of Man and Culture in Mexico.* Austin: University of Texas Press, 1962.

Womack, John Jr. *Zapata and the Mexican Revolution.* New York: Alfred A. Knopf, Inc., 1969.

## The Mexican American in the Southwest—General

Acuna, Rudolph. *A Mexican American Chronicle.* New York: American Book Co., 1970.

Carranza, Eliu. *Pensamientos on Los Chicanos: A Cultural Revolution.* Berkeley: California Book Co., Ltd., 1969.

Galarza, Ernesto. *Merchants of Labor.* Santa Barbara: McNally & Loftin, 1964.

Galarza, Ernesto, Herman Gallegos, and Julian Samora. *Mexican Americans in the Southwest.* Santa Barbara: McNally & Loftin, 1969.

Galarza, Ernesto. *Spiders in the House and Workers in the Field.* South Bend, Ind.: University of Notre Dame Press, 1970.

Greenwood, Robert. *The California Outlaw: Tiburcio Vasquez.* Los Gatos: The Talisman Press, 1960.

Griffith, Beatrice. *American Me.* Boston: Houghton Mifflin Co., 1948.

Hernandez, Luis. *A Forgotten American.* New York: Anti-Defamation League of B'nai B'rith, 1969.

Jenkinson, Michael. *Tijerina.* Albuquerque, New Mexico: Paisano Press, 1968.

Matthiessen, Peter. *Sal Si Puedes Cesar Chavez and the New American Revolution.* New York: Random House, 1969.

McWilliams, Carey. *The Mexican in America.* New York: Teacher's College Press, Columbia University, 1968.

Moore, Joan W. *Mexican-Americans: Problems and Prospects.* Madison: University of Wisconsin Press, 1967.

Moore, Joan. *Mexican Americans.* Englewood Cliffs, N.J.: Prentice-Hall, Inc., 1970.

Pitt, Leonard. *The Decline of the Californios.* Berkeley: University of California Press, 1966.

Robinson, Cecil. *With the Ears of Strangers.* Tucson: University of Arizona Press, 1963.

Ruiz, Ramon. *The Mexican-American War: Was it Manifest Destiny?* New York: Holt, Rinehart and Winston, 1963.

Rubel, Arthur J. *Across the Tracks, Mexican Americans in a Texas City.* Austin: Univ. of Texas Press, 1966.

Singletary, Otis S. *The Mexican War.* Chicago: University of Chicago Press, 1960.

Samora, Julian (Ed.). *La Raza, Forgotten Americans.* South Bend, Indiana: University of Notre Dame Press, 1966.

Sanchez, George. *Forgotten People: A Study of New Mexicans.* Albuquerque: University of New Mexico Press, 1940.

Taylor, Paul. *An American-Mexican Frontier.* Chapell Hill: University of North Carolina Press, 1934.

### The Mexican Americans in the Southwest—Educational

Carter, Thomas P. *Preparing Teachers for Mexican American Children.* Albuquerque: New Mexico University Press, 1969.

Carter, Thomas P. *Mexican Americans in School: A History of Educational Neglect.* New York: College Entrance Examination Board, 1970.

Hershel, Manuel T. *Spanish Speaking Children of the Southwest: Their Education and Public Welfare.* Austin: University of Texas Press, 1965.

Johnson, Henry S. and William J. Hernandez-M. *Educating the Mexican American.* Valley Forge, Pa.: Judson Press, 1970.

Rosenthal, Robert and Lenore Jacobson. *Pygmalion in the Classroom.* New York: Holt, Rinehart and Winston, 1968.

Stone, James C. and DeNevi Donald (Editors). *Teaching Multi-Cultural Populations, Five Heritages.* New York: Van Nostrand Reinhold Co., 1971.

## JOURNALS AND NEWSPAPERS

*Aztlan, Chicano Journal of the Social Sciences and the Arts.* Mexican American Cultural Center, University of California, Los Angeles, 1970.

*Con Safos: Reflections of Life in the Barrio.* P.O. Box 31085, Los Angeles, California, 90031.

*El Grito, A Journal of Mexican American Thought.* P.O. Box 9275, Berkeley, California, 94719.

*Bronze.* 1560 34th Avenue, Oakland, California, 94601.

*Compass.* 1209 Egypt Street, Houston, Texas, 77009.

*Coraje.* C/o Mexican American Liberation Committee, Tucson, Ariz.

*El Chicano.* 4021 First Avenue, San Bernardino, California.

*El Deguello.* P.O. Box 37094, San Antonio, Texas.

*El Gallo.* 1567 Downing Street, Denver, Colorado, 80218.

*El Grito Del Norte.* Route 2, Box 5, Espanola, New Mexico, 87532.

*El Malcriado.* P.O. Box 130, Delano, California, 63215.

*El Ojo.* 1700 K Street, N.W., Suite 1207, Washington, D.C., 20006.

*El Paisano.* P.O. Box 155, Tolleson, Arizona, 85353.

*El Papel.* P.O. Box 7167, Albuquerque, New Mexico, 87104.

*El Yaqui.* P.O. Box 52610, Houston, Texas, 77052.

*Hoy.* Newsletter, Cabinet Committee on Opportunities for Spanish Speaking People, 1707 H Street, N.W., Washington, D.C., 20506.

*La Causa.* 4715 East Olympic Blvd., Los Angeles, Calif., 90033.

*La Raza.* P.O. Box 31004, Los Angeles, California, 90033.

*La Revolución.* Box 1853, Uvalde, Texas.

*La Verdad.* P.O. Box 13156, San Diego, California, 92113.

*La Voz Mexicana.* P.O. Box 101, Wautoma, Wisconsin, 54982.

*Lado.* 1306 North Western Avenue, Chicago, Illinois, 60622.

*Nuestra Lucha.* 110 NW 5th Avenue, Del Rey Beach, Florida, 33444.

## RESEARCH REPORTS

### Mexican-American Study Project

(Division of Research Graduate School of Business Administration, University of California, Los Angeles, 1967)

Advance Report #1. *Education and Income of Mexican-American in the Southwest* by Walter Fogel.

Advance Report #2. *Mexican Immigration to the United States: The Record and Its Implications* by Leo Grebler.

Advance Report #3. *Revised Bibliography.*

Advance Report #4. *Residential Segregation of Minorities in the Urban Southwest* by Joan W. Moore and Frank G. Mittelbach.

Advance Report #5. *The Burden of Poverty* by Frank G. Mittelbach and Grace Marshall.

Advance Report #6. *Intermarriage of Mexican-Americans* by Frank G. Mittelbach, Joan W. Moore, and Ronald McDaniel.

Advance Report #7. *The Schooling Gap: Signs of Progress* by Leo Grebler.

Advance Report #8. *Mexican-Americans in a Midwest Metropolis: A Study of East Chicago* by Julian Samora and Richard A. Lamanna.

Advance Report #9. *The Spanish Americans of New Mexico: A Distinctive Heritage* by Nancie L. Gonzalez.

Advance Report #10. *Mexican-Americans in Southwest Labor Markets* by Walter Fogel.

Advance Report #11. *Health Status and Practices Among Mexican-Americans* by A. Taher Moustafa, M.D. and Gertrud Weiss, M.D.

Final Report. *Educational Achievement and Aspirations of Mexican American Youth in a Metropolitan Context* by C. Wayne Gordon and others, 1968.

## Mexican-American Education

**Mexican-American Education: A Search for Identity.** Superintendent of Documents, U. S Government Printing Office, Washington, D. C., 20402.

## EDUCATIONAL RESOURCES INFORMATION CENTER (ERIC)

### Bibliographies, Research Reports and Papers Pertinent to Mexican Americans

Adult Education, Syracuse University, 107 Roney Lane, Syracuse, New York, 13210. ERIC/AE is responsible for research and other documents on formal and informal adult and continuing education in all settings.

Counseling and Personnel Services, 611 Church Street, Ann Arbor, Michigan, 48104. ERIC/ CAPS focuses on information relevant to personnel work at all levels and in all settings, including college student personnel work, school psychology, school social work, elementary and secondary school counseling, school health work, school psychiatry, employment counseling, and personnel work research. Included are materials on pupil, student, and adult characteristics; educational, occupational, and community settings; and the types of assistance provided by personnel workers.

The Disadvantaged, Teachers College-Box 40, Columbia University, New York, New York, 10027. ERIC/IRCD is responsible for research reports and other documents on the educational, psychological, social, and general development of urban children and youth who are socially or economically disadvantaged.

Early Childhood Education, University of Illinois 805 West Pennsylvania Avenue, Urbana, Illinois, 61801. The Clearinghouse is responsible for research documents on the physiological, psychological, and cultural development of children from birth through primary grades.

Educational Administration, Hendricks Hall, University of Oregon, Eugene, Oregon, 97403. ERIC/CEA focuses on information concerned with leadership, management, and structure of public and private educational organizations at all levels. Included are documents on the practice and theory of administration, generated from the fields of educational, public, and business administration and from the humanities and the social and behavioral sciences. Such topics as the pre-service and in-service preparation of administrators, tasks and processes of administration (finance, planning, personnel, etc.) methods and varieties of organization, organizational change, and social context of the organization are covered. Not included are documents dealing specifically with educational facilities or junior colleges.

Educational Facilities, University of Wisconsin, 606 State Street, Room 314, Madison, Wisconsin, 53703. ERIC/CEF focuses on information about sites, buildings, and equipment used for educational purposes; included are the efficiency and effectiveness of related activities, such as planning, financing, constructing, renovating, maintaining, operating, insuring, utilizing, and evaluating educational facilities.

Educational Media and Technology, Institute for Communication Research, Stanford University Stanford, California, 94305. ERIC at Stanford is responsible for information on application of new media and technological innovation to education, including such subjects as instructional television, computer-assisted instruction, and programmed learning.

Exceptional Children, The Council for Exceptional Children, 1201 Sixteenth Street, N.W., Washington, D.C., 20036. ERIC/CEC is responsible for documents on educating children and youth who require special services—those who are gifted, mentally retarded, visually impaired, deaf, hard of hearing, physically handicapped, emotionally disturbed, or speech and language-impaired.

Higher Education, George Washington University, Washington, D.C., 20006. ERIC/CHE is responsible for research documents on higher education, with the exception of reports on both teacher education and teaching English in higher education.

Junior Colleges, University of California at Los Angeles, 405 Hilgard Ave., Los Angeles, California, 90024. ERIC is responsible for information about public and private, community, and junior colleges, including studies on students, staff, curricula, programs, libraries, and community service.

Library and Information Sciences, University of Minnesota, 2122 Riverside Avenue, Minneapolis, Minnesota, 55404. ERIC/CLIS if responsible for research documents on the operation of libraries and information centers, the technology used to improve their operations, and the education and training of library and information specialists.

Linguistics, Center for Applied Linguistics, 1717 Massachusetts Avenue, N.W., Washington, D.C., 20036. CAL/ERIC is responsible for research reports on linguistics and all related language sciences, uncommonly taught languages, and teaching of English as a foreign or second language, and the teaching of English as a native language to speakers of non-standard dialects.

Reading, 200 Pine Hall, School of Education, Indiana University, Bloomington, Indiana, 47401.

ERIC/CRIER focuses on information related to all aspects of reading behavior with emphasis on physiology, psychology, sociology, and the teaching of reading. Included are reports on the development and evaluation of instructional materials, curricula, tests and measurements, preparation of reading teachers and specialists, and methodology at all levels; the role of libraries and other agencies in fostering and methodology at all levels; the role of libraries and other agencies in fostering and guiding reading; and diagnostic and remedial services in school and clinic settings.

Rural Education and Small Schools, New Mexico State University, Box 3AP, University Park Branch, Las Cruces, New Mexico, 88001. ERIC/CRESS is responsible for research documents on organization, administration, curriculum, instruction, innovative programs, and other aspects of small schools and rural education in general, as well as outdoor education, migrant education, Indian education, and Mexican American education.

Science Education, Ohio State University, 1460 West Lane Avenue, Columbus, Ohio, 43221.

ERIC/SEIAC is responsible for reports on all levels of science and mathematics education, and on adult and continuing education in science and mathematics.

Teacher Education, 1156 Fifteenth Street, N.W., Washington, D.C., 20005. The Clearinghouse focuses on materials relative to the preparation of school personnel (nursery, elementary, secondary, and supporting school personnel); the preparation and development of teacher educators; and the profession of teaching. The scope includes recruitment, selection, life-long personal and professional development, and teacher placement.

Teaching of English, National Council of Teachers of English, 508 South Sixth Street, Champaign, Illinois, 61820. NCTE/ERIC focuses on research reports and other documents relevant to all aspects of the teaching of English from kindergarten through grade 12, the preparation of teachers of English for the schools, the preparation of specialists in English education.

Teaching of Foreign Languages, Modern Language Association of America, 62 Fifth Avenue, New York, New York, 10011. MLA/ERIC is responsible for research documents on teaching French, German, Italian, Russian, Spanish, Latin, and classical Greek at all instructional levels. It also is responsible for documents on the teaching of English in undergraduate and graduate education.

Vocational and Technical Education, Ohio State University, 1900 Kenney Road, Columbus, Ohio, 43212. The Clearinghouse focuses on research documents and related resources in vocational and technical education, new sub-professional fields, and the related fields of industrial arts education, manpower economics, occupational psychology, and occupational sociology.

# APPENDIX B*

## State Programs for Migratory Children Allotments for Fiscal Year 1971

| State | Amount | State | Amount |
|-------|--------|-------|--------|
| TOTAL | $57,608,680 | Idaho | 636,138 |
| Alabama | 497,508 | Illinois | 494,104 |
| Alaska | | Indiana | 510,465 |
| Arizona | 1,471,798 | Iowa | 70,663 |
| Arkansas | 525,688 | Kansas | 452,163 |
| California | 7,368,421 | Kentucky | 53,766 |
| Colorado | 1,065,629 | Louisiana | 341,714 |
| Connecticut | 501,516 | Maine | 45,346 |
| Delaware | 208,219 | Maryland | 191,901 |
| Florida | 7,796,910 | Massachusetts | 216,830 |
| Georgia | 376,047 | Michigan | 3,024,378 |
| Hawaii | | Minnesota | 312,015 |

* From *American Education,* June, 1971.

| State | Amount | State | Amount |
|-------|--------|-------|--------|
| Mississippi ............... | 727,802 | Rhode Island ............... | 2,215 |
| Missouri ................. | 325,194 | South Carolina ............ | 450,543 |
| Montana ................. | 610,226 | South Dakota ............. | 26,235 |
| Nebraska ................ | 202,436 | Tennessee ................ | 225,433 |
| Nevada ................. | 20,081 | Texas ................... | 13,594,055 |
| New Hampshire ........... | 15,546 | Utah .................... | 163,244 |
| New Jersey .............. | 1,539,926 | Vermont ................. | 4,533 |
| New Mexico ............. | 711,283 | Virginia ................. | 544,799 |
| New York ............... | 2,074,282 | Washington .............. | 1,481,313 |
| North Carolina ............ | 1,081,176 | West Virginia ............. | 112,716 |
| North Dakota ............. | 533,462 | Wisconsin ................ | 370,972 |
| Ohio .................... | 1,060,771 | Wyoming ................ | 132,042 |
| Oklahoma ................ | 540,911 | District of | |
| Oregon ................. | 1,379,238 | Columbia | |
| Pennsylvania .............. | 417,027 | Reserved ................. | 3,100,000 |

For further information, write to the Title I Migrant Coordinator in the State Department of Education in any State capital, or to the Migrant Programs Branch, Division of Compensatory Education, U.S. Office of Education, Washington, D.C. 20202.

# APPENDIX C

## Bilingual-Bicultural Education Programs

### ARIZONA

PHOENIX: Wilson Elementary School District 7—1970
**Individualizing Bilingual-Bicultural Instruction**
(OE 7-00066-1)                                        Amount Recommended: $300,000
*Description:* A component of a bilingual education project has been established to develop formulas for grouping children in the second and third grades having varying language abilities through the existing bilingual curriculum. A product of the project will be a complete description of a program in classroom management using small groups. The project will seek to (1) destroy the myth that two separate language groups cannot be taught together to their mutual benefit and (2) demonstrate that classroom experience can serve as a socialization process. The project will have demonstration sites in three locations including Phoenix Wilson Elementary School.
*For further information:* Jack Null, Superintendent, Wilson School District No. 7, 2411 East Buckeye Road, Phoenix, Arizona, 85034. (602) 273-1207.

TUCSON: Tucson Elementary School District No. 1—1969
**Bilingual-Bicultural Project**
*Languages:* Spanish, English
(OE 97-310)                                                           Amount sought: $80,302
*Description:* A pilot bilingual-bicultural program will be conducted in two preschool and three first grade classes. Preschool children and their parents will meet with a bilingual teacher and a bilingual aide once a week for a two-hour session. During the session, teachers will demonstrate activities and equipment easily duplicated at home. Materials will be loaned to the parents to help them continue the preschool experience until the next week. First grade instruction will be carried out in Spanish for one-third of the day, and in English for the remainder of the day. A bilingual representative from the community will be employed to serve as a link between the school and the community and to encourage parental involvement in classroom activities.
*Students served:* 450, Grades K-1
*Counties served:* Pima
*Further Information:* Jewell C. Taylor, Project Director, P.O. Box 4040, Tucson, Arizona, 85717. (602) 791-6129.

## CALIFORNIA

SAN DIEGO: San Diego Unified School District—1970
**Acquisition, Evaluation and Dissemination of Instruction Materials in Spanish and Portuguese**
(OE 7-00412)                                                   Amount recommended: $475,000
*Description:* Instructional materials which may be useful in bilingual education projects throughout the United States will be acquired through this project from the Spanish- and Portuguese-speaking countries of Latin America and Europe. These materials will be made available to bilingual education classes at the elementary and secondary levels. The plan of operation for the project includes the following activities: (1) preparation, (2) search and acquisition of materials, (3) evaluation, (4) annotation, (5) purchase, (6) trial-use, (7) field-testing in San Diego and other operating bilingual projects throughout the Nation, (8) synthesizing reports, (9) publication, (10) dissemination, (11) distribution, (12) assessment of project, and (13) additional activities.
*For further information:* Jack Hornback, Superintendent, San Diego Unified School District, 4100 Normal Street, San Diego, California, 92103. (714) 298-4681.

SANTA CLARA: Santa Clara Office of Education—1969
**Spanish Dame School**
*Languages:* Spanish, English
(OE 97-103)                                                           Amount sought: $81,500
*Description:* Groups of five three- and four-year-old Spanish-speaking children will be instructed in their homes by bilingual teachers who are specially trained members of the community. These teachers also will spend one hour each week showing the mother of each child how to use the materials to further help her child. Two lead teachers will provide continuous inservice training in evaluating student progress and in developing curriculum and materials. In addition,

each lead teacher and four aides will be equipped with a van specially designed as a traveling workshop.
*Students served:* 40, Grade Preschool
*Counties served:* Santa Clara
*Further information:* Glenn W. Hoffmann, County Superintendent of Schools, Santa Clara County Office of Education, 70 West Hedding Street, Santa Clara, California, 95110 (408) 299-2131.

POMONA: Pomona Unified School District—1969
**Bilingual Leadership Through Speech and Drama**
*Languages:* Spanish, English
(OE 97-33)                                                          Amount sought: $30,500
*Description:* Dramatic arts and speech training in Spanish and English will be stressed in a program for Mexican-American students in an inner-city which is also designed to strengthen their self-images and develop their leadership abilities, as well as to improve their language ability. Two bilingual instructors will work with each class, one a teacher with unusual English language competencies and one a paraprofessional with Spanish language competencies. Dramatic arts interpretation relevant to oral language use of Spanish and English will comprise one semester of the program, and the development of public speaking-leadership qualities in English and Spanish will comprise the second semester of the program. Spanish-speaking teacher aides will serve with each classroom teacher. Tape recorders will be used for listening and practicing oral communication skills; and field trips will be made to plays, television stations, and public debates and panels. Personnel of the Padua Hills Theater, a local Mexican culture and drama center, will be used as resource persons, as well as Mexican-American community members and school district personnel.
*Students served:* 105, Grades 7-8
*Counties served:* Los Angeles
*Further information:* Farrett C. Nichols, 800 South Garey Avenue, Pomona, California, 91766. (714) 623-5251, Ext. 400.

ST. HELENA: St. Helena Unified Schools—1969
**Project Bilingual Education: Adelante!**
*Languages:* Spanish, English
(OE 97-220)                                                         Amount sought: $22,500
*Description:* A bilingual teacher and a bilingual aide will develop and teach a four-part high school curriculum which will include courses in the humanities, social studies and science taught in Spanish and English, and courses in English as a second language. Also included will be an honors course in humanities taught in Spanish; a course in Spanish communication skills for Spanish-speaking students; and a tutoring program providing individual instruction in courses such as math, science, and vocational education. Inservice training, community involvement, and continuing evaluation activities are planned. During the second year, the project will add an elementary school component.
*Students served:* 55, Grades 9-12
*Counties served:* Napa
*Further information:* William K. Noble, Project Director, Secondary School Level, 473 Main,

197

St. Helena, California 94574. (707) 963-3604; Margaret Hall, Project Director, Elementary School Level, 1325 Adams, St. Helena, California, 94574. (707) 963-2140.

STOCKTON: Stockton Unified School District—1970
**The Development of Instruments to Provide a More Adequate Assessment of Skills and Competencies of the Child Whose Dominant Language is Other Than English as well as Instruments that Identify His Unique Characteristics**
(OE 7-00282-1)                                          Amount recommended: $500,000
*Description:* A bilingual education project has been established to develop instruments for adaptation and/or norming of inter-American tests for Spanish-speaking children in the Southeast and East. The tests will be adapted (through an item analysis), normed, and revised (through field testing) for use in the project. The project will use interview forms to identify cognitive skills for children whose home language is other than English, and will develop and use interview instruments which identify areas of interest about which a child verbalizes in his home language to enable schools to draw up a profile for each child. In doing so, it is hoped that myths concerning the Mexican-American child's competencies can be destroyed, and that ways of showing individual differences among members of ethnic groups can be developed. Instruments will also be developed for Puerto Ricans. Additionally, the project will develop videotapes for inservice training which will demonstrate the use of the instruments in developing profiles for children.
*For further information:* James Shannon, Director of Research, 701 North Madison Street, Stockton, California, 95202. (209) 466-3911.

SANTA PAULA: Santa Paula School District—1969
**Santa Paula Bilingual Education program**
*Languages:* Spanish, English
(OE 97-169)                                          Amount sought: $71,500
*Description:* A curriculum, stressing the authentic presentation of Mexican-American culture, will be designed with the help of local artists and artisans. Faculty members will be given inservice training in activities and materials relevant to language development, with a special emphasis on early childhood education. The diagnosis and prescription process will be improved through inservice training for staff and through the employment of three full-time specialists. A community liaison specialist will design and develop strategies for involving parents and the community in school activities.
*Students served:* 1,200, Grade preschool
*Counties served:* Ventura
*Further information:* Leonard Heid, Project Director, P.O. Box 710, Santa Paula, California, 93060. (805) 525-2182.

FRESNO: Fresno City Unified School District—1969
**Bilingual-Bicultural Title VII Proposal**
*Languages:* Spanish, English
(OE 97-283)                                          Amount sought: $101,500
*Description:* Development of the competence needed to employ two linguistic systems separately and consciously as mediums not only for speaking, but also for thinking will be the core of

a curriculum-oriented program being developed to serve inner city kindergarten and elementary school children in an area with a large Mexican-American community. The curriculum will be redesigned for all elementary grades, beginning with kindergarten and first grade, and will include instruction in English-as-a-Second Language, lessons conducted in Spanish in specified subject areas, and reinforcement of English through other subject matter instruction. Those conducting the program will include a resource teacher, a teacher who also serves as a liaison between school and community, three bilingual teachers, and five bilingual aides. Inservice training will be provided for those involved in the program. Parents will be consulted before children are selected for the program, and activities designed to maintain their support will be initiated. These will include a "Dad's Club" and a close home-school liaison designed to both inform parents and obtain information from them about the progress of the program.
*Students served:* 110, Grades K-7
*Counties served:* Fresno
*Further information:* Harry C. Allison, Project Director, 3132 E. Fairmont Street, Fresno, California, 93721 (209) 224-4350.


## COLORADO

CORTEZ: Montezuma—Dolores Board of Cooperative Services—1970
**Project SUN: Bilingual Program to Enhance Educational Opportunity**
(OE 7-00363)                          Amount recommended: $108,000
*Description:* Speaking skills, listening skills, and writing skills in English and the vernacular will be developed in 245 Ute, Navajo, Spanish American and Anglo kindergarten children in six elementary schools during the first year of this project. This project has a five-year objective to enable these children to speak and write the standard variant of English at grade level in addition to maintaining their native language, and to perform at grade level in the content areas. The monolingual speakers of English (voluntarily) are expected to learn Spanish well enough to: speak, read, and understand spoken Spanish to communicate in everyday situations. Major components by which these objectives will be achieved are: Bilingual and English-as-a-second-language instruction, material modification and development, staff development and training, and community participation.
*Counties served:* Montezuma, Dolores, Montrose, San Miguel
*For information:* Robert L. Werner, Executive Director, Montezuma Dolores Board of Cooperative Services, Post Office Drawer 1420, Cortez, Colorado, 81321. (303) 565-3613.


## FLORIDA

MIAMI: Dade County Public Schools—1970
**Spanish Curricula Development Center**
(OE 7-00498)                          Amount recommended $500,000
*Description:* A national core curriculum for Spanish-speaking children in grades one through three will be developed and field tested in selected bilingual education programs throughout the Nation. Multimedia Spanish curricula kits will contain materials for teachers and for

pupils in Spanish in respect to language arts, social science, fine arts, science, mathematics, and Spanish as a second language for each grade level. Field testing of first grade materials will begin in September, 1971; the total effort will be completed in four years.
*Counties served:* Dade
*Further information:* E. L. Whigham, Superintendent of Schools, 1410 N.E. Second Avenue, Miami, Florida, 33132. (305) 350-3011.

## MASSACHUSETTS

BOSTON: Boston School Department—1970
**Bilingual Education Program**
*Languages:* Spanish, English
(OE 97-274)                                                      Amount sought: $108,000
*Description:* Two classes of Spanish-speaking children, ages six to eight, will receive instruction in English-language skills, reading skills in both languages, and content areas in both languages. Two classes of newly arrived Puerto Rican children, ages nine to twelve, with little or no English language ability, will participate in an oral-aural English-as-a-second-language program and will be instructed largely in Spanish in the content areas. Two classes of newly arrived Puerto Rican children, ages thirteen to sixteen, with little or no English language ability, will participate in an intensive English-as-a-second-language program which will emphasize understanding and speaking, and will be instructed in Spanish in the content areas. Classes will be conducted by a bilingual teacher, a Puerto Rican parent aide, and volunteers. Other components will include a health program, field trips, cultural activities, a drop-in-center to provide counseling, tutorial, cultural, and vocational information and activities for young men and women of the area, and training in Spanish for English-speaking teachers.
*Students served:* 325, Grades 1-12
*Counties served:* Suffolk
*Further information:* Martha J. Shanley, Project Director, 102 Boylston Street, Room 521, Boston, Massachusetts, 02116. (617) 426-5552.

## MICHIGAN

PONTIAC: School District of the City of Pontiac—1969
**Itinerant Bilingual Teaching Teams**
*Languages:* Spanish, English
(OE 97-50)                                                        Amount sought: $91,000
*Description:* Non-English speaking students and bilingual students with severe language handicaps will be given individual attention and instruction to aid them in overcoming their language problems. A team composed of one bilingual teacher and two bilingual aides will be assigned to each group of fifty students and will provide individual and small group tutoring, diagnosis of the problems which affect the student's achievement, compensatory programs utilizing school and community resources, and follow-up activities. Team teachers and aides will also conduct inservice training for classroom teachers who are working with language handicapped students

and will assist in the development of elementary school social studies units incorporating Spanish-American cultural and historical materials and Spanish language materials.
*Students served:* 100, Grades K-12
*Counties served:* Oakland
*Further information:* B. C. VanKoughnett, Project Director, 9 Victory Court, Pontiac, Michigan, 48058. (313) 338-9151.

## NEW MEXICO

GRANTS: Grants Municipal Schools—1970
**Recreating the Environment for Language Learning within the Classroom**
(OE 7-00022-1)                                              Amount recommended: $300,000
*Description:* This project will rearrange and program the existing bilingual curriculum in a sequence which will facilitate the learning of a second language by "grappling with the environment". Research completed by Dr. Daniel Dato of Georgetown University, will be built on for implementation at the first grade and possibly high school levels for Spanish- and English-speaking children. A product of the project will be a complete description of newly developed teaching materials and planned interaction of students and adults both within and outside the classroom. Language learning, theories confirmed by basic research will be used and more relevant materials on how a second language is learned will be developed. The project will have demonstration sites in four locations including Grants, New Mexico.
*For further information:* M. B. McBride, Superintendent, Grants Municipal School, P.O. Box 8, Grants, New Mexico, 87020. (505) 287-2958.

## NEVADA

LAS VEGAS: Las Vegas City School District—1970
**Joint Bilingual Program—Las Vegas Schools and West Las Vegas**
(OE 7-00418)                                                Amount recommended: $102,000
*Description:* A bilingual education program has been established to provide for 540 children in the first grade the development of language processes in both Spanish and English, improvement of cognitive functioning, development of positive self-concepts, and desire for academic achievement. This project will also establish effective parent-teacher-school-community relationships. Teachers and parents will receive training, with mothers serving as second educators of their children. Educational concepts will be presented in the mother tongue of the children, with reinforcement of concepts in the second language; independent learning will be stressed. The curriculum will include English and Spanish literacy skills, concept development, culturally oriented program and self-image development. Project components are instructional program, staff development, and parent involvement. The long range objectives are to: (1) develop cultural awareness of the two predominant cultures, (2) extend the program through the fifth grade by adding an additional level each year, (3) raise the achievement level of students to that of the national norm by completion of the fifth grade, (4) provide worthwhile programs that will enable participants to become more productive members of society, (5) prepare

teachers for bilingual education programs, and (6) develop evaluation methods and techniques that will provide a true picture of achievement.

*Counties served:* San Miguel

*For information:* H. Fred Pomeroy, Superintendent of Schools, 917 Douglas Avenue, Las Vegas, New Mexico, 87701. (505 425-6784; Ray Ledger, Superintendent of Schools, West Las Vegas, S.D., P. O. Drawer J, Las Vegas, New Mexico, 87701. (505) 425-9316.

## NEW YORK

BROOKLYN: City School District of the City of New York—1970
**Project BEST—Modeling Innovative Programs Unit**
(OE 7-00420-1)                                     Amount recommended: $85,000
*Description:* A component is being added to the existing bilingual education project to analyze approximately 130 programs to determine whether or not the kinds of evaluation being conducted in individual projects are providing: (1) evidence of the advantage of bilingual education for a child—education in both languages—and proof that no real linguistic problems arise as a natural phenomenon when a person deals with two languages at an early age; and, (2) evidence to prove that a bilingual program set up as a remedial program to make children monolingual in English as rapidly as possible is really a disservice to children with a potential for becoming bilingual. This component will catalog, for computer retrieval, the essential characteristics of the bilingual programs funded under ESEA Title VII. Graduate students, involved in some area of language learning and evaluation, recruited from Hunter and Lehman Colleges as well as other Metropolitan area colleges and universities, will assist consultants and a program coordinator in the data collecting and analysis. This combined with two more detailed stages of analysis will help to determine the validity of current evaluation with regard to establishing valid models of bilingual education and will indicate where lacunae exist. Suggested directions for future finding strategies may also emerge as a result of the study.

*For further information:* Seelig Lester, Deputy Superintendent of Schools, 695 Park Avenue, New York, New York 10021.

NEW YORK: Two Bridges Model School District—1970
**Building Bilingual Bridges**
*Languages:* Chinese, Spanish, English
(OE 97-7)                                     Amount sought: $139,000
*Description:* Providing bilingual education in an integrated classroom setting which emphasizes individualized instruction rather than segregating children by language is the aim of an inner-city program where forty-five percent of the target group children are Chinese and thirty-three percent are Puerto Rican. The program will open with two classes each of pre-kindergarten and kindergarten children and children in grades one and two and will eventually be expanded to all elementary grade levels. Chinese-American children in the pre-kindergarten and kindergarten classes will receive curricular instruction in Chinese and in English, while the Puerto Rican children will receive curricular instruction in Spanish and in English. Each group will also receive intensive instruction in oral English and reading readiness activities. English-speaking

children will have the opportunity to participate in non-English instruction of the other children. A similar format will be followed in grades one and two where the English component will consist of oral language, reading readiness and beginning reading, and the native language component will consist of an IPI (Individually Prescribed Instruction) mathematics program. Subject-matter instruction in the two languages will be conducted by bilingual teachers. Weekly inservice meetings will be held with the project staff, and periodic progress discussions will be held with the teacher aides and with the children's parents.

*Students served:* 270, Grades Preschool-2
*Counties served:* Kings
*Further information:* Daniel Friedman, Unit Administrator, 217 Park Row, New York, New York. (212) 962-1410.

## TEXAS

FORT WORTH: Fort Worth Independent School District—1970
**The National Consortia for Bilingual Education**
(OE 7-00110-1)                                                    Amount recommended:
*Description:* The National Consortia for Bilingual Education are proposed to meet the critical need in bilingual education programs for various types of materials. The Consortia will focus their activities on all aspects of bilingual education, including instructional materials and equipment, community and parental involvement, staff development, instructional techniques and strategies, testing instruments and curriculum, management, as well as evaluation designs. After systematically assessing the major needs of the country's bilingual education programs which can be partially met through making a variety of materials available. The Consortia will identify, evaluate, refine, install, and test existing materials and where necessary, develop new ones for broad dissemination. The Consortia will consist of a number of materials packaging centers in different parts of the country and a central planning and coordinating group designated as the National Support Team which will develop operational plans for the individual consortia and develop the functions the Center will perform during the program's second and third year of operation.
*For further information:* Julius Truelson, Superintendent of Schools, 3210 West Lancaster Boulevard, Fort Worth, Texas, 76107. (817) 336-0743 or 336-2451.

SAN ANTONIO: San Antonio Independent School District—1970
**Proyecto Bilingual Intercultural**
*Languages:* Spanish, English
(OE 97-60)                                                    Amount sought: $201,500
*Description:* A multimedia learning system will be designed to help alleviate the serious shortage of materials for Spanish-speaking children in Grades kindergarten to one. The system will include filmstrips, films, audio tapes, teachers' manuals and student materials and will use Spanish as the primary medium of instruction until the child's command of English is sufficient to enable him to communicate effectively in that language. Teaching Spanish as a second language will be a second focus of the system. A junior high school curriculum development

project will focus upon identifying, developing, improving, and adapting materials and techniques to assist Spanish-speaking children in becoming independent learners in English and to teach sufficient Spanish to English-speakers to prepare them for instruction in Spanish. A program to train high school students as bilingual secretaries and office workers will be a third component of the project.

*Students served:* 1,650, Grades K-1, 6-7, 9-12

*Counties served:* Bexar

*Further information:* Josue M. Gonzalez, Project Director, c/o Navarro Elementary School, 623 South Pecos Street, San Antonio, Texas, 78207. (512) 227-4195

# APPENDIX D

## Teaching Techniques During the Aural-Oral Phase: Devices for Presentation and Practice*

### Mimicry-memorizing presentation

*Presentation by the teacher*—clearly but not too slowly, from all parts of the room so that all pupils may hear and see. The teacher may mark the sentence melody on the blackboard as a guide to the pupil's accurate hearing and imitation. (Short and long dashes at different levels, of different intensity.)

*Responses by pupils*—

Full-choral response, single repetition—the teacher repeats his model pronunciation loudly, clearly, and at normal speed. The entire class imitates it as accurately as possible.

Full-choral response, double repetition—the teacher calls for double repetition of a new phrase or sentence about eight times.

Half-choral practice—One-half of the class responds to the teacher's model pronunciation; the other half monitors. The teacher calls for four or five double repetitions with each half.

Small-group practice—The teacher calls for two or three double repetitions from each row of pupils or each group of pupils.

### Dialog Practice

Dialog practice can proceed from 1) teacher to class; 2) teacher to individual pupil or indi-

---

* From *Modern Foreign Languages in High School: Pre-reading Instruction* by Patricia O'Connor, U. S. Department of Health, Education, and Welfare Bulletin No. 9-OE-27000, 1960.

vidual pupil to teacher; 3) pupil to class; 4) pupil to pupil. Dialog should be meaningful and sensible.

Material should be introduced through the mimicry-memory presentation and done from teacher-pupil then pupil-pupil dialog.

*Pupil-Pupil chain Dialogs*

T to P¹: My name is _____. What's your name?
P¹ to T: My name is _____.
P¹ to P²: My name is _____. What's your name?
P² to P¹: My name is _____.
P² to P³: My name is _____. What's your name?
P³ to P²: My name is _____.
P³ to P⁴: My name is _____. What's your name?
P⁴ to P³: My name is _____.
T:         Thank you.

Reversed role—the teacher interrupts the chain to correct the statements; he may pronounce the model answer himself and call for double repetitions by the entire class. The teacher interrupts with the statements "please ask me that question."

T: Is your friend here?
P: No, he isn't. He isn't here. He's in New York.
T: Please ask me that question.
P: Is your friend here?
T: (correcting the error) No, he isn't. He isn't here. He's in New York. (repeats model, calls for double repetition of model and begins chain again.)

*Reversed role*—to interrupt and change the order of question-answer chain.

P¹ addressing P²: My name is _____. What's your name?
P² answering P¹: My name is _____.
P² addressing P³: My name is _____. What's your name?
            (Chain continues through to P⁶ when teacher interrupts.)
T addressing P⁶: Please ask me that question.
P⁶ addressing T: My name is _____. What's your name?
T answering P⁶: My name is _____. What's your name? (to pupil 12)

*Reversed role*—to introduce new word or phrase. The following example illustrates the introduction of the new sentence, "I don't know":

First the teacher reviews questions about ages from the previous lessons:

T: How old are you?
P: I'm thirteen.

The teacher then questions a pupil about another pupil's age. If necessary, he permits a whispered inquiry:

T: How old is John?
P1: He's fourteen.

Then the teacher reverses the roles and calls for the question to be addressed to him:

T: Please ask me: How old is Frank?
P1: How old is Frank?
T: I don't know. How old are you, Frank?
P2: I'm thirteen.
T: Frank is thirteen.

This dialog is practiced six to eight times as P-T, with various pupils asking the first question and the teacher giving the answer, before the new sentence "I don't know" is presented for choral practice by the entire class.

*Reversed role*—to develop expanded answer form:

T: Do you have a French name?
P: No, I don't.
T: Please ask me that question.
P: Do you have a French name?
T: No, I don't. I don't have a French name, but I have an English name.

*Eliciting longer answers*

The teacher instructs the pupils to give two kinds of answers to the same question—first a full answer, and then a short answer—and finally to combine both the short and full answer forms into one longer statement.

Teacher instructs a portion of the class to give a full answer to the question.

T: Is Paul's book dark green?
P: Yes, Paul's book is dark green.

Teacher calls for a short answer.

T: Is Paul's book dark green?
P: Yes, it is.

Teacher calls for a combined short and full answer.

T: Is Paul's book dark green?
P: Yes, it is. Paul's book is dark green.

The teacher calls first for a full answer, then a short answer, then a combined answer with correction.

The teacher holds up a light green book. He first calls for a full answer, then a short answer.

T: Is Mary's book dark green?
P: No, Mary's book isn't dark green.

T: Is Mary's book dark green?
P: No, it isn't.

Combined answer with a correction.

T: Is Mary's book dark green?
P: No, it isn't. Mary's book isn't dark green. It's light green.

The teacher reverses roles to give an expanded answer and then drills the class on the new answer before returning to the T-Cl, T-P dialog practice.

T: At what time does the English class begin?
Cl: It begins at nine o'clock.
T: Please ask me that question.
P: At what time does the English class begin?
T: It usually begins at nine o'clock but sometimes it begins at eleven o'clock.
Teacher calls for descriptions of persons, objects, or processes which allow the students to combine in one short speech sentences which have been previously practices as separate statements.
T: Please tell us about _____.

*Pattern Drills*—drill on the structure of the sentence ifself by using it as the basis for an exercise in patterned substitution.

Choral exercises to make automatic the pattern "I don't have any. . . ."

T: I don't have any pencils.
Cl: I don't have any pencils.
T: Ink.
Cl: I don't have any ink.
T: I don't have any notebooks (and so on.)

*Nonverbal Clues*—An actual object or picture serves as the stimulus to the pupils' answer, their response is dominated more by what they see than by what they have just heard spoken by the teacher. The think itself, rather than its name, serves as a triggering action in the pupils' memory, evoking a realistic selection from a limited number of possible verbal responses. Nonverbal clues should be chosen so as to suggest to the students one and only one response until they have the ability for selection.

*Nonverbal Clues*—

Meaning without Translation—teacher presents the new item in a more elaborate framework—through a teacher-class or teacher-pupil dialog.

The teacher shows a bookbag to the class, and, as he has done in previous lessons, asks them to guess what he has in the bag. After pens, pencils, etc., have been named, the teacher asks the class:

T: What else do I have in the bag?
P: I don't know.
T: I have some paper in the bag. Do you know the word "paper"?

If no pupil thinks of saying "Please show us," the teacher asks if they would like to see "paper." If necessary, he suggests that the pupils ask him to show them "paper."

P: Please show us.
T: (holding several sheets of paper) This is some paper. (Holding one sheet) This is a piece of paper.

Then the teacher calls for choral practice of the new sentence, "This is a piece of paper."

Reinforcement of Already Learned Meanings—After new material has been introduced and practiced through mimicry-memorizing presentation, teaching aids can be used as non-verbal cues to reinforce learning.

Choral exercises for realistic practice of the pattern "I have a _____ and a _____." First the teacher, and then the pupils actually hold up and display the two objects named in the practice sentences.

T: I have a book and a notebook.
Cl: I have a book and a notebook.
T: I have a notebook and a pencil.
Cl: I have a notebook and a pencil.

Grammatical Drill with Practice in Variation—when the practice of a given structure has progressed to the point of allowing some variation in the pattern, the showing of different combinations of objects can provide realistic cues to various student responses. Pupils must listen for and respond to the variations in the teacher's directions.

The teacher places a French book, an English book, two notebooks, and a pencil on his desk. The pupils are instructed to do likewise. After choral practice of "I have a French book, an English book, two notebooks, and a pencil," with the pupils actually touching the named objects on their desks, there is a series of teacher-pupil requests. The teacher walks around the room asking individual pupils to give him the various objects. He accepts and holds each object briefly.

T: Please give me the pencil.
   Please give me the French book.
   Please give me the notebooks.
   Please give me the two books.

After considerable practice as teacher-pupil requests, the exercise is continued as pupil-pupil chain practice.

Classroom Games—must be adapted to need, size, ability of group; should be correlated to classroom work; should be simple; should be used only a few minutes each day.

Guessing game with Foreign Language Names—teacher writes name on the board and pupils attempt to guess whose name is written.

P: Is it _____?
T: No it isn't.

P: Is it _____?
T: Yes it is.

"I see something" (game #1. Pupil selects an object; teacher may ask the first questions.)
P: I see something.
P: Is it something in this room?
P: Is it something blue?
P: Is it something dark blue?
P: Is it a pencil? (and so on).

"I see something" (game #2. Pupil selected to leave room, class chooses item, pupil guesses.)
"I see something" (game #3. Teacher selects object, pupils try to guess. Teacher gives pupils short descriptive statements about the object as "clues.")

T: I see something.
   It is in this classroom.
   It is brown.
   It is near the blackboard.
   It has books on it.
   What is it?

If pupil thinks that he has guessed the object, he may volunteer a question:

P: Is it your desk?
T: Yes. It is my desk.

What time is it? Guessing game with a practice clock. Teacher turns the face of the practice clock toward him and manipulates the hands so the class can not see the time. Pupils guess individually.

P: Is it nine o'clock?
T: No it is not nine o'clock. (and so on) Pupil who guesses the correct time sets the next time to be guessed.

Do you have a Book and a Pencil? Pupils are instructed to have on their desks four objects, such as a book, a notebook, a pencil, and a pen. Then each pupil is to select and hold out of sight any two of the four objects. The teacher asks individual pupils:

T: Do you have a book and a pencil?

If the teacher happens to guess correctly, the answer is:

P: Yes, I do. I have a book and a pencil.
If the answer is not correct, the answer is:

P: No, I don't. I do not have a book and a pencil. I have a book and a notebook.

How many Pencils? (practice of the foreign language equivalent of "There are and there is." The teacher shows four pencils, then puts both hands behind his back, out of sight of the class, and asked:

T: Are there any pencils in my right/left hand?

The pupils guess when called on:

P: There are three pencils in your right hand.

After each guess, the teacher displays the hand asked about and says:

T: Yes, there are. There are three pencils in my right hand. The other is in my left hand. (or)
T: No there aren't. (Pupils may take the teacher's role.)

# APPENDIX E

## Diagnostic Sound Test

### Developed For Use With *"Shuck Loves Chirley"*\*

By: LEONARD OLGUÍN
Copyright 1968
University of California
Irvine, California

\* Used by permission of Leonard Olguín.

| CHECK BELOW | | | DOMESTIC TEST FOR SOUND PROBLEMS | Name_____<br>Grade_____Age_____<br>Language spoken at home_____<br>Tested by_____<br>Staff position_____<br>Date tested_____ | |
|---|---|---|---|---|---|
| NO PROBLEM | INCONSISTENT | PROBLEM | | | |
| | | | TESTING THE SOUND OF | PROBABLE PROBLEM | TEST SERVICE |
| | | | 1 schwa –ə (uh) | ah or eh instead of ə | This is a girl. |
| | | | 2 short a | ah or eh instead of ă | The pig is fat. |
| | | | 3 intervocalic b (between vowels) | sounds like v | Babies are cute. |
| | | | 4 final b | unvoiced-unaspirated (not fully produced) | Water is in the tub. |
| | | | 5 initial c | unaspirated (not enough air) | Cars go fast. |
| | | | 6 intervocalic and final c (or k) | unvoiced-unaspirated | I look at a book. |
| | | | 7 intervocalic d | will sound like the "th" in the or the "tt" in butter. | This is a lady. |
| | | | 8 final d | omitted or made as a t | The world is big. |
| | | | 9 ch | sounds like sh | I sit in a chair. |
| | | | 10 sh | sounds like ch | My shoes are new. |
| | | | 11 hard intervocalic g | becomes glottal fricative (buzzed in the throat) | We went days ago. |
| | | | 12 final g | unvoiced-unaspirated | I see a bug. |
| | | | 13 h | becomes glottal fricative | I see a house. |
| | | | 14 short i | becomes long or short e | The dog is in the house. |
| | | | 15 j | sounds like ch or y | I like to jump. |
| | | | 16 l | omitted or distorted in final positions | It is a big ball. |

| NO PROBLEM | INCONSISTENT | PROBLEM | | | | |
|---|---|---|---|---|---|---|
| **CHECK BELOW** | | | DIAGNOSTIC TEST FOR SOUND PROBLEMS | | | |
| | | | **TESTING THE SOUND OF** | **PROBABLE PROBLEM** | **TEST SERVICE** | |
| | | | 17 final m | unvoiced in final position | His name is Tom. | |
| | | | 18 ng | says n instead of ng, also low aspiration level | He sang a song. | |
| | | | 19 long o (ou) | glide-off sound omitted | We go to the show. | |
| | | | 20 initial and inter-vocalic p | unaspirated | Puppies are cute. | |
| | | | 21 final p | unsounded | It's time for a nap. | |
| | | | 22 r* | distorted weak | Run like a rabbit. | |
| | | | 23 voiced intervocalic s ("z" sounding s) | sounds like a "hissed" s | The rose is pink. | |
| | | | 24 initial s blends | e is placed before s | Snails stroll at night. | |
| | | | 25 all t's | unaspirated or distorted (often sound like d) | The water is hot. | |
| | | | 26 voiceless th | becomes s or t or f | We thank you. | |
| | | | 27 voiced th | becomes d | This is fun. | |
| | | | 28 schwa u (uh) | becomes ah or oh | My feet are under the table. | |
| | | | 29 intervocalic v | sounds like soft b | I count to eleven. | |
| | | | 30 final v | unvoiced | I count to five. | |
| | | | 31 initial w | takes g characteristics | We play with toys. | |
| | | | 32 y | takes on j characteristics | The yellow bird sings. | |
| | | | 33 z | sound like voiceless s's (unless followed by voiced consonant.) | The bees will buzz in the trees. | |

* Asterisked items do not apply to children grades K-2.

# Diagnostic Test

## PART II

Test for fluency.
1. Select a picture appropriate to grade level.
2. Tell the child you would like him to tell you all about the picture.
3. Show and listen for about a minute.
4. Rate degrees of ability:

|         | Poor |   |   |   |   |   |   |   |   | Good |   |
|---------|---|---|---|---|---|---|---|---|---|----|---|
|         | 1 | 2 | 3 | 4 | 5 | 6 | 7 | 8 | 9 | 10 |   |
| Fluency |   |   |   |   |   |   |   |   |   |    |   |

5. Other speaking problems noted.

## PART III

Comments_____

_____

_____

_____

_____

# NOTATIONS

## Chapter 1

[1] Arturo Cabrera, *A Survey of Spanish Surname Enrolled Students, San Jose State College, 1963-64* (Washington, D.C.: Educational Resource Information Center, U. S. Office of Education), p. 1. (ED 020 031)

[2] Richard A. Lamonna and Julian Samora, *Recent Trends in Educational Status of Mexican Americans in Texas* (Washington, D.C.: Educational Resource Information Center, U. S. Office of Education, 1965), p. 22. (ED 020 813)

[3] U. S. Office of Education, National Advisory Committee on Mexican American Education, Armando Rodriguez, Chief, *The Mexican American: Quest for Equality* (Albuquerque: Southwestern Cooperative Educational Laboratory, 1968), p. 1.

[4] Herschel T. Manuel, "The Educational Problem Presented by the Spanish Speaking Child of the Southwest," *School and Society,* XL (November, 1934), p. 695.

[5] Octovio Ignacio Romano, V., "Minorities, History and the Cultural Mystique," *El Grito, A Journal of Contemporary Mexican American Thought* (Berkeley: Quinto Sol Publications, Inc., Fall, 1967), p. 7.

[6] Carlos Conde, *A New Era* (Cabinet Committee on Opportunities for Spanish Speaking People, Fall, 1970), p. 8.

[7] Inter Agency Committee on Mexican American Affairs, *Mexican American Newsletter,* I (December, 1969), p. 3.

## Chapter 2

[1] John Burma, *Spanish Speaking Groups in the United States* (New York: Book Craftsmen Association, 1961), p. 65.

[2] *Ibid.,* p. 60.

[3] Good Neighbor Commission of Texas, *Texas Migrant Labor, The 1966 Migrants* (Austin: Educational Resource Information Center, U. S. Office of Education, March, 1967), p. 3. (ED 013 157)

[4] H. H. Fisher and George Mair, *The Helping Arm, The Bracero in California Agriculture* (Los Angeles: Town Hall, Industrial Relations Section, 1966), p. 25.

[5] For a full discussion of this topic see, Octovio Ignacio Romano, V., "The Anthropology and Sociology of the Mexican Americans; The Distortion of Mexican American History," *El Grito, A Journal of Contemporary Mexican American Thought* (Berkeley: Quinto Sol Publications, Inc., Fall, 1968), p. 1.

[6] Peter Matthiessen, *Sal Si Puedes,* quoting Cesar Chavez (New York: Random House, 1969), p. 177.

[7] *Ibid.,* p. 196.

[8] Michael Verdugo, Organizer of the United Mexican American Students (UMAS) in Southern California. Currently Director of the Educational Opportunities Program, San Fernando Valley State College.

[9] *Ibid.*

[10] *Ibid.*

[11] *Ibid.*

[12] *Ibid.*

[13] *Ibid.*

## Chapter 3

[1] Cary McWilliams, *North from Mexico* (New York: Greenwood Press, 1948), p. 8.

[2] C. Wayne Gordon, *et al.*, *Educational Achievement and Aspirations of Mexican American Youth in a Metropolitan Context* (Los Angeles: Center for the Study of Evaluation of Instructional Programs, University of California, Los Angeles, 1968), p. 90.

[3] Octovio Ignacio Roman V., "Minorities, History and the Cultural Mystique," *El Grito, A Journal of Contemporary Mexican American Thought* (Berkeley: Quinto Sol Publications, Inc., Fall, 1967), p. 7.

[4] Joan W. Moore, *Mexican Americans* (Englewood Cliffs, New Jersey: Prentice-Hall, Inc., 1970), p. 100.

[5] Frank Del Olmo, "A Week in the Life of a Poor Migrant Family," *Riverside* (California) *Press Enterprise,* August 17, 1969. (Used by permission of the publisher.)

[6] Reverend William E. Scholes, "The Migrant Workers," in *La Raza, Forgotten Americans,* ed. by Julian Samora, quoting Bureau of Labor Standards, "Coverage of Agricultural Workers Under State and Federal Labor Laws," U. S. Department of Labor, *Bulletin,* 1964. (264)

[7] Louise F. Harvey, "The Delinquent Mexican Boy," *Journal of Educational Research,* XLII, No. 8 (April, 1949), p. 583.

[8] M. Terry Rusk, "A Study of Delinquency Among Urban Mexican American Youth" (unpublished Ph.D. dissertation, University of Southern California, 1969).

[9] Celia S. Heller, *Mexican American Youth: Forgotten Youth at the Crossroads* (New York: Random House, 1966), p. 68.

[10] Joseph W. Eaton and Kenneth Polk, *Measuring Delinquency, A Study of Probation Department Referrals* (Pittsburg: University of Pittsburg Press, 1961), p. 32. (Used by permission of the publisher.)

## Chapter 4

[1] George W. Mayeske, "Educational Achievement Among Mexican Americans: A Special Report from the Educational Opportunities Survey," in *Integrated Education,* VI, No. 1, ed. by Meyer Weinberg (Chicago: Integrated Education Associates, 1968), p. 33.

[2] Robert Rosenthal and Lenore Jacobson, *Pygmalion in the Classroom, Teacher Expectation and Pupils' Intellectual Development* (New York: Holt, Rinehart, and Winston, Inc., 1968), p. 172.

[3] *Ibid.*, p. 175.

[4] *Ibid.*, p. 177.

[5] *Ibid.*, p. 178.

[6] *Ibid.*

[7] *Ibid.*, p. 179.

[8] *Ibid.*, p. 180.

[9] Jane Case Williams, *Improving Educational Opportunities for Mexican American Handicapped Children* (Washington, D.C.: Educational Resource Information Center, U. S. Office of Education), p. 8. (ED 018 326)

[10] C. Wayne Gordon, *et al.*, *Educational Achievement and Aspirations of Mexican American Youth in a Metropolitan Context* (Los Angeles: Center for the Study of Evaluation of Instructional Programs, University of California, Los Angeles, 1968), p. 100.

[11] Mayeske, *loc. cit.*

[12] *Ibid.*

[13] Williams, *op. cit.*, p. 5.

[14] Mayeske, *loc. cit.*

[15] *Ibid.*

[16] James Coleman, "The Concept of Equality of Educational Opportunity," *Harvard Educational Review*, XXXBIII, No. 1 (1968), p. 18.

[17] Mayeske, *op. cit.*, p. 35.

[18] Uvaldo Palomares, *Assessment of Rural Mexican American Students in Grades, Preschool— 12th* (Kern County: Research Project, Educational Resource Information Center, U. S. Office of Education, 1967), p. 1. (ED 013 690)

[19] Ronald Henderson, *Environmental Stimulation and Intellectual Development of Mexican American Children* (Washington, D.C.: Educational Resource Information Center, U. S. Office of Education, 1966), p. 170, quoting A. H. Maslow, *Motivation and Personality* (New York: Harper and Row, 1954). (ED 010 587)

[20] Rumalod Z. Juarez, *Educational Status Orientations of Mexican American and Anglo American Youth in Selected Low Income Counties of Texas* (Washington, D.C.: Educational Resource Information Center, U. S. Office of Education), p. 1. (ED 023 511)

[21] Gordon, *et al.*, *op. cit.*, p. 91.

[22] Henderson, *loc. cit.*

[23] Uvaldo Palomares, "The Education Gap: Why Mexican-American Children Fail in School," *The Mexican American Heritage: Developing Cultural Understanding, First Papers on Migrancy and Rural Poverty* (Los Angeles: Teacher Corps, Rural Migrant, University of Southern California, 1968), p. 23.

[24] Henderson, *loc. cit.*

## Chapter 5

[1] Report of the President's Commission on National Goals, *Goals for Americans* (Englewood Cliffs, New Jersey: Prentice-Hall, Inc., 1960), p. 3.

[2] John Plakos, *Mexican American Education Research Project Report, California State Department of Education* (Washington, D.C.: Educational Resource Information Center, U. S. Office of Education, 1967), p. 11. (ED 018 281)

[3] Bruce Joyce, *Strategies for Elementary Social Science Education* (Chicago: Science Research Associates, Inc., 1965).

[4] Benjamin S. Bloom, *et. al., Taxonomy of Educational Objectives The Classification of Educational Goals Handbook I: Cognitive Domain* (New York: David McKay Company, Inc.. 1956).

[5] David R. Krathwohl, *et al., Taxonomy of Educational Objectives The Classification of Educational Goals Handbook II: Affective Domain* (New York: David McKay Company, Inc., 1964).

## Chapter 6

[1] John Macnamara, "Bilingualism in the Modern World," *The Journal of Social Issues,* XXIII, No. 2 (April, 1967), p. 5.

[2] Bruce Gaarder, *et al., Bilingualism, From the Viewpoint of the Administrator and Counselor* (Washington, D.C.: Educational Resource Information Center, U. S. Office of Education), p. 18, ED 018 286, quoting, R. B. LePage, *The National Language Question—Linguistic Problems of Newly Independent States* (New York: Oxford University Press, 1964).

[3] *Ibid.,* quoting, J. Vernon Jensen, *Bilingualism—Effects of Childhood Bilingualism* (Champaign, Illinois: National Council of Teachers of English, 1962), p. 18.

[4] *Ibid.,* p. 20.

[5] Carl Rosen and Philip D. Ortego, *Problems and Strategies in Teaching the Language Arts to Spanish Speaking Mexican American Children* (Washington, D.C.: Educational Resources Information Center, 1969). (ED 025 368)

[6] Constance Amsen, *A Reading Program for Mexican American Children* (Washington, D.C.: Educational Resource Information Center, U. S. Office of Education, revised April, 1965), p. 100. (ED 016 757)

[7] Macnamara, *op. cit.,* p. 5.

[8] Texas Education Agency, *A Resource Manual for Implementing Bilingual Education Programs, The Regional Educational Agencies Project on International Education* (Austin: Texas Education Agency, 1969), p. 3.

[9] Robert P. Stockwell, *The Grammatical Structures of Spanish and English* (Chicago: University of Chicago Press, 1965), p. 5.

## Chapter 7

[1] Robert P. Stockwell and J. Donald Bowen, *The Sounds of English and Spanish* (Chicago: University of Chicago Press, 1965), p. 19.

[2] M. A. K. Halliday, *et al., The Linguistic Sciences and Language Teaching* (Bloomington: Indiana University Press, 1964), p. 71.

[3] Robert Lado, *Linguistics Across Cultures* (Ann Arbor: University of Michigan Press, 1964), p. 39.

[4] *Ibid.*, p. 80.

[5] *Ibid.*, p. 82.

[6] Robert P. Stockwell, *et al., The Grammatical Structures of English and Spanish* (Chicago: University of Chicago Press, 1965), p. 4-5.

    a. "Grammar is a classification of the signals which differentiate one sentence from another. This is sometimes called SIGNALS GRAMMAR, FORMALISTIC GRAMMAR, . . . or TAXONOMIC GRAMMAR. It consists of a description of those surface respects in which one sentence differs from another and of a classification of those differences . . .

    b. "Grammar is a finite number of sentence patterns, each pattern containing one or more slots within which a corresponding class of lexical units may replace one another. This kind of grammar is sometimes called SLOT-AND-SUBSTITUTION GRAMMAR . . . Fundamentally, it consists of a list of abstract patterns, like

Determiner + Noun + verb + Adverb
     (intransitive)        (postverbal)

This is the pattern of . . . *That horse runs fast.* Along with the patterns, there must be a lexicon that specifies which words belong to each class designated in any of the patterns . . .

[7] *Ibid.* "Grammar is a description of the degrees of closeness—or clustering—of lexical units in sequence . . . It is called IMMEDIATE CONSTITUENT ANALYSIS or PHRASE STRUCTURE GRAMMAR. It postulates that given any sequence of lexical units that constitute a sentence, it is possible to determine which items are closely related to which others and to specify the degree of relationship. Thus, given the sentence

*The two boys were playing in the yard.*

a phrase structure description postulates a close relationship of *the two boys,* on the one hand, and of *were playing in the yard,* on the other. These, then are two IMMEDIATE CONSTITUENTS of the sentence. Each of these, in turn contains further immediate constituents."

Step 1    *the two boys were playing in the yard.*

Step 2    *the two boys PAST be-ing in the yard.*

           (The "ing" of playing is more closely related to BE; therefore, it is placed with BE. The past form of BE is used in the sentence.)

[8] Ralph F. Robinett, "A Linguistic Approach to Beginning Reading for Bilingual Children," reprint from *Perspectives in Reading,* No. 5, International Reading Association, available from (Boston: D. C. Heath and Company, 1965). (Reprinted by permission of D. C. Heath and Company.)

[9] R. Sjolseth, *Instructional Aid ESL* (Los Angeles: Los Angeles City Schools, 1967).

[10] Elizabeth H. Ott, *A Study of Levels of Fluency and Proficiency in Oral English of Spanish-Speaking School Beginners* (Austin: University of Texas, 1967), p. 123.

[11] Frank Angel, *Program Content to Meet the Educational Needs of Mexican Americans* (Washington, D. C.: Educational Resource Information Center, U. S. Office of Education, 1968), pp. 5, 8, 9. (ED 017 392)

# Index